A PILLAGE OF ART

Read by
Gary M. Rowland
1/15/90

A PILLAGE
OF ART

JUDITH GRANT

Illustrated

ROY PUBLISHERS, INC.
New York 10021

Library of Congress Catalog Card No. 68–12417

PRINTED IN GREAT BRITAIN

CONTENTS

ILLUSTRATIONS

ACKNOWLEDGEMENTS

For special assistance in making this book possible I would like to thank Richard Hewins, Eddie Cotsis and Mr. Francis R. Walton, Director of the Gennadius Library in Athens.

To
JASON

INTRODUCTION

THERE is no subject in the world of art which has produced a
greater mass of literature than Greek statuary and no other can be
compared with it as the goal of wealthy and fashionable collectors.
This collectors' passion has an almost unbroken history—the Roman
Emperors, the Renaissance nobles, princes of the Church, the British
and French aristocracy of the seventeenth century and onwards, the
petty courts of Germany, the rising commercial princes of northern
Europe—all competed for the statuary of ancient Greece almost as
if its possession were a portent of nobility. There is no doubt that
the participants in this scramble were guided more by acquisitive
than aesthetic impulses and that the whole business has been heavily
set about by a considerable amount of misrepresentation and fraud.

Many civilizations have been characterized by a passion for the
production of statuary but nowhere did it reach greater heights than
in Greece between the sixth and the second century B.C. There is a
considerable body of evidence to support the belief that public
buildings, sports stadia, etc. were covered with an absolute forest
of statuary of various kinds. There was an immense production of
carved marble statuary, both for public and private use and it is
probable that every citizen employed this type of sculpture to
decorate his own house. The total number of statues produced in
Greece and the Greek colonies may well have amounted to considerably more than the total human population. In addition to the
life or larger than life-size works there was a vast production of
small terracotta sculpture employed as votive offerings and for other
purposes.

Contemporary records indicate that the most highly valued
sculptures were chryselephantine and bronze. The chryselephantine

sculpture was built up of ivory and precious metals around a wood core and not a single example has survived, while less than half a dozen bronze sculptures have yet been discovered. The position of carved marble statuary in ancient Greece is extremely complicated and controversial. It would appear from the evidence of contemporary records that the carving of marble statuary could not have been very highly regarded as the carvers themselves were only paid at the rate of day labourers and under these circumstances it seems highly improbable that the famous sculptors of the day ever worked directly in marble although they may have employed artisan copyists. A considerable number of marble carving workshops existed in Athens and were employed in the production of copies of bronze or chryselephantine sculptures or even copies of copies of the works of the great masters of the period. It is obvious that a workshop employed to reproduce a chryselephantine sculpture set up in a temple would be dependent purely on memory in the making of it. It is inconceivable that these copyists would have been allowed to scramble around the temples taking detailed proportional measurements or in any other system of accurate reproduction. In addition to which the transfer of a sculpture from one medium or set of dimensions to another always results in considerable aesthetic loss. In some cases as many as half a dozen different examples of copies of a single sculpture have been discovered which show such a large variation from one to another as scarcely to be recognizable. The Greeks, like many other peoples in history, were impressed not only by aesthetic considerations but also by the intrinsic value of the materials used in sculpture and it is not generally recognized that marble has never been a valuable material in Greece and that its use for sculpture depends on the fact that no other stone is easier to carve, since it is both soft and tenacious. All marble carvings were painted over rather in the manner of modern drapers' shop models and it is not unlikely that most of them were no more highly regarded than the painted plaster dogs etc. which are sold in market-places today.

The looting and collecting of Greek statuary has continued since Roman times and there can be no doubt that shiploads of it were exported by the Romans and all the subsequent conquerors of Greece. During the course of history most of the chryselephantine sculptures were stripped of the ivory and precious metals with which they were embellished. Bronze was always a scarce and valuable material, with the result that the bronzes were subsequently melted down for the metal which they contained. Marble is in its very nature a fragile material and there is no doubt that the larger part of it found its way into the lime burner's kiln as it is well known that, for instance, the Temple of Zeus in Athens formed a lime burner's quarry for centuries.

As the supply of statuary for the collectors decreased, fakers entered into the trade to supply the deficiency. Fragments were collected and assembled regardless of whether or not they all formed part of the same work and missing pieces were fabricated in order to produce apparently intact originals. Around this lucrative industry there developed a host of "scholars" whose prime function was to "authenticate" and thus enhance the value of works acquired by wealthy patrons. This situation evolved more or less continuously over the last two thousand years with the result that any real knowledge of the sculpture of the period has become hopelessly clouded. There is no doubt that the Greeks evolved the art of sculpture to an exceedingly high level but under the circumstances of the time it is equally certain that there was a production of work much of which was valueless from an aesthetic standpoint, and that the merit of Greek statuary has been enormously inflated owing to the fact that the possession of any form of Greek statuary became a symbol of status and prestige.

The pursuit of the collectors' passion has frequently been coloured by an obsessive fury which at times amounted almost to mania. Constantine the Great in his megalomaniac obsession to adorn the city which he created must have employed armies of men and fleets of ships to transport the forest of sculpture with which he decorated the city, while the transport of the famous porphry column from Delphi to Constantinople must have required the most highly organized moving job in the history of the times. The obscene figure of Lucius Cornelius Sulla looting Athens for treasures which he neither understood nor appreciated for the purpose of producing the largest triumphal procession in Roman history—the pillage of Athenian treasures in Constantinople by the Crusaders who arrived there by a series of accidents and whose activities were almost entirely destructive—the parvenu courtiers of the court of James I who competed in the collection of Greek statuary which had no other purpose than the enhancement of their own personal prestige —the absurd squabbles of subsequent dilettanti and "scholars"— leave the impression of a special kind of "Greek madness". All this was followed in the nineteenth century by the ridiculous and frequently obscene competition of governments to obtain objects which were felt to enhance their national prestige, while the deliberate and calculated deceits practised by archaeologists whose principal purpose appears to have been the denigration of their rivals, all present a picture of megalomaniac behaviour almost amounting to dementia.

Chapter I

THE LOOT OF SULLA

In 81 B.C. the Roman dictator Sulla celebrated his return from the wars in the East with a magnificent triumphal procession and for more than a week, scores of chariots were drawn through the streets of Rome laden high with the loot which this victorious general had gathered in the course of his campaigns in Greece. Sulla's booty included not only the usual treasures of gold, silver and precious gems but also an immense quantity of marble sculpture which he had plundered from Greece. This remarkable triumphal procession astonished the citizens of Rome and established a precedent for the strange passion for collecting ancient Greek sculpture as a method of vaunting an individual's cultural pretensions and power.

Lucius Cornelius Sulla, one of the most ruthless tyrants ever to rule the Roman Empire, was an exceedingly ugly man with a large and brutish physique and a face so covered with grotesque birthmarks that it was described by a contemporary as "a mulberry sprinkled over with meal". The revulsion which people could not help but express against his repellent appearance undoubtedly contributed to the growth of Sulla's pathological ambition and cruelty, and even in this age of extreme cruelty and corruption he was regarded as being unusually heartless and dissolute. He seized control of the government by civil war and then solidified his position as dictator by systematically exterminating his rivals in a reign of terror which spread from Rome throughout the Italian peninsula.

One of the consequences of this struggle for power within Rome was the development of a serious threat to the eastern part of the Empire. Mithridates, King of Pontus, a kingdom on the coast of the Black Sea, took advantage of the civil war in Rome to occupy the Roman provinces of Asia Minor and to massacre some eighty thousand Roman residents there. He then sent an army and a considerable fleet to Greece, including a contingent of Pontic soldiers to the city of Athens under the command of Aristion, an Athenian Greek turned Pontic.

By the summer of 87 B.C. Sulla felt himself sufficiently secure as ruler of the Empire to leave Rome in order to deal with Mithridates and he proceeded to Greece with a considerable army. He marched through central Aetolia and Boeotia whose Greek inhabitants willingly provided him with provisions and tribute and then entered Attica. When Sulla and his legions reached Athens, they were refused permission to enter the citadel of the Acropolis by Aristion who tried to conceal the fact that two thousand Pontic soldiers were quartered there. Sulla was informed about the presence of this Pontic garrison and determined to punish the Athenians for their defiance of Rome. Leaving some forces on the outskirts of Athens, he proceeded to the port of Piraeus, six miles to the south, where he found several ships of Mithridates' fleet at anchor. He decided to take Piraeus first and then deal with Athens.

The defenders of Piraeus were well ensconced behind massive fortifications and Sulla realized that he would require catapults and other engines of war to successfully breach these fortifications. He therefore ordered his soldiers to cut all the sacred trees lining the famous Academy of Plato for timber with which to construct catapults and commanded the demolition of every structure remaining outside the walls of Piraeus for rubble with which to build huge platforms on which to mount them. While these engines of war were being completed, Sulla attempted to destroy the fortifications of Piraeus by mining and his Roman soldiers excavated tunnels under cover of darkness, hidden behind the catapult platforms. Sulla's intention was to dig tunnels under the walls of the city which would be supported by internal timbering and filled with a highly combustible mixture of hemp, sulphur and pitch. When they were completed, he planned to set fire to these tunnels in order to burn out the supporting timber, thus causing the collapse of the tunnels and the walls above them. This plan failed, as the tunnellers encountered a solid mass of rock which they were unable to penetrate.

Several months passed while the Roman armies prepared for their assault on Piraeus and Sulla used this time to his personal advantage. Accompanied by a small party of his best soldiers he visited the Greek temples at Epidaurus, Olympia and Delphi, none of which were able to offer any resistance, and pillaged a vast quantity of the sacred treasures for which they were widely renowned, including much gold, silver, ivory and precious gems. In addition he also seized many pieces of Greek sculpture which caught his fancy on these expeditions, for he was an enthusiastic admirer of sculpture, although not endowed with a particularly refined taste.

Although his immediate objective was the port of Piraeus, Sulla had also left enough of an army encamped outside the city of Athens to effect a siege and by January Athens was suffering from a dreadful famine. Access to their fields and livestock having been denied them for several months, the Athenians could not hope to feed themselves, let alone the large garrison of Pontic soldiers with which they were encumbered. It is said that when they had devoured all their existing provisions, they proceeded to boil their sandals and leather flasks for soup. Despite all this suffering, the traitor Aristion conducted himself in a shamelessly irresponsible manner. There was no lack of food or drink at his table, and while the Athenians huddled together at night, sleepless in their hunger, the city echoed with the noise of Aristion's endless drunken feasts where he revelled, caroused and frolicked in his armour. So little did he care for the feelings of his people that he permitted the sacred lamp of the Goddess Athena to be extinguished for lack of oil. In spite of the suffering of the populace, life seemed to be one continual party for Aristion, and when the Chief Priestess of the Temple of Athena begged him for a bushel of wheat, Aristion laughed and sent her a bushel of pepper. When the Priests of the Temple arrived to beg him to take pity on the starving people by coming to terms with Sulla, Aristion howled with glee as his guards dispersed the priests with a volley of arrows.

It was Aristion's unfortunate sense of humour which finally brought about the fall of Athens. Early one winter morning Aristion caught sight of Sulla inspecting his armies outside the walls of Athens and exhibited himself to the Roman General by performing

2

a ludicrous dance on the walls of the Acropolis while shouting rude remarks about Sulla's repulsive appearance. This spectacle put Sulla in such a rage that he ordered his troops to an immediate attack and the assault was so violent and unexpected that it succeeded and Athens fell into Sulla's hands. Aristion and the Pontic garrison were quickly murdered by the people they had failed to protect, while Sulla encouraged his Roman soldiers in their rape and slaughter of the Athenians, too weak with famine to resist or escape. His wrath still not spent, Sulla ordered a similar surprise assault on Piraeus which also capitulated before the end of the day. The infuriated Roman dictator then commanded that every building and every fortification in Piraeus be levelled to the ground and his orders were carried out so thoroughly that the city was completely destroyed. Piraeus was not rebuilt until modern times and for two thousand years all that remained of this famous port was a mound of rubble and a ten-foot marble statue of a lion overlooking an empty harbour.

After conquering Athens and destroying Piraeus, Sulla proceeded to defeat the Pontic armies in Boeotia and to drive the enemy from Greece. In 84 B.C. he was forced to conclude a treaty with Mithridates in order to return to Rome as his rivals had regained control of the capital. During his three years in Greece, Sulla spent a large part of his time busily engaged in systematically looting the country of everything which appealed to his unrefined and flamboyant taste. There is no record of exactly what Sulla pillaged from Greece but it is known that his loot included not only gold and precious metals but large quantities of Greek paintings, statues, busts and inscribed stones as well as marble columns and architectural decorations from buildings.

On his return to Rome Sulla successfully defeated his rivals and once again became absolute master of the city and the Empire. It was at the beginning of 81 B.C. when he staged the famous triumph for his victories in the Mithridatic War and displayed his incredible quantity of spoils from Greece in a procession through Rome. For several days chariots and cartloads of ancient Greek sculpture were paraded through the streets of Rome to the amazement of the incredulous and terrified Romans. However Sulla did not live long to enjoy his power and possessions. In 78 B.C. this repellent and ruthless dictator died of pediculosis—an infestation of lice—and was solemnly conveyed to his funeral pyre behind a huge image of himself, moulded from frankincense and cinnamon.

Two thousand years after the mortal remains of this hideous tyrant were cremated in Rome, a crew of Greek sponge divers discovered a most unusual shipwreck off the coast of Africa which appeared to be connected with Sulla. Sponge diving is one of the few professions of ancient times which has survived throughout the centuries as the principal source of revenue for the peoples living on many of the infertile Aegean islands. When these divers eventually scavenged all the sponges from the seas around Greece they were forced to seek new areas to fish. They discovered that there were relatively shallow seas off the flat coast along certain sections of North Africa, particularly Tunisia, and that these seas have a long shelf covered by a thin layer of mud in which sponges flourish. They began to visit these North African sponge beds annually towards the end of the nineteenth century in their fleets of caiques, ships which in size, shape and equipment hardly differed from those which had sailed the Mediterranean in ancient times. It was the custom for each caique to single out one section of the coast as its private fishing ground and for this reason only one Greek caique regularly fished the seas off Mahdia, a small Tunisian fishing village in the gulf of Gabes, between Sousse and Sfax.

This particular caique arrived to fish its traditional area off Mahdia in the spring of 1907 equipped for the first time with modern diving gear, and they were therefore able to try fishing further from the shore than usual. This equipment enabled the divers to go deeper and remain longer on the bottom than in previous years, when they fished by the primitive method of holding a heavy stone to sink themselves and staying down as long as they could go without drawing breath.

Several days after they started fishing in this new area further from the shore, one of the divers announced that he had seen "a lot of big guns" on the bottom of the sea. The captain of the caique descended to investigate this curious report and found a large mound almost directly beneath the caique which had a number of barrel-like objects projecting from it. Scraping the mud from one of these "guns" he discovered that it was in fact a marble column. He then realized that this could be a shipwreck containing ancient marbles and became very excited, for seven years previously another caique from the Greek sponge diving fleet, driven off course to the barren island of Cerigotto off the south-eastern tip of the Peloponnese, had become famous and earned considerable wealth from its discovery of the wreck of an ancient ship carrying a cargo of marble and bronze statues of the Augustan period.

By working all day these divers were able to extract several fragments of broken pottery from the half-buried wreckage. At sunset they sailed to Mahdia, about an hour away from the diving site, and took these fragments to the Tunisian authorities. There was great excitement in Mahdia and the news reached the ears of Alfred Merlin, Director of Tunisian Antiquities, later to become Curator of the Greek and Roman Antiquities of the Louvre Museum. Merlin immediately recognized the possible importance of this wreck and accompanied the caique back to the site the following day. A few more exploratory dives left no doubt in Merlin's mind that this was the wreckage of a ship dating from Roman times whose cargo was, at least in part, one of art treasures. He was wildly enthusiastic and reported to the French press that: "Nothing comparable has come to light since Pompeii and Herculaneum".

Determined to procure the money and equipment necessary for a thorough investigation and salvage of what he now considered to be "his" shipwreck, Merlin succeeded in getting the assistance of the Maritime Prefect of Bizerta and several wealthy patrons of archaeology, as well as the promise of financial aid from the Tunisian government and several French governmental agencies. However these negotiations were not completed until September and they had to wait until the following spring to start their excavations as the winter seas off the North African coast are so turbulent as to preclude diving and underwater work.

Salvage operations on this wreck began in the spring of 1908 and continued through five summers. The crews of Greek caiques of the sponge diving fleet were almost exclusively employed as divers as they were the only men willing to work at such depths, although a French naval tug and tender stood by at all times to assist these caiques when necessary. As the site was some three miles from Mahdia Point and therefore outside the shelter of the harbour of Mahdia, these ships and divers were at the mercy of the strong winds and heavy seas which are frequent along this coast even in the summer months. On several occasions storms carried off the buoys marking the site which caused them the considerable trouble of relocating the wreck.

The centre of the site was a mound containing the "guns" which had been noticed by the original sponge divers at a depth of approximately one hundred and twenty feet. These "guns" turned out to be sixty marble columns neatly laid out in six rows and covering an area some thirty-five yards long and seventeen yards wide. There was a mass of marble fragments scattered around the periphery of this mound, including several capitals and bases of columns and a number of square blocks which had apparently come from buildings. There was also a profusion of broken earthenware mixed in with these architectural fragments, especially at the northern end of the site, and this broken earthenware was apparently all that remained of the pottery which had been on board the ship—amphorae, very few of which had remained intact, and receptacles of many different types which had been used to transport the oil, wine, water, food-stuffs and other provisions needed by the crew during the voyage. A few smaller marble columns, blocks, amphorae and five anchors were found under a separate layer of mud adjacent to the central mound.

The sixty marble columns proved to be so unwieldy and of so little archaeological value that it was decided to leave them on the bottom. However the salvagers had to shift them in order to get at the rest of the cargo, a very difficult and painstaking operation which took more than a year. Every time they disturbed the central mound, however slightly, the water became so clouded that the divers could not see what they were doing and they were only able to stay down in this "infernal cloud of black ooze and bubbles" for thirty to forty minutes at a time, groping in a churning mass of liquid sludge for objects which they could not see. Once they located an object which felt as if it might be interesting, it required an infinite amount of time and patience to secure it with ropes and hoist it to the surface. It was incredibly slow and often very discouraging work.

Once they shifted the marble columns from the mound they came upon a layer of rotten timber about eight inches thick which they assumed to be the remains of the deck on which the columns had been placed. When they cleared away this rotting timber they found a number of small bronze and marble sculptures along with fragments of ornaments for furniture which apparently had been stored in the hold of the ship. From the general pattern of the wreckage they were able to determine that the ship was a merchant sailing craft of a type which had been widely used in the Mediterranean as a cargo carrier by the Romans. It was a notoriously clumsy type of vessel and one that was difficult to manage in heavy seas. As one naval critic explained: "With her square canvas and excessive super-structure she was markedly inferior to her Greek and Phoenician forebears, but almost certainly her capacity was greater."

It seemed clear that this particular ship had met with a storm off Mahdia Point and too heavily laden with a cargo of marble, plunged straight to the bottom without breaking up or capsizing. All five anchors—including the heavy sheet anchor which was used only in cases of extreme danger—lay considerably outside the central mound of the wreck, along one side, which suggested that they had been dropped in a desperate effort to save the ship from foundering.

All of the objects salvaged from this wreck were taken to the Bardo Museum in Tunis, with the exception of two anchors, an Ionic capital and a nail which were subsequently salvaged and taken to France. The cargo consisted primarily of Greek sculpture in bronze and marble. The bronze works included a four-foot statue of Cupid, a small bust of Dionysus, two large cornices adorned with busts of Dionysus and Ariadne, several statuettes which had ap-parently been fashioned as decorations for furniture and a group of small comic statues which included two grotesque dancers, a clown with a huge head, a cupid and a satyr. The marble pieces were in very poor condition, having been so corroded by the sea, nibbled and bored by various types of marine life and encrusted with shell-fish that it was barely possible to discern their shapes. Aside from the sixty columns which were left to rest on the bottom of the sea, the marble works included what appeared to be a "bust of Aphro-dite, a small Pan, a Niobe, two Niobids, two satyrs, one youth, two torsos of young boys and several statuettes". The divers also brought up from the wreckage several bronze lamps, a bronze candelabra, a number of bronze ornaments for furniture, a few sections of a marble bas-relief and several inscribed marble slabs. In addition they salvaged bones of rabbits, sheep and pigs as well as a human skull.

Since the cargo was almost entirely composed of Greek sculpture Merlin, the archaeologist in charge of the salvage operations, felt that this ship must have sailed from Greece on her fatal journey, probably from the port of Piraeus. To substantiate this theory he cited the fact that they had found several marble slabs inscribed with decrees issued by the Paraloi, the crew of the sacred ship *Paralos* which was permanently anchored in Piraeus harbour, as well as several ingots of pig lead which could easily have come from the lead mines at Lavrium, near Piraeus. Furthermore, he argued, the two heavy bronze cornices adorned with the busts of Dionysus and Ariadne appeared to be trophies from the prow of a ship, and as such were likely to have originated from a port such as Piraeus.

Having established in his own mind that this ship of probable Roman origin had sailed from Piraeus, Merlin then attempted to ascertain the date of its last voyage by a careful examination of its cargo. He was considerably aided by the fact that the small bronze bust of Dionysus contained the name of its sculptor cut into the base: Boethus of Chalcedon, who was known to have lived during the late second century B.C. The presence of this sculpture in the wreckage therefore determined that the ship could not have sailed earlier than 150 B.C. When he invited several students of Greek architecture to see the salvaged cargo, they pronounced that the general artistic character of the architectural decorations, such as the unusual Ionic capitals and the capitals with griffon heads, were characteristic of architectural decorations in fashion in Greece at the end of the second and beginning of the first century B.C. They also pointed out that one small terracotta lamp had been found with its flaxen wick in a carbonized condition, thus proving that it had been in actual use during the voyage and not an item of cargo. Lamps of this particular type, according to these experts, were used in ancient Greece at the end of the second century B.C. Furthermore they added that although the twelve lead ingots were signed, three of these signatures did not include a cognomen or family name and cognomens were in regular use in Greece after 75 B.C. Merlin then consulted experts of naval history who pronounced that the huge six-ton anchors found in this wreck were commonly used by ships sailing the Mediterranean during the first century B.C.

Merlin and the other archaeologists involved in the salvage operations used all this relatively vague and flimsy evidence to pinpoint the date of the wreck of this ancient ship at 86 B.C., the year in which Lucius Cornelius Sulla had plundered Greece. Once they made up their minds that this shipwreck contained Sulla's loot, they dis-regarded any evidence which might disprove this theory and advanced arguments of the wildest sort to prove their point. They cited Pliny, the Roman historian, who reported Sulla as having ordered the columns of the Temple of Zeus in Athens to be transported to Rome for a sanctuary which he planned to build there and argued that the columns found in the Mahdia wreck were in fact these very columns. They quoted a story by the ancient writer Lucian which mentioned that a ship carrying Sulla's spoils had been sunk off Cape Maleas and claimed that the Mahdia wreck was in fact this very wreck—although Maleas is situated on the opposite side of the Mediterranean, almost one thousand miles from Mahdia. They also argued that:

> The very character of the cargo of the Mahdia wreck—art works of reasonably good value along with those of definitely mediocre worth—was typical of the taste of the Roman dictator . . . the statue of Cupid is very similar to a statue which Sulla is known to have had in his dining room and the odd collection of grotesque statuettes—the bronze buffoon of repulsive ugliness, the lump of a woman dancer with a trivial and sensual face and a shameless expression who seems to be fidgeting with reckless liveliness, and the ridiculous dwarf . . . all these are pieces which would have pleased a man who was outstandingly ugly himself, and who was given to the pleasures of the theatre. And most certainly Sulla, who had been labelled the New Dionysos in Greece, would have wanted a statue of Dionysos for his garden in Rome.

All this is certainly not convincing evidence and it is regrettable that these salvagers succumbed to the temptation to exaggerate the importance of their discovery by stating as fact that which could not be more than conjecture. The mystery of this wreck is likely to remain unsolved and no one will ever be able to state definitely whether or not the wreck found off Mahdia was one of Sulla's ships. Perhaps this is for the best—how it would have enraged Sulla to have his spoils displayed in a museum in Tunis, only twelve miles from Carthage, Rome's greatest rival.

Chapter II

THE SACK OF CONSTANTINOPLE

FOLLOWING the precedent which Sulla set, the Romans pillaged countless thousands of statues from Greece. The later Emperors spent huge sums on immense public monuments—temples and baths, aqueducts and markets, amphitheatres, stadiums and triumphal arches—and decorated these monuments of self-glorification with pillaged Greek sculpture. All too frequently they were sufficiently insensitive to the aesthetic beauty of a sculpture to remove the original head and substitute their own likeness, usually carved with greatly inferior craftsmanship and from poorer stone. Moreover the possession of Greek sculpture became the fashion amongst the Roman aristocracy and wealthy Roman villas became veritable museums of original Greek sculpture as well as of its copies, for clever artisans had developed a thriving business fabricating faked Greek sculpture. The quantity of original and faked Greek art found in the ruins of Italian cities such as Herculaneum testifies to the magnitude of this pillage of Greek sculpture by the Romans. In the city of Rome alone, at the height of the Empire, it is recorded that there were 3,785 bronze statues, 80 gilt statues, 22 equestrian statues, 2 colossi more than a hundred feet tall and uncounted thousands of marble statues publicly displayed, most of which were Greek.

Most of these sculptures did not stay in Rome but were moved to Byzantium by Constantine the Great when he transferred the capital of the Empire to this city. The shipment of this incredible quantity of ancient sculpture to the new capital of Constantinople was a project which involved vast expense and labour as well as fantastic feats of engineering in the dismantling, shipping and re-erecting of these massive and often fragile sculptures with the primitive means of transportation available in these times. The fact that Constantine went to such an immense trouble to move these sculptures indicates that he regarded them as symbols of Imperial wealth and power. But virtually all of this magnificent collection of ancient sculpture amassed in Constantinople by Constantine was destroyed by an army of French and Venetian Crusaders in 1204. It is one of the great ironies of history that these Crusaders, who set out with such a high spirit of idealism, failed to ever reach the Holy Land and accomplished instead the sordid destruction of the capital of a fellow Christian state and the almost total destruction of the greatest collection of Greek art ever assembled.

The Crusade began with the best intentions under the direction of Pope Innocent III who ascended the Papal throne at the age of thirty-five determined to recapture the Holy Land for the Christian world. He felt that this aim could best be accomplished by an expedition led by feudal barons whom he assumed would be responsive to the biddings of the Church rather than Kings whom experience had shown to be so jealous of their rights and powers that they had reduced the previous Crusades to chaos. The Fourth Crusade was therefore composed of feudal barons from Northern Europe including Tibald, Count of Champagne and his cousin Louis, Count of Blois, as well as Baldwin, Count of Flanders and his brother Henry, Count of Hainaut. It was a Crusade noted for the youth of its principal participants, many of whom were still in their twenties. These young feudal barons pledged not only themselves but the vassals who served them, and in fact a large proportion of the soldiers of this expedition were French peasants who had been pledged to go to the Holy Land without their consent, in accordance with the nature of the feudal system. Most were men from the provinces of Champagne and Burgundy, although there were also large contingents from Flanders and Northern Germany.

It was decided to transport these men by sea to the Holy Land rather than to risk the delay and dangers of an overland trek of several thousand miles by horse and by foot to Jerusalem. The Republic of Venice agreed to provide the necessary ships and provisions and it was agreed that the cost of this fleet would be met by contributions from all the participants in the expedition, according to their feudal rank. The Crusaders began to congregate in Venice during the late spring of 1202 and were quartered on the small island of the Lido in the bay. By June this island had become so crowded that living conditions for the knights and their vassals were exceedingly difficult. But less than half of the expected number of Crusaders arrived in Venice and as a result, they had less than half of the necessary funds to pay for the ships which lay ready and waiting at anchor outside the arsenal of Venice. Once it became apparent that the absentees were definitely not coming to the rendezvous, the Crusaders approached the Doge of Venice to explain their predicament. The blind octogenarian Doge refused to discuss the matter and stated that he would not deliver them a single ship until they paid him the full amount which had been stipulated at the time of the original agreement. The Crusaders managed to augment their treasury by additional contributions but they still fell far short of the required sum. As the summer wore on, conditions on the Lido became appalling. There was an acute scarcity of all provisions and this fact plus the unbearable heat and shocking sanitary conditions brewed such sickness and misery that morale steadily declined. By late August it was evident that a large-scale desertion of Crusaders was going to occur at the first opportunity.

It was at this critical and opportune moment that the Doge of Venice proposed his compromise. He informed the Crusaders that he would deliver the ships to them for the sum which they had in their treasury and would even strengthen the expedition by sending a contingent of manned Venetian galleys with them to the Holy Land, on condition that they would first accompany the Venetians on a brief expedition to Dalmatia, a province which had recently refused to acknowledge its homage to Venice. The Crusaders were faced with no real alternative but to accept the Doge's offer. The pact was sealed and orders given to outfit and load the ships.

The departure of this expedition from Venice was a magnificent spectacle. Fifty Venetian galleys headed the armada, behind the bright red galley of the blind Doge, whose throne had been placed under an ornate vermilion tent on the main deck. (Venice was a long-standing enemy of Papal expansion and the Doge's decision to accompany the Crusade personally marked the end of Innocent III's control of this expedition.) One hundred and sixty large "nefs"

followed the galleys filled with the bulk of the Crusading armies
and decorated with a glittering display of the shields of the knights.
Several hundred "hussiers" came next with the Crusaders' horses
and "engines of war" for which these ships had been especially
constructed with hinged bows that opened to form landing and
loading platforms. As the Crusaders shouted themselves hoarse,
trumpets blew, drums sounded and the priests gathered on the stern
castles of the ships to chant the "Veni Creator Spiritus".

When they arrived at Zara, the capital of Dalmatia, they found it
necessary to assault and defeat this city in order to re-establish
Venetian rule. Following the capitulation of Zara, the Crusading
armies, both Venetian and French, entered the defeated city to
indulge in an unrestrained orgy of slaughter, rape and pillage. This
sordid treatment of a Christian city and the completely undisci-
plined and violent behaviour of the French Crusaders was undoubtedly partly a reaction to the frustration and deprivations which
they had suffered the previous summer on the Lido although it is
probable that many of the uneducated peasants from France mistook Zara for Jerusalem.

The Crusaders then decided to remain in Zara until spring in
order to avoid risking the loss or damage of their ships during the
violent storms to which the eastern Mediterranean and Aegean Seas
are liable in winter. As they were preparing to leave Zara the following March they were joined by a young Byzantine prince, Alexis,
who claimed that he and his father, the Emperor Isaac, had been
dethroned and incarcerated in the dungeons of Constantinople by
a usurper. Alexis had finally managed to escape, determined to seek
assistance to regain his throne and it was for this reason that he had
sought out the Crusaders. He announced that the usurper only
enjoyed the support of a limited part of the population of Constantinople and asked of the Crusaders only that they escort him back to
the gates of the city as the very sight of their superior forces would
undoubtedly force the usurper to capitulate immediately. Alexis
added that his father, Isaac, had been blinded in prison and this
blindness by tradition invalidated him from holding the throne so
that he, Alexis, was now the legitimate Emperor.

Prince Alexis tempted the Crusaders with magnificent promises.
If they would agree to assist him to regain his throne of Byzantium,
he agreed to provide them with a fabulous sum of gold, whatever

provisions they required and a large contingent of Byzantine soldiers to assist in their conquest and subsequent garrisoning of the Holy Land. As a further inducement, he undertook to place the Greek Orthodox Church in subservience to the Pope, thus ending one of the major divisions of Christendom.

These promises were sufficient to persuade the Crusaders. Alexis' proposal was strongly supported by the Doge of Venice who was fully alive to the commercial possibility of a Byzantine Emperor who owed his throne to Venetian assistance and who would therefore assist Venice to oust Pisa and Genoa from the valuable commerce of Constantinople. The French feudal barons, on the other hand, whose treasury was now virtually bankrupt, saw in Alexis' plan the possibility of remounting the Crusade enriched not only by Byzantine gold but with Byzantine military assistance, while the more religious supporters were attracted by the promise of a Roman controlled church. The proposal was strongly opposed by the Pope when he learned of it, on the grounds that an expedition to Constantinople could only serve to further delay their arrival in Jerusalem, but the Crusaders were no longer responsive to commands from Rome.

The compact between Alexis and the Crusaders was quickly sealed and the expedition left Zara in April of 1203—headed for Constantinople. They sighted their destination in July and were astounded, for although the Byzantine Empire had long since passed its prime, Constantinople had remained the largest and richest city of the entire mediaeval world. When Constantine the Great had taken his decision to move the capital of the Roman Empire to the East in A.D. 326—a decision based not only on personal preference but on the economic and political history of the declining Empire— he had chosen a site which combined a proximity to the frontiers of the Empire with a control of the wealthy Black Sea trade. The garrison town of Byzantium which he selected was an almost impregnable fortress, being surrounded on the three sides by water with only a narrow neck of land as its defensible frontier and in fact Constantinople subsequently proved to be the most siege resistant city in history. Furthermore the Bay of the Golden Horn provided an excellent anchorage where ships were sheltered from all prevailing winds so that when the Crusaders arrived, almost a thousand years after the city's foundation, Constantinople still controlled the bulk of the trade between East and West.

The Crusaders stared incredulously at Constantinople, whose formidable walls had been built on the orders of Constantine himself at the cost of some sixty thousand pounds weight of gold. Constantine had imported a population of some half a million people to populate his capital, for whom he had constructed, in the space of a decade:

> . . . a capital school of learning, a circus, two theatres, eight public and one hundred and fifty-three private baths, fifty-two markets, five granaries, eight aqueducts, four halls, two pagan temples, fourteen churches, fourteen palaces, and four thousand three hundred and eighty-three fancy houses.

The subsequent growth and prosperity of the city exceeded even Constantine's wildest dreams and the Crusaders, as they sailed past the city walls, could not believe that such a city was possible. They crowded on deck to gape at the thousands of wealthy houses built on terraces, the huge palaces, the vast cathedrals with their gilded domes, and last but not least, at the many monuments and forests of sculpture in marble and bronze which Constantine had brought to lavishly adorn his capital. According to Cedrenus, a historian of Constantine's time:

> Statues were to be found everywhere in great abundance . . . the trophies of memorable wars, the objects of religious veneration, the statues of Greek gods and heroes, of the sages and poets of ancient times filled the city . . . nothing seemed wanting except the souls of the illustrious men whom these admirable monuments were intended to represent.

Constantinople was in fact littered with ancient statues, mostly Greek. The porticoes which extended the length of the Forum were thick with statues on every side, including a group of Muses from Helicon, and the centre contained a huge column which had been transported with great difficulty from Delphi in Greece. On the summit of this porphyry column there stood a colossal bronze statue of Apollo by Phidias, brought from Athens, whose original head had been removed in order to substitute a bronze likeness of Constantine. The Hippodrome which Constantine built for the circus games was filled with other statues—the top of the seats was virtually solid with statues and there were many others between the goals, under the arcades, above the stalls and even under the seats, several hundreds in all, coming from all parts of the Greek and Roman world. The holy tripod of Delphi, reputed to be the source of the famous oracle of Delphi, was placed in the centre of the Hippodrome while the several palaces built by Constantine and his successors were also decorated with statues and the public and private baths contained scores of bronze sculptures. In front of the first church of St. Sophia which Constantine erected there was a veritable forest of more than four hundred statues, including the Pythian Apollo, the Simnthian Apollo, the Samian Hera, the Olympian Zeus, the Pallas of Lindos, the Zeus of Dodona, the four bronze horses of Rome and Phidias' immense bronze statue of Athena from the Acropolis in Athens. Many of these statues had been set on new pedestals, some had been given new titles and a few new heads but most of them had survived otherwise unaltered until 1204.

When the Crusaders sailed past this fabulous city and anchored at nearby Chalcedon, they were expecting to be immediately greeted by the supporters of Prince Alexis whom the young Prince had so often described as eagerly awaiting his return. However not one solitary Byzantine noble emerged from the capital to address them. After a few days of fruitless waiting, they moved their ships to a better anchorage at Scutari and outfitted ten galleys which they sailed along the city walls, with Prince Alexis prominently displayed on the deck of the leading galley. When this gambit failed to evoke a response from the friends of the Prince, the Crusaders called a conference to discuss their situation. They had to face the fact that they had insufficient provisions to permit them to remain for any length of time outside Constantinople waiting for the Byzantine decision to rally to the support of Prince Alexis. On the other hand they were most reluctant to leave Constantinople and proceed to the Holy Land without having secured the supplies, men and gold which Alexis had promised them. After days of heated debate, the leaders of the Crusade decided on a dangerous course of action—to feint an assault on Constantinople with the hope that this would frighten the Byzantines to revolt against the usurper and take back Prince Alexis. They did not actually intend to attack the city at this stage of events and their elaborate preparations to do so were intended merely as a bluff.

In accordance with this plan the Crusaders brought their fleet inside the Bay of the Golden Horn and ranged their armies, seven battalions strong, outside the north-western walls of Constantinople. Trumpets blew and cymbals crashed and the Crusaders armed every man who could stand, including the cooks who were covered with quilted mattresses and advanced with sticks, stones and cooking pots. Fortunately for the Crusaders, who were then subsisting on minimum rations of bread and water, their colossal bluff succeeded. A small party of Byzantine nobles came out from the city to invite Prince Alexis to return and explained that the usurper had fled Constantinople, taking with him the Imperial Jewels, one thousand pounds weight of gold and his favourite daughter.

Alexis was thus restored to his throne but subsequent events did not follow the course which the Crusaders had anticipated. The Byzantines mistrusted Alexis whom they considered as a "mere youth, having neither character, nor knowledge of affairs", and having unearthed his father, the blind Isaac, from the dungeons of Constantinople, they insisted that father and son be crowned Co-Emperors. The Crusaders were somewhat uneasy at this unexpected development as Isaac had shown himself in the past to be bitterly opposed to the Catholic West. However they enjoyed the provisions which Alexis sent to their camp and settled down to wait for the gold which the Prince had promised them.

Days passed and then weeks but no gold was forthcoming. Alexis made the excuse that the state treasuries had been emptied by the absconding usurper and that he was therefore forced to raise the sum by various means of taxation. The Crusaders continued to wait, more and more distressed by reports that the old Emperor, Isaac, was determined not to recognize his son's commitments to the "uncouth barbarians of the West" and that Alexis' attempts to tax the wealthy and the Church were raising not gold but a violent reaction of resentment. Winter came and there was still no solution in sight. Just before Christmas there was a serious riot in Constantinople of the Byzantine populace, enraged by the burden of providing food for the foreign armies encamped outside their walls and by Alexis' taxes. A thirty-foot ancient bronze statue of Athena was destroyed by the mob during these riots because its right arm "pointed to the West from whence the barbarians had come". This statue was in fact the famous sculpture by Phidias which had for-

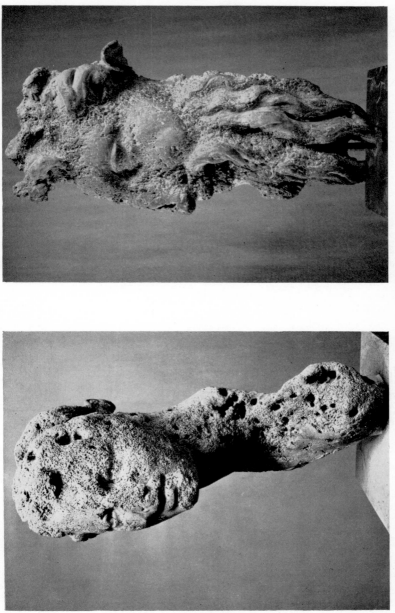

Sculptures found off Mahdia in 1908.

Marmora Arundeliana at Oxford. (From Ackermann: *History of the University of Oxford*.)

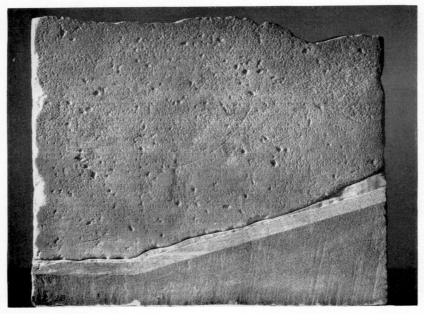

"Marmor Parium" carrying an inscription (not visible in the photograph) listing principal events in Greece for 1,318 years up to 245 B.C.

merly stood on the Acropolis of Athens, visible on a clear day to ships rounding the Cape of Sounion. It was the first of countless hundreds of priceless classical sculptures to be destroyed as a result of the Fourth Crusade.

Shortly after this riot Alexis learned of a plot to dethrone him and in his fright turned for assistance to a powerful Byzantine noble, Murzuphle, who responded by throwing both Alexis and Isaac in prison and proclaiming himself Emperor of Byzantium. One of his first acts as Emperor was to poison Isaac and strangle Alexis, after which he turned his energies to rebuilding the armies of the Empire which his predecessors had sadly neglected.

The Crusaders were horrified when they learned of these events and realized that they could no longer hope to receive the money, soldiers and supplies for which they had been waiting so long. On the other hand they knew that it would be courting disaster to embark on the rest of their journey to the Holy Land in mid-winter without provisions or funds. It was also apparent to them that the new Emperor, Murzuphle, was strengthening the Byzantine armies with the intention of attacking them and that it was only a matter of time before he would muster a sufficient force to defeat them. They therefore decided that the only course left open was for them to attack first. It was a dangerous plan—Constantinople had never been taken by assault since its foundation by Constantine the Great —but it carried the force of a decision taken in anger. The Crusaders later rationalized their actions by arguing that the ruling Byzantine hierarchy was so thoroughly dishonest and corrupt that the Christian world could only benefit from its destruction and that, furthermore, a Western controlled Byzantium would do more in the long run to ensure permanent Christian control in the Holy Land than their own immediate presence in Jerusalem. When they actually decided to attack, however, the Crusaders were not reasoning but raging. Two long years had passed since they had gathered in Venice full of ideals and enthusiasm for liberating Jerusalem and the wrath resulting from the frustration of their purpose was now directed against the Byzantines—"a dishonest, treacherous, corrupt, heretical, effeminate, weak and degenerate people"—who certainly didn't deserve their wealth.

Confident of victory, the Crusaders drew up an agreement for the division of the Byzantine Empire amongst themselves and issued stern warnings on the "Evils of Unchristian Behaviour". Each Crusader was required to take an oath that:

> He would bring all spoils to a specified centre, that he would not use force with any woman or despoil her of any garment, that he would not lay hands on any monk or priest unless it be in self-defence and that he would not break into any church or monastery.

The Crusaders then attacked Constantinople. The first assault failed but the second succeeded after a small party of French soldiers crawled through an old drainage hole and opened one of the city gates from within. Victory was declared at sunset on the twelfth of April, 1204, when the Emperor Murzuphle was seen fleeing the city through the fabled Golden Gate, which by tradition was opened only to receive an emperor returning from victory in his chariot of gold. The Crusaders' capture of Constantinople was followed by one of the most appalling ravages of a city in the history of warfare. For more than a week fifty thousand enraged Crusading soldiers ran wild through the streets of the Byzantine capital pillaging, murdering, raping and destroying everything in their path while a fire raged which consumed "more houses than there were to be found in the three largest cities of France". The howling mobs snatched up everything that glittered and destroyed whatever they could not carry, slaughtering and raping the Byzantines who tried to stop them. Neither palaces nor churches, nor monasteries nor libraries were spared, while the wounded and the dying lay neglected in the streets.

Both French and Byzantine reports agree on the frightful destruction perpetrated by these French and Venetian rioters who, in addition to their slaughter of the Byzantine population and pillage of the wealth for which this city was famous, accomplished the most wanton and disastrous destruction of the vast collection of ancient sculpture which Constantine the Great and his successors had imported to adorn their capital. "From the very commencement," wrote one Byzantine historian, "they displayed all their national covetousness and struck out a new system of rapine which surpassed all the former despoilers of cities." Mobs ransacked the great Byzantine palaces, smashing the chandeliers for their silver, chiselling the gold and silver from the columns, gouging the gilt from the walls, tearing apart the inlaid furniture to retrieve their jewels. They spared not one room out of the five hundred rooms of the Bucoleon Palace and the three hundred rooms of the Blachernae Palace. Other mobs pillaged the churches without fear of Divine Reprisal, for they considered the Byzantines as heretics. "The western barbarians", moaned Nicetas Chionates, brother of the Bishop of Athens, "spared neither the living nor the dead, but began with God and His servants." The Byzantines regarded their Emperors as Divine and were therefore horrified when the Crusaders sacked the Imperial tombs in the Heroum and Church of the Holy Apostles and:

> Sacrilegiously laid their hands upon every golden ornament and every chalice which had been studded with pearls and precious stones. They gazed with admiration at the body of Justinian, which after so many centuries exhibited no mark of decay, but they refrained not from appropriating to themselves the sepulchral ornaments.

The sack of the cathedral of St. Sophia was so extensive that the Crusaders brought horses and mules into the main body of the church in order to cart off their hoard of sacred vessels, silver chalices, chandeliers, pieces of bronze doors and even the gold and silver which had adorned the Patriarchal throne. They smashed the altar in order to extract its rubies and diamonds and ripped the veil of the sanctuary in order to remove its golden border. As a background to this scene, peasants from Champagne and Burgundy swung from the silken hangings and trampled the age-old parchment gospels while a prostitute entertained them by sitting on the remains of the Patriarchal throne singing lewd French songs.

As the rioting continued the Papal emissaries who accompanied the Crusaders threatened excommunication but few Crusaders heeded this warning. Many felt that their considerable plunder of religious treasures would more than compensate for their sins. More than three hundred relics were sent to France after the sack of Constantinople including the head of Saint Anne which was sent by Count Louis of Blois to the cathedral of Chartres, the Veil of the Virgin which was sent by Archbishop Nivelon to Notre Dame of Soissons and a section of the Belt of the Virgin, sent by Robert of Clery to the Abbey of Borbie. Other relics sent to France included many Pieces of the Cross, innumerable Sections of the Cloth, several

Vials of His Blood and at least ten Authentic Heads of John the Baptist. In addition, the treasury of St. Mark's Cathedral in Venice is filled with relics from Constantinople.

The rioters were certainly not restrained by their feudal overlords who, far from feeling any compulsion to control their men, were themselves actively engaged in plunder. There is no record of what the knights took for themselves but certainly it was well over and above what they declared and deposited in the centres set up for receiving official plunder. According to Villehardouin, a French witness, no one could count the value of the loot brought to these centres in the form of gold and silver, plate and jewels, samite and silks and garments of fur, vair, silver-grey and ermine, adding that "never since the world was created, had so much been taken in a city". This loot was divided according to the agreement: three-eighths to the French, three-eighths to the Venetians and two-eighths reserved for the future Latin Emperor of Byzantium, to be chosen by the Crusaders.

It is a great pity that the feudal barons did not try to restrain the rioters who were smashing ancient marble statues for their amusement and dismantling ancient bronze sculptures with the intention of melting them down for the value of the metal which they contained. There is no longer any doubt that these rioters destroyed most of the finest works of ancient Greek sculpture. One of the earliest English Ambassadors to Constantinople, Sir Thomas Roe, found a number of manuscripts in this city containing the works of the thirteenth-century Byzantine historian, Nicetas Chionates, which he sent back to England in 1628. These manuscripts were deposited in the Bodleian Library at Oxford and were not translated into English until the nineteenth century when it was discovered that one of them contained a list of some of the best ancient sculptures which were destroyed during the riots of April, 1204. The account is shocking. Chionates describes how the mobs of angry Crusaders broke up the colossal bronze statue of "Apollo" by Phidias which had stood in the Forum of Constantine, a sculpture so immense that "four oxen could scarcely draw its head to the furnace" and then relates how they turned to dismantling "The Shepherd of Ida" which stood with "Venus" in a scene representing "the presentation of the Golden Apple of Discord". He recounts that the rioters next brought down the "Four-sided Monument of

Brass" whose height "rivalled the loftiest pillars in the whole city":

> On whose sides were represented birds pouring forth their vernal
> melody, the ploughman's toils, the shepherd's relaxations, the very
> bleating of the sheep, the frisking of the lambs. The sea itself was en-
> graven and multitudes of fish were beheld, some in the act of being
> taken, others overpowering the nets and again dashing into the deep.
> In another section a troop of naked Cupids were sporting, pelting
> apples at each other whilst laughter shook their sides. The monument
> itself terminated in a pyramid on whose apex stood a female figure
> which turned at the slightest impulse of the air and hence was denomi-
> nated as "The Hand Maid of the Winds".

"The Crusaders", wrote Chionates, "had no love of what was
beautiful but coined art into money, exchanging what was precious
for what was vile." His list concerns only bronze sculptures and he
does not catalogue the immense quantity of marble statuary which
the rioters destroyed in the Hippodrome, the Forum and the square
of St. Sophia. The sculptures which Chionates mentions include
the "Equestrian Figure of the Forum" which contained a sacred
image within the horse's hoof, the "Hercules Trihesperus" of
Lysippus—"a sculpture so immense that its thumb was equal to
the waist and its leg to the size of an entire man", "The Ass Loaded
and the Ass Driver Following", "The Hyaena", "The She-Wolf",
"The Man Wrestling with the Lion", "The River Horse of the
Nile", "The Elephant Shaking his Proboscis", "The Sphinxes",
"The Unbitted Steed", "The Brazen Eagle" of Apollonios Tyaneus
with outstretched wings that served as a sundial, "Scylla and her
Group", "The Victorious Charioteers" and "The Basilisk and the
Asp". Chionates particularly lamented the destruction of the statue
of Helen which he felt indicated the Crusaders' abysmal lack of
culture:

> What shall I say of the statue of Helen? How shall I describe the
> white-armed daughter of Tyndarus with her taper neck and well-
> turned ankles? . . . Did she soften these barbarians? Did she subdue
> these iron-hearted? No, verily! . . . yet Venus though cast in bronze
> seemed fresh as the descending dew. Her swimming eyes provoked
> love. Her lips, like a rose-bud, were just opening as if to speak and a
> grateful smile met and enraptured the beholder . . . But, O Helen,
> where were your irresistible philtres? Why did you not employ them?

And he added, with great bitterness:

> Those verses which Homer sang in thy praise, O beauteous Helen,
> were in vain addressed to illiterate barbarians, ignorant even of the very
> alphabet.

In fact there were some Crusaders who admired the history of
ancient Greece and appreciated the beauty of ancient Greek sculpture, although those who sought to preserve rather than to destroy
were unfortunately the rare exceptions. A few Venetians sent works
of ancient Greek sculpture back to Venice and several busts, marble
slabs, sections of columns and capitals were incorporated at this
time into the structure of St. Mark's Cathedral in Venice. The best
known of the Venetian spoils resulting from this sack of Constantinople are the four bronze horses which today adorn the façade of
St. Mark's. These horses have an extraordinary history as symbols
of victorious conquest. They were originally brought from Greece
to Rome by Julius Caesar, to be placed on top of his triumphal arch
in the Roman capital and they were later displayed on top of the
triumphal arches of Nero, Domitian and finally of Trajan. Constantine removed them to Constantinople and the Venetian Crusaders
sent them to Venice. Napoleon took them to Paris to adorn his
triumphal Carrousel and they were restored to Venice after Waterloo. At the beginning of every major European war since this time
these horses have been carefully taken down from the façade of St.
Mark's and hidden away.

Unfortunately the Crusaders spared only a few works from Constantine's magnificent collection of ancient sculpture. One can only
estimate the extent of their destruction of ancient art by comparing
the descriptions of ancient sculpture displayed in Constantinople
during the twelfth century with the pitifully few works which have
survived. The discrepancy is appalling. A fragment of the bronze
tripod from Delphi remains as a forlorn relic in front of the Mosque
of Sultan Ahmet and there is a mutilated fragment of the porphyry
column which once held the "Apollo" of Phidias near the University
of Istanbul. The forest of statues in front of St. Sophia have vanished
together with those of the Hippodrome and the Forum.

The Crusaders never went on to the Holy Land. They were ousted
from Constantinople after a brief rule of fifty years although one

group of French Crusaders remained in control of the Greek Peloponnese for over a century and the Venetian occupation of a number of Greek islands continued up until the fifteenth century. The capture of Constantinople by the Fourth Crusade did not in any way benefit the cause of Christendom in the Holy Land but on the contrary, by seriously weakening the Byzantine Empire, definitely assisted the later Moslem conquests of the Near East and south-eastern Europe. The sack of Constantinople was certainly not justi-fied by future events and in fact the only real benefit resulting from this appalling pillage was the discovery and removal to the West of a great quantity of manuscripts containing the works of forgotten ancient writers as these manuscripts played an important role in the development of the Renaissance. Ironically, it was as a result of the renewed interest in the ancient world during the Renaissance that Europeans came to regret the careless destruction of ancient sculpture by their enraged ancestors.

On the other hand, many of the ancient monuments which Con-stantine the Great left behind in Rome survived, while those which he built in Constantinople were destroyed. This phenomena was due to the curious fact that several decades before the fall of Rome to the Gothic tribes, a Roman ruler levied a special tax on pimps and prostitutes of both sexes in order to create a fund for the repair of ancient monuments. In this way were preserved for posterity such monuments as the Theatre of Marcellus, the Circus Maximus, the Stadium in the Campus Martius and even the Colosseum.

Chapter III

THE FAVOURITES OF JAMES I

GUNPOWDER was introduced into Europe a few decades after the knights of the Fourth Crusade had conquered and sacked Constantinople and in the centuries that followed uncounted thousands of ancient bronze sculptures from all parts of the Hellenic world were melted down by Christians and Moslems alike to make cannon. During the same period an even greater number of ancient marble statues were broken up for the lime burners' kilns. Only with the advent of the Renaissance did the people of Europe come gradually to appreciate the beauty of ancient sculpture and seek to preserve rather than to destroy it.

The Renaissance passion for collecting ancient Greek and Roman sculpture began to manifest itself during the last decades of the fifteenth century in Rome. Pope Sixtus IV gathered together in the Capitol a large quantity of ancient sculpture which had previously been scattered in and about the city and in 1471 he donated this valuable collection to the people of Rome. A few years later Pope Julius II established the Belvedere Court collection of ancient art in the summer palace of the Vatican. A number of powerful Cardinals and representatives of the great Italian families of Rome and Florence were quick to take up this fashion for ancient statuary and in many instances they financed private excavations of ancient ruins in order to obtain new and valuable items for their collections. A strong ecclesiastical reaction against graven images occurred during the sixteenth century which resulted not only in the end of Papal collecting but in the closure of the Belvedere Court. However this reaction did not dampen the enthusiasm of the collecting Cardinals and in fact one of the finest collections of ancient sculpture ever assembled—over three hundred works, many of them of very considerable merit—was amassed by Cardinal Ludovico Ludovisi at this time.

By the middle of the sixteenth century the passion for owning ancient sculpture had spread from Rome to Venice, Paris, Madrid, Munich and Prague. When the wealthy Roman families became impoverished during the later Renaissance they sought to sell their inherited collections to this expanding market as a means of bettering their financial condition. The Giustiniani family were the first to sell and the Chigi and Albani were quick to follow. In the beginning the courts of Madrid and Dresden were the principal buyers of this ancient sculpture but wealthy Englishmen soon entered the field. The fashion for owning ancient art took hold in England at the beginning of the seventeenth century, during the reign of James I, amongst the young men who were regarded as royal favourites of this unfortunate Stuart monarch. One of these favourites who became deeply involved with this passion for collecting was Thomas Howard, Earl of Arundel.

Unlike most of the other favourites of James I, Thomas Howard was certainly not handsome nor "beautiful". He was described by a contemporary as being "tall of stature and grave of countenance, with a long face, large black piercing eyes, a hooked nose, a beard which was thin of hair and cheeks which were covered with warts and moles".

Moreover, his manner was so brusque and cold that few men other than the King cared for his company and he was frequently depicted in the following terms: "Arundel is a snob who is not loved at all, nor cares for the affections of men"; and "Arundel prefers to let the Common People know their Distance and Due Observation."

Thomas Howard came of an old Norfolk Catholic family which had suffered reverses during the reign of the Tudors. His grandfather had been executed for attempting to assist the imprisoned Mary Queen of Scots to escape and his father, in his turn involved in the Catholic intrigues, had been committed to the Tower where he subsequently died. It was at this juncture that Elizabeth I had

deprived the Howards of their titles and most of their estates, so
that Howard and his sister were brought up by their ardent Catholic
mother in relatively straightened circumstances, imbued with the
belief that they had been unjustly dispossessed of their rightful
position in English society.

Howard was only eighteen when James I assumed the throne of
England but he was mature enough to recognize that this presented
him with an opportunity to regain the Howard honours and estates.
He applied himself diligently to the court and person of the new
monarch who, in his vanity, appreciated the attentions showered on
him by an English youth. Howard pointed out that his family had
suffered deprivations because of their support of James I's mother,
Mary Queen of Scots, and requested that this injustice should be
rectified. The King responded by restoring a large part of his family
titles and estates and appointing Howard as companion to the royal
heir, Prince Henry.

In 1606 Howard, now the Earl of Arundel, married the daughter
of the Earl of Shrewsbury and his first son, born a year later, was
christened James by the King himself. His second son, born in 1608,
was named Henry in honour of the Prince. It was at this time that
Arundel felt himself threatened by tuberculosis, which had taken
the life of his sister, and sought out the milder climate of Italy as a
cure. He spent several months in Italy after his second son's birth
and returned there for a longer visit in 1612. His second sojourn
in Italy was abruptly terminated when he received the news that the
heir to the throne, Prince Henry, had succumbed to a fever, and he
hastened back to England to console the King and ensure his continued favour in the court. In this he was successful and when James I
arranged the marriage of his daughter Elizabeth to a German prince,
Arundel and his wife received the honour of being among those
selected to escort the young Princess to her new home. The Arundels
and some of the other members of this party who escorted the
Princess to Germany proceeded afterwards on an extended tour of
Italy. In a very leisurely fashion they visited Venice, Padua, Florence
and Rome and one member of their party was Inigo Jones, later to
become famous as an architect but who then held the appointment
of designer for the theatrical masques of the court. Lady Arundel
was an enthusiastic patron of the theatre and frequently travelled
with a suite of private entertainers, including a dwarf and a jester.

It was apparently at her request that Inigo Jones was chosen to accompany them on this tour.

Inigo Jones took this opportunity to study assiduously Italian art and architecture, particularly that of Palladio, and it is probable that his enthusiasm for the works which they saw inspired Arundel to become interested in collecting paintings and sculpture. Collecting works of art was just beginning to become fashionable among the members of the English court at this time. The recently deceased Prince Henry had himself gathered a small collection consisting of eighteen small ancient sculptures as well as an assortment of ancient coins and jewels and the Earl of Somerset had managed to accumulate a considerable collection of paintings before his downfall as a favourite of the King. The idea of possessing unusual works of art appealed to Arundel's snobbish instincts and he decided to take advantage of Inigo Jones's knowledge of artistic merit to secure for himself some valuable items during this tour of Italy. Arundel—or more accurately his wife—had a considerable fortune, a prerequisite for any successful collector, and on Inigo Jones's advice they purchased many paintings and several ancient sculptures in Italy. At the end of their tour Inigo Jones made arrangements with several Italian art dealers to act as purchasers of worth-while paintings and sculpture for Arundel's growing collection, so that Arundel returned to England in 1615 with a reputation as a "collector". James I presented him with the paintings which had belonged to the ill-starred former favourite, the Earl of Somerset, and this sizeable addition to his purchases in Italy permitted Arundel to set himself up as the foremost collector in England at this time. His enemies, of whom he had many, criticized his motives in forming this collection and commented that he had not the slightest appreciation of the beauty or aesthetic value of the items which he bought. Clarendon, in his *History of the Rebellion*, describes Arundel as:

being willing to be thought a scholar and to understand the most mysterious parts of antiquity because he made a wonderful and costly purchase of excellent statues whilst he was in Italy and in Rome . . . whereas in truth he was only able to buy them, never to understand them . . . and moreover his expenses were without any measure, and always exceeded very much his revenue.

Arundel was unperturbed and in fact flattered by this criticism. On Christmas Day in 1616 he renounced his Catholic upbringing to become a member of the Church of England in a move which seems to have been motivated by reasons of social expediency rather than moral conviction. As a result, he now felt himself completely secure in his position in the court of James I but in truth he was not. Not only did Prince Charles, the heir to the throne, have little use or respect for his dead brother's snobbish mentor, but a new face had made its appearance in the King's entourage—George Villiers, born the son of a kitchen maid and endowed with "remarkable beauty, gracefulness and becommingnesse of person", had captured the fancy of the ageing, debauched monarch. James I became so completely besotted over Villiers whom he created Viscount Villiers in 1616, Earl of Buckingham in 1617 and Duke of Buckingham in 1623, that he once informed Parliament:

> I, James, am neither a god nor an angel, but a man like any other. Therefore I act like a man, and confess to loving those dear to me more than anyone else, and more than you who are here assembled. You may be sure that I love the Earl of Buckingham more than anyone else. I wish to speak on my own behalf, and not to have it thought to be a defect. Jesus Christ did the same, and therefore I cannot be blamed. Christ had His John, and I have my George.

As Buckingham rose in royal favour, Arundel declined and quite naturally these two men detested one another. As long as James I was alive Arundel remained ostensibly "in favour" and the monarch sought to assuage the wounded pride of his favourite by reinstating him in the post of Earl Marshal of England, a dignity which had been hereditary in the Howard family until revoked by Elizabeth I. In his turn, Arundel attempted to demonstrate his cultural superiority to the "common Duke of Buckingham" by enlarging his artistic collection and in 1621 hired Sir Thomas Roe, Ambassador to the Ottoman Court, as his agent for the purchase of ancient Greek sculpture in the Levant. Sir Thomas Roe had come under the patronage first of Prince Henry and subsequently of Arundel who secured him a knighthood and the appointment as Ambassador to the Court of Jehângîr, the Mogul Emperor of Hindustan. When Roe returned to England in 1620, Arundel was instrumental in securing him his next appointment as Ambassador to the Ottoman

Court on condition that he "look for treasures of antiquity, works of art and manuscripts in those partes of the world" and purchase any items which he felt to be worthy of Arundel's collection. Roe agreed to "do this bidding and look back on antiquity even though my job is the other end of the circle, to attend to new things" and he assured his patron that he was himself "a lover of such virtues, although no great connoisseur of the quarry and stone business".

As soon as he was settled in Constantinople, Roe made inquiries concerning the places which were most likely to contain any ancient ruins of value and sent Arundel an account of the results of his investigations. He reported to his patron that he had ordered the various British consular agents in the Mediterranean to search for antiquities and that he had conferred with the Bishop of Andros, "a man of good learning and great experience" who advised him that the search "after old and good authors was utterly vaine" but that there were many "antiquities in marbles in divers parts", especially on the island of Delos which had served as a sanctuary for the ancient Greeks and that these could be easily procured "for the charge of digging and fetching". For his own part Roe added that he was certain:

. . . many statues are buried, to secure them from the envy of the Turks, and I will starte a searche for these as soon as I am warme here . . . Coynes wilbe had from Jewes, but very deare . . . I have already secured one antiquitie, a stone taken from the olde palace in Troy which is cutt in horned shape . . . but I can neither tell of what it is, nor if it hath any other beauty, but only the antiquity and truth of being a piece of that ruined and famous building.

After a year of searching around Constantinople, Roe discovered and purchased several pieces of ancient sculpture which he then shipped to Arundel. He found his assignment difficult for not only did he have to reckon with Turkish objections to his removing pieces from ancient ruins, but he was frequently approached by Turks with ostensibly ancient objects for which they demanded large sums of money. Roe was completely ignorant concerning the value of these objects, except on the basis of their "completeness" and the extent of the "damage which they had suffered from time" and he was constantly afraid of offending his patron by purchasing something at a high price which Arundel might declare to be worthless. He wrote to Arundel at the same time that he sent the first shipment of sculptures about this plight:

> I beseech Your Lordship to believe that it was very difficult to procure so much and I hope the effects thereof will content you . . .
>
> I have found other antiquities in gold and silver of the ancient Greeks, from Alexander downward, and many Roman more ancient but they are so deare, by reason the last French Ambassador made great search and some Italians are ready to buy, that I know not whether Your Lordship will esteem them at such rates . . .
>
> In particular, I have been offered a lyon to the wast, of pure white, holding a bulls head in his clawes, but I know not if Your Grace would want it since the very nose and mouth are defaced . . .
>
> I have also learnt of innumerable pillars, statues and tombstones of marble with inscriptions in Greeke, but I know not if Your Lordship is willing to pay the cost of fetching them at charge and secretly.

By this time, however, Arundel's dreaded rival, the Duke of Buckingham, also sensitive to the dictates of fashion, had become an ardent collector, especially of paintings. Whereas Arundel's collection of paintings included a number of valuable Holbeins, the Duke of Buckingham's collection was one of the greatest English collections of paintings of this century, including the works of Titian, Raphael, Tintoretto, Correggio, Giorgione and Leonardo. In 1622 Buckingham had purchased the entire personal collection of Peter Paul Rubens which contained many magnificent paintings and also a number of ancient vases, medals and sculptures which aroused the Duke's enthusiasm for ancient sculptures. In 1623 Buckingham, then the pampered favourite of the ailing King, wrote to Sir Thomas Roe in Constantinople and asked him to find and purchase ancient sculptures for his collection. He was very specific in his requirements and instructions to Roe, cautioning the Ambassador against the purchase of works which were not genuine antiquities and stating that: "Neither am I so fond of antiquity as to court it in a deformed or misshapen state, but where you shall meet beauty with antiquity together in a statue, I shall not stand upon any cost your judgment shall value it at."

Roe found himself in a great dilemma when he received Buckingham's communication, as he was now commissioned by two avowed enemies to act on behalf of each of them and he dared not offend either because of their wealth and influence at court. He decided to attempt to please both men, on the supposition that they would hardly be expected to exchange information on his activities, and replied to Buckingham—taking care not to mention Arundel's commission:

> The antiquities which I conceive Your Grace doth desire are either columns or statues in stone, or books, or ancient coynes, or medals. I confess my ignorance in choosing or knowing any of these; yet, for the reverence I bear to them, either as lights or reliques of ancient learning or noble sciences, I have a little endeavoured to search and inform my selfe. . . .
>
> I have found that there are many antiquities in marble on the island of Delos which I can take without trouble or prohibition, whatsoever His Grace pleased. . . .
>
> In particular I know of a lyon to the wast, of pure white, holding a bulls head, which might please Your Grace . . .
>
> All antiquities I can performe or find are freely presented to Your Grace for I have as much affection to serve Your Grace as any man living.

Unfortunately for Roe, Arundel learned that Buckingham had commissioned the Ambassador to collect antiquities and he was incensed at Roe for accepting this commission. Determined not to be outdone by the "impudent upstart who calls himself Duke of Buckingham", Arundel promptly despatched the Reverend William Petty to Constantinople for the sole purpose of buying antiquities for Arundel House. Petty, who had been educated at Cambridge, had served as chaplain to the Arundel household since the Earl's timely conversion to Protestantism and had previously been sent by his employer to purchase antiquities in Italy. He had a superior knowledge of ancient history and was much more capable of judging the value of classical remains than Roe.

Roe learned of Petty's impending arrival from various sources and was more than a little disturbed by the news. However when Petty presented himself in Constantinople in 1624, Roe was extremely affable in his welcome. In fact Roe was impressed from the very beginning with Petty's knowledge of ancient history as well as by his determination to "discover" valuable antiquities and decided that it was greatly to his advantage to have this man as his friend rather than as his rival. They discussed the question openly of Roe's dual commission from Arundel and Buckingham and came to the conclusion that the most sensible course was for them to co-operate in this work. Petty had both the time and temperament to travel in search of antiquities as well as the ability to judge their value. On the other hand, Roe, by virtue of his official position, was able to provide Petty with the necessary documents from the Ottoman authorities to travel freely throughout the Empire and remove any antiquities which he wished. They agreed finally to work together— Petty to search and Roe to assist—and then to divide the fruit of their joint labours between their two patrons. With this in mind, Roe wrote to the Duke of Buckingham, describing Petty's skills and abilities in glowing terms:

> There was never a man so fitted to an employment, that encounters all accident with so unwearied patience, eates with the Greeks on their worst days, lies with fishermen on planks at their best, is all things to all men, that he may obtain his ends.

He then went on to present his proposal:

> Therefore that we (Petty and myselfe) may not prevente one the other, I have mooved him, and he is well content, yf Your Grace and the Earle Marshall approve yt, to joyne, and whatsoever both can recover, to put into one stocke; and so to divide them, when they come to England, by lotts, or any other way that shall seem best to Your Grace.

There is no record of Buckingham's reaction to this proposal but Arundel, to whom Roe had not written, was enraged. He was determined not to be associated in any way with Buckingham, who was then turning his attentions from the aged and failing King to the young Prince Charles. He first wrote to Petty instructing him specifically not to enter into any agreements with Roe and then wrote to Roe, hinting that it was not in his best interests to serve the Duke of Buckingham for he, Arundel, was a man both powerful and wealthy. He added: "Money I know does any thinge, and I am willinge to bestowe it. . . . Furthermore I am resolved that Mr. Petty shall search only for me, because he knowes what will fitte me beste."

Bronze horses, removed by Crusaders from Constantinople in 1204, in their present position above the entrance to St. Mark's Cathedral, Venice.

Contemporary painting of Admiral Francisco Morosini.

Marble lion, removed by Morosini from Piraeus, in its present position outside the arsenal, Venice

Contemporary painting of part of the fleet employed in Morosini's conquest of Greece

When this rebuff reached Roe, Petty had already left Constantinople on an extended tour of Asia Minor and Roe saw no reason to change their arrangements until this tour was completed. When Petty wrote from the Greek island of Samos that he had "so far found only trifling spoil, a few fragments of no considerable value" Roe was distressed for he had heard from other sources that Petty had gathered a large quantity of antiquities, including the valuable "Marmor Parium", an inscription listing the principal events in Greece throughout a period of 1318 years, which he had shipped directly to Arundel without informing his partner. Roe was forced to conclude that Petty was not adhering to their agreement and was, in fact, deceiving him. He wrote to Buckingham concerning these suspicions:

> Petty is a close and subtill borderer, who does not bragg of his prizes, but although Petty has the advantage of being able to make search with his owne eyes, and is not sparing to spend, I will not let myselfe be cheated . . .
> He shall not out-buy mee.

In the same post Roe complained to Arundel about Petty's behaviour, saying that he had gone to great trouble to keep his part of the arrangement by providing Petty with the necessary papers from the Ottoman authorities. Roe was particularly distressed about some sculptures which he and Petty had discovered in Constantinople and agreed to share between the two patrons:

> I perceive that Petty hath entitled Your Lordship to them all, by some right, and this is not possible. Your Lordship shall never find me to write you an untruth, nor dissemble the truth . . . Mr. Petty did not discover them . . . If I do manage to procure them . . . a very difficult task . . . I will send Your Grace your parte, but only that, without Mr. Petty or any other help.

Roe ended this letter to Arundel by explaining that as a servant of the King he felt that he could not in all propriety refuse the Duke of Buckingham's commission to gather antiquities. He added that it was unjust of Arundel to ask this of him.

It was then that James I died and his son, still very much under the influence of the Duke of Buckingham, succeeded to the throne

4

as Charles I. Within a few weeks after the accession, Buckingham managed to secure the "eclipse" and "disgrace" of Arundel. When he learned of these occurrences, Roe decided to devote all his energies towards collecting antiquities for the apparently victorious Buckingham, although he was cautious not to inform Arundel of this decision. His technique was simply to write Arundel from time to time that he was unfortunately unable to find any antiquities for various reasons. In one letter he wrote: "I am tyed to my residence almost as to a prison and therefore cannot make search myselfe." In another he said: "Those that I am forced to employ to search for antiquities send me heavy stones at great charge, that prove newe images where I seek old idolls." As an example of the worthless pieces which his agents sent him, Roe cited:

> A statue from Angory which is a half-woman in marble, brought eighteen days by land, upon change of mules, which wants a hand, a nose, a lip, and is so deformed that she makes me remember a hospital.

At the same time as he was despatching these gloomy reports to Arundel, Roe was describing in glowing terms his success in locating and purchasing antiquities to the Duke of Buckingham. He wrote Buckingham that:

> I have sent agents to the chief towns of Asia Minor, including Ankyra, Bursa, Troy and Pergamon; and to the islands of Greece, and to the mainland of Greece, and these agents are sending me many valuable antiquities.

In another letter he reported that:

> My agent in the Peloponnese has discovered a greate many whole statues, beautiful and well-preserved which I am preparing to ship to England.

And this shipment included:

> A fine statue, in marble, of a half-woman which has come from Angory by mules and which would serve Your Grace well, I thinke.

Roe had good reason to curry favour with the Duke of Buckingham for he was very dissatisfied with his appointment in Constantinople and longed to return to England. In 1628 Buckingham, pleased

with Roe's reports of the many antiquities which he had purchased
on his behalf, secured Roe's recall and the Ambassador arranged to
return on a ship which was loaded with the many sculptures which
he had "discovered" for the Duke of Buckingham. However when
he arrived in London, Buckingham had already been assassinated.
The final disposition of this shipment of antiquities which Roe
brought with him is uncertain but it appears that Arundel, who
quickly regained favour in the court after Buckingham's death, was
successful in procuring these ancient sculptures for himself. There
is evidence of this in a letter from Arundel to his wife which was
written during the summer of 1628:

> I desire you woulde presently, by some meanes, knowe what Sir.
> Tho. Roe hath brought of antiquities, Goddes, vases, inscriptions,
> medalles, or such like . . .
> I wish it were done before Friday, for I feare my Lord Chamber-
> layne; and nowe I think they might easily be had.

In the end, despite Roe's decision to favour Buckingham, Arundel
secured a considerable quantity of ancient sculptures from the
Levant, particularly as his agent Petty succeeded in purchasing
many valuable items on his tour of Greece and Asia Minor. The
antiquities which Petty bought began to arrive at Arundel House in
1627 and caused great excitement. Arundel erected a colonnade in
his garden for the statues, many of which were restored by an anony-
mous sculptor, and set the inscribed marble slabs in the walls of his
house. King Charles I and many others came to see his collection,
some to admire it and a few to criticize. Osborn scoffed that "It was
ridiculous to give so many hundred crowns for an urn a mason
would not have valued at a penny", while Sir Francis Bacon, on
seeing the nude statues in the colonnade, cried out, "The Resurrec-
tion", caught a chill, and died at Arundel House. Henry Peacham
in his well-known seventeenth-century book of etiquette, *The Com-
pleat Gentleman*, wrote that:

> I cannot but with much reverence mention the every way Right
> Honourable Thomas Howard, Lord High Marshal of England, as great
> for his noble Patronage of Arts and ancient learning, as for his birth
> and place, to whose liberall charges and magnificence this angle of the
> world oweth the first sight of Greeke and Roman statues, with whose

admired presence he began to honour the gardens and galleries of Arundel House about twenty years agoe, and hath ever since continued to transplant old Greece into England.

Arundel's collection contained, according to an early catalogue:

> 37 statues in the house and garden
> 128 busts decorating the gallery
> 250 inscribed stones set in the walls, including the
>   famed "Marmor Parium"
> 138 cameos
> 133 intaglios
> uncounted coins
> unspecified quantities of sarcophagi and fragments
>   of altars, etc.

By 1641 Arundel feared for his safety during the growing civil strife because of his long and close connection with the Royal family. He secretly shipped all the family jewels and a considerable sum of money to Holland and proceeded with his wife and sons to Italy where he remained until his death in Padua five years later. His sculptures stayed at Arundel House and although Parliament laid the entire estates of the Howard family under attachment during the Civil War, no steps were taken to appropriate them. At the time of the Restoration, Arundel's grandson Thomas was reinstated in the family titles and estates by King Charles II but Thomas was unfortunately insane and never returned from Padua to resume his inheritance. The management of Arundel House fell to his younger brother Henry:

> A man of little artistic appreciation who ignored the most valuable collection of ancient sculptures which were miserably neglected and scattered up and down the garden and in other parts of Arundel House, in a state of being exceedingly impaired by the corrosive air of London.

Many sculptures were destroyed or stolen during this period and some were actually used as building material in the repair of the house. The upper half of the "Marmor Parium" was found in the backing of a new chimney by a horrified classical scholar who finally persuaded the incumbent Lord Arundel to donate all the inscribed marbles—but not the sculptures—to Oxford University. Only one hundred and thirty-six of the original two hundred and fifty inscribed marbles could be found in 1667 and these went to Oxford where they were given the honourable title of "Marmora Arundeliana" and where they still remain.

In 1678 Lord Arundel decided to pull down Arundel House with the intention of laying out streets and developing the area as a housing estate, only a portion of the garden near the river being reserved for the new Town House. Some of the ancient statues were sold at this time, including most of the busts, to the Earl of Pembroke, while most of the remainder were transferred to the new establishment and forgotten, until they were discovered in fragments many years later in the cellars of the new Town House in Norfolk Street. Lord Arundel gave a few sculptures to one of his servants, Boyder Coper, who used them to decorate his "Cupid's Gardens" and some pieces were moved to a plot of ground which the Howard family owned at Kennington where they were extracted a century later from beneath a thick layer of rubbish. One ancient column was used for several decades as a roller for Mr. Theobald's bowling green at Waltham Place, Berkshire. A few sculptures ended up with the Earl of Pomfret who had them badly restored. Pomfret's share of Arundel's collection was seen by Horace Walpole in the early eighteenth century who described this experience in the following terms:

> In an old green house there is a wonderful statue of Tully haranguing a numerous assembly of decayed Emperors, vestal virgins with new noses, colossos, Venuses, headless carcasses and carcasseless heads, pieces of tombs and hieroglyphics.

This greenhouse assembly was presented by the Earl of Pomfret to Oxford University in 1755.

In these various ways Arundel's collection of antiquities was dispersed and virtually destroyed. In fact all of the great collections of ancient Greek sculpture—as well as those of invaluable paintings—amassed during the reign of the Stuarts suffered a similar fate. Whereas the collections gathered by Arundel and the Earl of Somerset were lost in England, the many fine sculptures and paintings owned by King Charles I and the Duke of Buckingham were sold at public auctions, for the most part to Europeans who carted them off to all corners of the Continent and in most cases subsequently concealed or destroyed them. The favourites of James I were actually responsible not for "preserving antiquitie" but for destroying what must have been many of the best pieces of ancient Greek sculpture to have survived until the seventeenth century. Arundel's collection undoubtedly contained many excellent and irreplaceable sculptures and in the end the only monument left at Arundel House was the ridiculous statue of Thomas Howard, Earl of Arundel, in accordance with the directions given in his will:

> I desire that my Tombe bee my owne Figure (of white marble or Brasse designed by Signr Francesco Fanelli) sitting and looking upwards (according to the Last Clause of the Epitaphe), leaning upon a Lyon holding an Esconchion upon which the Epitaph to bee engraven, and at the feete the Marshalls Staffee with a Cornett or the like.

Chapter IV

MOROSINI'S LIONS

THE ancient ruins of Greece suffered irreparable damage from the greed of early collectors and also from the misfortunes of war. The Parthenon, which was undoubtedly the most famous of all the monuments of ancient Athens, survived intact for more than eighteen centuries, only to be reduced to ruins during an inconclusive war between the Venetians and Turks during the late seventeenth century.

The Ottoman Turks, driven by their religious enthusiasm, completed their conquest of the remains of the Byzantine Empire by capturing Constantinople in 1453. The Turkish army was by far the most efficient military organization of the age and spearheaded by its dread Janissary divisions, it subsequently overran what is now Greece, Rumania, Bulgaria, Albania, the Ukraine and the Crimea. Taking advantage of the political disunity prevailing in late medieval Europe, the Turks then proceeded to conquer Yugoslavia and most of Hungary, capturing both Belgrade and Budapest, so that by the mid-sixteenth century only the dominions of Austria, under the rule of the House of Hapsburg, served as a barrier between central Europe and the threatened advance of Turkish power.

Europe, however, was spared at this time by the death of the brilliant, ambitious Ottoman ruler, Suleiman the Magnificent, which was followed by a period of decline within the Turkish Empire which lasted for several decades. The successors of Suleiman showed no interest in leading their armies into battle, being preoccupied with "passing their lives in the enervating atmosphere of the harem, thus becoming the puppets of female intrigue".

The iron discipline which had held the invincible Turkish army together was relaxed during the reign of these degenerate Sultans and its character gradually changed as the Janissaries, once celibate, were now permitted to marry and each sought to secure a military sinecure for his sons. Favouritism and corruption also took its toll in the civil administration of the Empire and for nearly eighty years Turkish power ceased to expand. It was fortunate for Europe that this decline occurred during the chaotic period of the Thirty Years War when the Christian continent would hardly have been able to withstand the pressure of a Turkish invasion.

The situation was reversed when an Albanian septuagenarian, Mohammad Kiuprili, became Grand Vizier and founded a ministerial dynasty which revived the Empire and rekindled its ambitions for expansion. In the middle of the seventeenth century the Christian world of Europe once again found itself threatened by the Turkish army which, although it was no longer as efficient as in the days of the great Sultans, was still a formidable enemy. In 1663 the Turks declared war on the Austrian Hapsburg Empire and their army, led by the Grand Vizier himself, slowly marched across Hungary, capturing the various fortresses which defended the course of the Danube and its tributaries to ensure their control of the river valley. Europe was sufficiently alarmed to unite and a coalition French, German and Austrian army succeeded in defeating the Turks in a decisive battle which secured them a truce of twenty years.

When this truce expired the Turks, with an enormous army estimated as containing five hundred thousand men, again marched across Hungary with Vienna, capital of the Hapsburg Empire, as their declared objective. The Austrians appealed to all the powers in Europe for assistance in defeating this Moslem invasion. Although Louis XIV cynically remarked that "Crusades have been out of fashion since the days of St. Louis", there was a considerable response to this Austrian plea. Pope Innocent VI sent money, the Republic of Venice promised aid, Duke Charles of Lorraine, brother-in-law of the Austrian Emperor, vowed assistance and, most important of all, Jan Sobieski of Poland pledged to furnish an army of forty thousand men for the defence of the Austrian capital.

The Turkish army reached Vienna without difficulty in July,

1683, and blockaded the city. The Austrian Emperor, Leopold I, fled, leaving the defence of the besieged city in the hands of its governor, Count Rüdiger von Starhenberg. The impending doom of Vienna, capital of the Holy Roman Empire and one of the greatest cities in Europe, filled the whole of the Christian world with the most real sense of danger which it had ever known, for it seemed that if Vienna could be lost, all of Europe could well follow. Under these circumstances Jan Sobieski of Poland hastily assembled an army of twenty-six thousand men and, without waiting for additional troops, moved by forced marches to the relief of the city where he was joined by Duke Clarence of Lorraine and ten thousand men. This combined force defeated the Turkish army and succeeded in putting them to flight.

This victory, however, was followed by a series of disputes over future policy by the powers who had come to the relief of Vienna and these disagreements continued until the following spring when on 5th March, 1684, a so-called Holy Alliance was signed by the Austrian Hapsburg Empire, Poland and Venice. Under the terms of this alliance, these three powers pledged themselves to carry on the war against the Turks and to conclude no separate peace with the Infidel. Each power was to retain any conquests which it might make and the Pope was recognized as the patron and protector of the alliance, Austria, Poland and Venice all swearing a solemn oath to carry out its terms. Austria and Poland were already officially at war with the Turks but the Venetians felt it necessary to present their Declaration of War against the Ottoman Empire to the court in Constantinople. The Venetian Ambassador was terrified when he received his orders and made elaborate preparations before executing this assignment. His plans laid, he presented himself to the court of the Sultan where, after several hours of leisurely tea drinking and compliments, he presented the sealed Declaration and bowed himself out of the assembly before it had been opened and read to the Sultan. Once outside the palace, "he leapt onto his horse, raced to a pre-arranged hideout, changed into rags, shaved his head completely and made a successful escape from Constantinople disguised as a sailor on a merchant vessel."

The members of this Holy Alliance pursued their war against the Turks for fifteen years, until the Peace of Carlowitz effectively freed Europe from the threat of further Ottoman invasion. Austria, Poland

and Venice for the most part engaged in separate campaigns against the Turks in different areas and their contributions to the ultimate success of this war were unequal in merit and extent. The Poles joined the Austrian Hapsburgs in their pursuit of the Turkish armies back through Hungary and Yugoslavia until political difficulties forced Jan Sobieski to return to Poland, leaving Austria to bear the brunt of this campaign. The Venetians, on the other hand, taking full advantage of the fact that the main Turkish forces were occupied in Hungary, planned an expedition to outflank the enemy by attacking Greece.

Venice, whose prosperity depended on trade, had frequently been at odds with Turkey over the control of various islands and ports in the eastern Mediterranean and in fact this war of the Holy Alliance was the fifth "official" Venetian-Turkish war since 1500. Venice had originally secured a number of important islands, including the "Dodecanese Empire" of Naxos, Crete and Euboea as her share of the victory by the Crusaders over Byzantium in 1204 and had also taken over at this time many of the key ports of the Peloponnese, including Coroni, Modon, Patras and Nauplia. All of these islands and ports, which served as important trading depots and ports of call, had subsequently been lost to the Turks. Euboea had been taken by the Turks in 1470, Naxos and the "Empire of the Dodecanese" in 1566 and Coroni, Modon, Patras and Nauplia were lost during the same period. By the mid-seventeenth century the island of Crete was the only possession in the eastern Mediterranean which Venice retained. The Republic had been desperately anxious to hold Crete as her commercial position had been seriously weakened on the one hand by the discovery of the Cape route to the Indies which had diverted the stream of trade from the Mediterranean to the Atlantic, and on the other by the appearance of English and Dutch trading companies in the Mediterranean.

When a Turkish fleet laid siege to Crete in 1665, a Venetian armada under the command of Admiral Francisco Morosini was sent out to break the siege but failed and Crete was also lost to the Turks. The Venetians were so disheartened by this final defeat that they brought Admiral Morosini to trial for his conduct of the naval campaign but he was vindicated and later became considered a hero for his efforts to save Crete.

Venice was still smarting from this loss when the Holy Alliance was formed after the battle of Vienna and greeted with enthusiasm this new opportunity to attack the Turks. When the Venetian expedition to Greece was finally ready to set forth it was Admiral Francisco Morosini who was designated as commander-in-chief, despite his advanced age of sixty-six years. As the Venetian constitution prohibited the Republic from raising or maintaining an armed force, Venice provided only ships and sailors and the army was composed of some nine thousand troops gathered throughout Europe, the largest contingents being French and German. One small party of troops were designated as "bombisti" and were given charge of the heavy artillery, consisting of twenty-three cannon and four mortars. The "bombisti" were commanded by an engineer, Antonio Mutoni, Count of San Felice, an Italian who had studied mathematics, ballistics and the construction of fireworks in France and who had been, for a brief period, the official Builder of Fireworks for the King of France. Mutoni constructed his own weapons and explosives and a large quantity of these were purchased by the Venetians for this expedition.

The Venetian armada which sailed from Venice in late June of 1685 is described as having contained twenty-six galleys, fourteen galeots, six galeasses, eighty-seven fly boats and pinks.

The embarkation was festive and gay as Venetian tradesmen and artisans, arrayed in the traditional ornate costumes of their various guilds, lined up along the ten-foot walls of the famed arsenal of Venice, wherein the great Venetian galleys were built. There were master silversmiths with garlands on their heads, furriers dressed in samite and scarlet silk with mantles of ermine, master tailors in white set off with crimson stars, fustian workers in robes of fur and quiltmakers in white cloaks sewn with fleurs-de-lis overlaid with garlands of gilt beads. There were butchers in scarlet; glass workers in red with gold fringed hoods and rich garlands of pearls; goldsmiths with their wreaths of gold and silver necklaces heavy with sapphires, emeralds, diamonds, topazes, jacinths, amethysts, rubies, jaspers and carbuncles. Every guild had its special ornate costume— locksmiths and joiners, painters and stone masons, shipbuilders and carpenters, spice dealers and bakers, fish-mongers and wine merchants. The occasion was marred only by a display of Mutoni's explosives which was such a fiasco that it resulted in a bitter debate in the Venetian Senate over the fact that public funds had been expended on ineffective explosives and on an engineer who was obviously incompetent.

The expedition sailed directly to Greece and attacked Coroni, a fortress on the south-western tip of the Peloponnese which served as an important port of call for ships plying the Mediterranean trade and as such had formerly been controlled by Venice. They stormed and captured Coroni early in August and spent the next few weeks subduing the surrounding countryside in order to solidify their foothold in the Peloponnese. In the autumn they installed a small permanent garrison to hold Coroni and set sail for the Ionian island of Zante where they landed without encountering any opposition. Since the winter winds and seas around the Peloponnese are frequently so violent as to be exceedingly dangerous for small sailing craft, the expedition remained on the island until the following spring. This long, enforced idleness on Zante bred discontent and friction among the various national contingents which had been quartered in camps on opposite ends of the island. A bristling antagonism developed between the French and Germans who considered themselves as independent self-governing forces, responsible only to their own leaders and not to Morosini's central command. The French commander, the Comte de St. Paul, was constantly in a violent state of disagreement with the German commander, the Chevalier de Degenfield and both of these men consistently disregarded orders sent them by the aged Venetian commander-in-chief. Morosini was determined that he would not continue the war with such an ineffective and potentially explosive basis of command and sent a message to the Venetian Senate requesting that they send him someone to serve as commander of all the troops and as his liaison officer with the national contingents. After considerable debate the Venetian Senate contacted Count Otto William de Koenigsmark, a Westphalian general then serving as Marshal of the Swedish army, and offered him a substantial salary under contract to command the land forces of the Venetian expedition. General Koenigsmark accepted the offer and proceeded to Zante, accompanied by his wife and servants, in the spring of 1686.

The second campaign of the war, conducted during the summer of 1686, went well and the Venetians captured the Peloponnesian ports of Navarino, Modon and Nauplia. Up to this point they had encountered very little resistance, apparently because the bulk of the Turkish army was then heavily engaged in Hungary and the Turks had no soldiers to spare for the defence of the Peloponnese. In the few engagements which they had fought, however, Mutoni's artillery had functioned poorly and the "bombisti" troops complained bitterly that his bombs failed to function correctly, that they were dangerous and that he was thoroughly incompetent to handle them. The expedition returned to their winter quarters in Zante following the capture of Nauplia in August, well satisfied with their gains.

The most important campaign of this war occurred during the third summer, in 1687. The expedition was delayed in leaving Zante until the late spring due to "Some little Heats and Contentions among the troops which resounded much to the Honour of His Excellency, Lord Admiral Morosini". However they compensated for this delay by capturing the city of Patras on the 23rd of July in spite of a determined resistance by the Turkish garrison. Flushed with their first real military victory, they advanced along the northern coast of the Peloponnese to storm the city of Corinth in a second impressive battle in mid-August.

Morosini was now faced with the necessity of making a difficult decision. If he wished to concentrate on the further conquest and occupation of the Peloponnese, he would have to stop the advance and fortify the isthmus at Corinth, a narrow neck of land only five miles wide joining the Peloponnese to central Greece. However the ultimate objective of the Venetian expedition was the island of Euboea which lay to the north and east of the mainland, not far from Athens. Euboea, a rich island well situated as a depot for ships trading in the eastern Mediterranean, had been taken from Venice by the Turks in 1470 and Morosini felt that its recapture would serve as a great victory for Venetian prestige in the Mediterranean and would compensate for the loss of Crete. He therefore decided not to attempt the fortification of the isthmus of Corinth and complete the conquest of the Peloponnese but to press on into the province of Attica in northern Greece with Athens as his first objective.

However it was necessary to shift the fleet from the western to the eastern coast of the isthmus before he could advance into northern Greece. There was no canal across the isthmus at this time but there existed the traces of a special track, the "diolokos", which had been used in medieval times for the transport of ships of low tonnage across the five-mile isthmus. Morosini attempted to construct a system by which his ships could be towed across this "diolokos", but met with such difficulties that he abandoned the project and set off with the fleet to sail the whole way around the Peloponnesian peninsula. This circumnavigation took a full three weeks and it was mid-September when Morosini brought the ships to anchor on the eastern coast of the isthmus. It was then so late in the summer, with the troops so depleted by casualties suffered in the battles of Patras and Corinth as well as by a severe outbreak of dysentery, that Morsoni decided to postpone the proposed attack on Euboea until the following spring. On the other hand he felt that he could safely count on several more weeks of good weather which would give him sufficient time to advance into Attica and perhaps to secure Athens before retiring once again to winter quarters. He reasoned that it would be greatly to his advantage to be in control of Athens during the winter as it would enable him to organize the assault on Euboea early in the spring. He sent a despatch to the Venetian Senate advising them of his plans for advancing into Attica and requesting reinforcements for the projected invasion of Euboea the following May. He also informed them that he had arranged to quarter the bulk of the army in Corinth and Nauplia during the winter instead of returning with them to the island of Zante.

The fleet sailed from Corinth during the night of 21st September with all of the troops, listed as nine thousand, eight hundred and eighty soldiers and eight hundred and seventy horses, crowded into five of the galleys. The rest of the ships were sent, lightly manned, to the coast of Euboea in an attempt to confuse the Turks about their real intention. They reached Piraeus by dawn and found the port deserted, for Piraeus had never been rebuilt or resettled after its destruction at the hands of Sulla. As they disembarked they were confronted only by a statue of a colossal lion which overlooked the empty harbour and gave to it the medieval name of Porto Leone. On the flank of this statue was cut, in runic script, an inscription by the Viking Harald Hadrada who had visited Porto Leone in 1040 while in the service of the Byzantine Emperor. This was the same Harald who in 1066 appeared in English history as the defeated leader at the battle of Stamford Bridge.

They then proceeded to march, unopposed, along the six-mile route which connected Piraeus to Athens. Those who were familiar with the ancient history of Greece were bitterly disappointed when they reached the outskirts of Athens, for the great city which had given birth to so much of western civilization and culture had almost entirely vanished during the long centuries of Roman, Byzantine and Turkish occupation. What they found was no more than a poor, shabby village built on the fringe of the hill of the ancient Acropolis. The ancient monuments which remained on top of the Acropolis— the Parthenon, Erechtheum and the Propylae—had been reconstructed to serve as quarters for a Turkish garrison of three thousand soldiers, while some five thousand Greeks lived in appalling poverty in the cluster of dilapidated stone huts which formed the village. The Turkish garrison had moved their families, along with all their goods and chattels and most of the available livestock, inside the citadel of the Acropolis when they learned of the Venetian landing in Piraeus, leaving the terrified Greeks to fend for themselves. The Venetians immediately occupied all of this Greek village and Morosini sent an order to the Turkish garrison on the Acropolis to surrender.

When Morosini received the Turks' refusal, he ordered the armies to prepare for an assault on the citadel which, however, presented a difficult military problem. The Acropolis, a solid rock plateau situated on the top of a steep hill, was protected by formidable walls which had originally been constructed in Mycenaean times and strengthened by successive civilizations over the centuries. As these walls rose in a continuation of the steep stone cliff on the north, south and east of the Acropolis, the only feasible approach to the citadel was by the west and this western entrance had been heavily fortified by the Turks. The huge marble columns on the Propylae, just inside this western entrance, were thick with Turkish guns behind the new battlements which had been constructed by the Turks from the ruins of the ancient Temple of Nike.

Morosini decided that it was inadvisable to attempt a direct assault on this western entrance in consideration of the relatively small size of his depleted army and ordered Mutoni to bring the artillery from the ships in order to subject the Acropolis to a bombardment. The twenty-three cannon and four mortars were brought up from Piraeus and placed into position. One battery of cannon was situated on the

Hill of the Muses, aimed at the fortifications inside the western entrance, while a second battery was placed on the Pnyx Hill and aimed at some additional fortifications which the Turks had constructed on the western slope outside the entrance. The four mortars were placed at the bottom of the Areopagus Hill for the purpose of shelling the citadel at random, a tactic which Morosini hoped would bring about a general panic among the families of the Turkish garrison encamped in the open on the Acropolis.

Mutoni's "bombisti" began their bombardment of the Acropolis on the morning of the twenty-fourth and ceased on the following afternoon in order to assess the effectiveness of their barrage. The cannon on the Hill of the Muses and the Pnyx Hill had succeeded remarkably well, considering their distance from the targets and the impossibility of effecting accurate control over the primitive gunpowder of that time. They had considerably damaged the Turkish guns in the Propylae as well as the fortifications which were located outside the western entrance. On the other hand the mortars had completely failed, for not one of their missiles had even reached the citadel. This failure was brought to Morosini's attention and he immediately summoned Mutoni and reprimanded him for the ineffectiveness of his weapons. Mutoni was enraged by this criticism and promptly moved his mortars to a new location east of the citadel and began to fire them in the direction of the Parthenon. This famous ancient temple was the largest and most complete structure on the Acropolis and for this reason was used by the Turks as a storehouse for their munitions. It is impossible to say whether Mutoni had been informed of this fact and deliberately aimed his mortars at the Parthenon—if it was possible for him to aim his inventions at any specific target—or if it was only by accident that one of these mortars scored a direct hit on the Parthenon on the afternoon of 26th September, 1687.

There was a frightful and terrifying explosion when the store of Turkish munitions inside the Parthenon exploded and the roof, the massive walls of the cella, eight columns from the northern side and six columns from the southern side as well as great quantities of the sculpture which had adorned this magnificent ancient monument crashed to the ground. Eye-witnesses describe a cloud of thick black smoke which covered the Acropolis while fragments of carved marble were spewed out over an area of several hundreds of yards.

The Venetians regarded this explosion as a Divine Blessing and wildly cheered as Mutoni was hoisted to the shoulders of his excited "bombisti" troops and carried through the ranks. There were no signs of distress over the destruction of the greatest ancient Greek temple. Even General Koenigsmark, who had received so thorough a classical education that he was fluent in Latin and Greek and frequently regaled his family with the tales of Homer and the philosophy of Aristotle, apparently experienced only a small pang of regret, according to one of his staff:

> Reluctantly His Excellency saw himself compelled to destroy this beautiful temple which has stood some three thousand years and is called the Temple of Minerva. But it could not be helped.

Contrary to Venetian expectations, the Turkish garrison did not immediately surrender after this disaster but held on, hoping that the small Turkish army which was advancing on Athens from the north of Greece would arrive in time to relieve them. The garrison finally capitulated when they received the news that General Koenigsmark had intercepted these reinforcements and had defeated them in battle near Thebes. One of the terms of the surrender was the evacuation of the entire Turkish population from the citadel which was promptly executed, so that Morosini was able to take official possession of the Acropolis and to hoist the flag of Saint Mark over the Propylae on the eighth day following the explosion. While his soldiers hastily disposed of the three hundred Turkish dead which they discovered amid the rubble of the Parthenon, the aged Admiral notified the Senate of Venice that he had captured Athens.

Morosini's report of the victory was received in Venice with great excitement. The Venetians, who were as gifted in the art of propaganda as they were in matters of commerce and trade, interpreted the capture of Athens as a proof of the "right and might of the marvellous Queen of all the cities and republics of the world". An account of the arrival of the news in Venice was carried in one of the first modern newspapers ever printed:

> The people of Venice crowded round the messengers with shouts of victory. The news immediately spread with the swiftness of the wind, and soon a humming noise of Joy ran through the streets while the

5

people gathered in clusters to give ear to the speaker who undertook to give a relation of the victory.

The author went on to comment on Venetian glory:

That this wise Republick has sometimes been seen in Troubles and Disorder is no more to be wondered at than that Clocks and Watches should be sometimes amiss: not for any defect of Act, but by reason of the moisture or other intemperateness of the weather.

Morosini was hailed as a hero and the Senate decreed that his statue be erected in the Hall of the Council of Ten, "on a pedestal adorned with an inscription of the victory in golden letters", an honour never before granted to a living Venetian. For his contribution to the victory, General Koenigsmark was given a large increase in salary and his contract as commander of the land forces of the expedition was extended for five years.

The Turks, on the other hand, were greatly distressed by the news of the fall of Athens, particularly as this defeat happened during a period when their armies were also suffering serious reverses in Hungary at the hands of the Austrians. An uprising occurred in the Turkish army in Thrace which then mutinied, marched on Constantinople and disposed of Sultan Mehmed IV on 9th November, placing his younger brother, Suleiman II on the Ottoman throne. The new Sultan immediately sought to remove the corrupt influences from the court and the army, to strengthen the Turkish forces on all fronts and to draw plans for stemming the tide of Christian advances into Turkish territories.

Morosini was unaware of these changes in Constantinople which did not, in fact, affect his position in Greece for many months. Once he had secured Athens and the surrounding countryside, Morosini turned his attention to the pressing problem of establishing the armies in winter quarters. The original plan to quarter the different national contingents in separate towns in the Peloponnese was now in question as a result of rumours of plague throughout the Peloponnese. Morosini was very reluctant to establish winter quarters in Athens due to the insufficient housing available, the shortage of food in the area and the danger of counter-attack by Turkish forces which were known to exist to the north of Attica. However he was eventually forced to conclude that it was wiser to stay in Athens than to leave as more and more cases of plague were reported in the south. He therefore ordered the fleet to be secured in Piraeus harbour and the route from Athens to Piraeus to be fortified in order to secure a line of retreat in case of a Turkish counter-attack. The troops were quartered in the Greek village and the officers installed in those buildings which had remained intact on the Acropolis.

By December the supplies of food were seriously depleted while efforts to replenish them through raids on the surrounding country-side were unsuccessful. Morosini realized that if the situation did not improve, it might be necessary to leave Athens in mid-winter and he made tentative plans for this departure. He did not wish to leave the Turks a citadel which they could reoccupy and therefore drafted an order that all structures on the Acropolis—including the ancient monuments—were to be completely destroyed when and if they were forced to abandon Athens. As a first step in meeting this eventuality Morosini began to study possible sites to which he could move the army if it became necessary and ordered a plan to be drawn up for the deportation of the Greek population of Athens to the Peloponnese. He intended to leave Athens ruined and depopu-lated and never once doubted his right to destroy the antiquities of this famous ancient city.

Despite these elaborate preparations for departure, the Venetian expedition remained in Athens for three more months, principally because they could not decide on an alternative. Shortly after the new year the plague epidemic spread to Corinth and there were reports of suspicious deaths in northern Greece. The first cases of plague in Athens occurred in February and the epidemic rapidly spread through the debilitated Greek population. Morosini ordered all troops to be moved onto the Acropolis where living conditions quickly became insupportable for ten thousand men encamped in the open air in mid-winter on less than four acres of barren rock. Within a few weeks, plague had broken out amongst the armies on the Acropolis and in the ensuing panic there was a real danger of mutiny. Morosini immediately abandoned his plans to destroy the fortifications on the Acropolis and evacuate the Greek population and concentrated his efforts on effecting an immediate withdrawal from Athens before a mutiny did occur. He decided to move the army to Poros, an island in the nearby Saronikos Bay which had apparently escaped the epidemic and ordered the ships to be prepared and loaded. There were several tense days, however, before the fleet was ready to sail.

Despite the gravity of the situation with which his army was faced, Morosini was determined that he would not leave Athens without some ancient sculpture as a trophy of his victory. For this purpose he chose a sculpture of Jupiter in a chariot drawn by two fierce horses which had remained intact on the western pediment of the Parthenon and appeared to him as a representation of "a God making his entry into an assembly of Gods". No doubt he drew an analogy with his own triumphal return to the Venetian Senate, to whom he wrote concerning this choice, "One remarks the majesty of Jupiter . . . the celestial fire which animates the horses . . . the grace in the movement of victory . . . the white and fine marble in which it is done."

This sculpture was smashed while it was being removed from the Parthenon, according to Morosini's report to the Venetian Senate:

In the plans for abandoning Athens, I conceived the project of taking some of the beautiful ornaments, especially those which could add to the splendour of the Republic. With this intention, I instigated the first steps for detaching from the façade of the Temple of Minerva —where there are the most beautiful sculptures—a statue of Jupiter and the reliefs of two magnificent horses. But hardly had the workers started to remove the large cornice than it all fell from this extraordinary height, and it is a miracle that no harm came to the workers.

The blame for this accident lies in the construction of the temple, built with stones placed one on top of the other, without mortar and with a marvellous art, but which were all dislocated by the shock resulting from the explosion.

The impossibility of erecting scaffoldings and of taking yard arms from the galleys and other machines to lift heavy weights up to the top of the Acropolis, makes any other attempt difficult and dangerous. I have forbidden it, so much the more that having deprived it of that which was the most remarkable, all that remains seems to me inferior in some limb by the corrosive action of time.

Distressed by the loss of this sculpture from the Parthenon, Morosini then decided that he would take back to Venice a sculpture of a lion, as lions by tradition were the symbol of St. Mark. He therefore sent some twenty officers to scour the countryside for lion statues and they brought him two sculptures, one from the Temple of Theseus and one from the Academy of Plato. He was still not satisfied and before leaving Piraeus succeeded in removing and loading on his galley the famous ten-foot lion which dominated the empty harbour. As they set sail for Poros the aged Admiral, clad in a richly embroidered morning coat, a golden toga and a round red velvet cap, sat proudly on the deck of his vermilion galley surrounded by his marble lion trophies.

Although the incidence of plague among the troops gradually decreased on Poros, the expedition was seriously weakened by the events of the winter and adequate reinforcements failed to arrive from Venice in time for the projected assault on the island of Euboea. Moreover, as a result of the reforms carried out by the new Ottoman Sultan, the Turkish army on Euboea had been considerably strengthened and reorganized. As a consequence, the assault on Euboea was soundly repulsed, General Koenigsmark was killed and Morosini was forced to order a retreat to the Peloponnese.

The Turks did not pursue them beyond the isthmus of Corinth and they were subsequently able to retain their control of the main Peloponnesian ports although they never succeeded in subduing the entire peninsula. Morosini, who became Doge of the Republic, remained with the armies in the Peloponnese until his death in Nauplia in 1694.

The Venetians were able to hold the Peloponnese for several decades after Morosini's death but they profited little from this nominal control and, under the terms of the peace in 1718, the ports of the Peloponnese were returned to the Turks. The Venetian expedition to Greece has generally been forgotten except by those who happen on the lion of Piraeus set up in front of the arsenal in Venice and read the following inscription cut in Latin in the base:

> Francisco Morosini
> Peloponnesiacus
> Having Conquered Athens by Storm
> Removed by His Own Hand These Triumphal
> Marble Statues of Lions
> From the Piraeus
> And Transported Them to His Own Country
> To Be the Property

Of the Lion of Venice
As They Had Been the Ornaments of Athenian Minerva.

Athens Trophies of the Venetian Fleet
By Decree of the Venetian Senate
Erected in the Naval Quarter.

Chapter V

THE ABBÉ FOURMONT

THE French did not seriously begin to collect ancient Greek sculpture in the Levant until the late eighteenth century, despite the English Ambassador's report to the Earl of Arundel that his counterpart in Constantinople "had made great searche for antiquities" during the 1620s. It is understandable that the highly decorative and romantic taste of the court of Louis XIV found no place for ancient sculptural fragments from Greece. The aristocratic Frenchmen of this age preferred the wholesale production by their own carvers of pseudo-classical sculpture with a far more romantic character than the time-worn fragments of the Levant.

There is no doubt that the French were better informed than the English about the presence of ancient ruins and sculpture in the Levant as a result of their long and active history in this part of the world. Most of the French knights from Champagne and Burgundy who had participated in the Fourth Crusade were involved in the subsequent invasion and conquest of Greece in 1206 when a prosperous French principality was established in the Peloponnese which flourished for over a century. Even after the collapse of this principality, French religious missions had survived throughout Greece and the Levant, for the French had always aspired to convert the adherents of the Eastern Orthodox Church to Catholicism and for this reason maintained an intricate series of Jesuit and Capuchin hospices wherever they were permitted to do so, first by the Byzantine and later by the Moslem authorities. Aside from these religious interests, the French from a very early date maintained an active economic interest and trade with the ports of the Eastern Mediterranean and were exploiting the Levant at a time when the English regarded this area as composed of unknown and essentially dangerous lands to be quickly passed through on their pilgrimages to the Holy Land. There was a French Ambassador regularly posted to Constantinople as well as French consuls and consular agents permanently established in several Levantine ports by the early sixteenth century.

Although the French showed little interest in acquiring specimens of ancient classical art and architecture until quite late, they did have a passionate interest in ancient manuscripts. While the agents of the seventeenth-century English collectors were busily searching the Levant for ancient statues, contemporary Frenchmen were combing the same area for old manuscripts and their interests rarely conflicted—except on the subject of ancient inscribed stones which the French wanted for the content of their inscriptions, while the English regarded these as particularly genuine bits of decorative ancient marble, ideally suited for insertion in garden walls.

The first French King to interest himself in ancient manuscripts was Francis I who established the "King's Library" to house his personal collection. This collection of ancient manuscripts in the King's Library was greatly enlarged in the early seventeenth century through the efforts of the historian Jacques-Auguste de Trou who brought to Paris a considerable number of ancient and rare manuscripts from Italy and the Levant. De Trou not only collected manuscripts on his own travels but he commissioned the French Ambassador in Constantinople as well as the French consular agents and Capuchin missions in the Levant to search for ancient manuscripts and inscriptions for the King's Library. The French Ambassador and his agents were busily engaged in this search when Sir Thomas Roe arrived in Constantinople. One of the men employed by de Trou was a certain Provençal scholar, Claude Peiresc who, in his turn, hired a series of agents to tour the Levant. It was one of Peiresc's agents who discovered an important cache of inscribed marbles on the Greek island of Paros, including the "Marmor Parium". However the agent unwisely attempted to smuggle these inscribed marbles off Paros without paying for them and he was imprisoned by the Moslem authorities on this account. The marbles then fell into the hands of the English agent, Petty, and much to the chagrin of Pieresc and de Trou the precious "Marmor Parium" was sent to England to decorate the gardens of Arundel House. When the "Marmor Parium" was discovered decades later mending a hole in the Arundel chimney, the French were indignant. So much, they said, did the English appreciate the value of ancient inscriptions.

One Frenchman who was very much interested in ancient manuscripts was Cardinal Richelieu and he acquired manuscripts as much for his own personal collection as for the King's Library. Richelieu commissioned the French Ambassador in Constantinople to purchase manuscripts on his account, as is shown in a letter written to him by the Ambassador in 1638:

> Monseigneur, after serving the King my greatest duty is to serve Your Eminence. It seems to me that the greatest memorials of antiquity have survived the ravages of time for so many centuries only in order that they could be judged great enough to be placed in your library. . . .

The Ambassador concluded:

> I have already written everywhere in the Levant, and given the necessary orders in all places where there are Consuls of France to gather up all manuscripts that could be considered worthy of Your Taste. As long as Your Eminence considers me capable of remaining in this place, I will see to His wishes.

Mazarin shared the passion of his predecessor for collecting ancient manuscripts and inscriptions and shortly after coming to power, wrote to Jean de la Haye, the French Ambassador in Constantinople:

> I assure myself that you will not refuse me the assistance which I ask of you to satisfy the passion which I have to fill my library with curious books.

De la Haye was not only obliging but resourceful and sent a Greek priest to search for ancient manuscripts in the monasteries of the Holy Sanctuary of Mt. Athos in Greece, where all manner of valuable treasures and writings were reputed to have been hidden away to escape the notice of the Ottoman authorities. This priest returned with more than five hundred valuable manuscripts, including not only religious writings but works of the ancient Greek philosophers and Byzantine historians. (Two years later the Russian Patriarch sent a Russian priest to Mt. Athos for the same purpose and another three hundred valuable manuscripts were discovered and sent back to the Library of the Synod in Moscow. These two expeditions removed virtually all valuable manuscripts from the Holy Sanctuary of Mt. Athos, although the myth of valuable treasures and manuscripts hidden there has persisted until the present day.) De la Haye's Greek priest was an indefatigable worker and when he was over seventy he spent a full decade searching for ancient manuscripts in Cyprus, Greece and Constantinople, in particular in the monasteries of Thrace, Thessaly and Macedonia. He sent many manuscripts to the French authorities but apparently felt that he was not adequately reimbursed for his labours, for when he was ninety-one he sent the last of a series of pathetic letters to the French King requesting payment.

Both Cardinal Richelieu and Mazarin were also interested in ancient sculpture but for some reason they accumulated their considerable collections of sculpture from sources in Italy and apparently never acquired any ancient statuary from the Levant, nor requested the French Ambassador in Constantinople to search for ancient works. Mazarin also purchased a great many sculptures from the collections of King Charles I and the Duke of Buckingham when these were sold at public auction by Parliamentary decree after the Civil War and his collection at the time of his death was reputed to contain some four hundred ancient sculptures, at least half of which were inherited by his niece, the Duchess of Mazarin. Unfortunately her husband, the Duke of Mazarin, was a "hysterically jealous man who lived in a perpetual state of quarrel with his wife". One morning during an unexplained absence of his wife, the Duke entered the sculpture gallery of their ancestral home armed with a large hammer and he proceeded to bludgeon the nude statues in a fit of enraged prudery. The same evening he returned to the gallery with five assistants, all armed with hammers, to complete his work of destruction. The collection was totally demolished and the English, when they heard of this, were indignant. So much, they said, did the French appreciate ancient art.

It seems a paradox that the greatest of the seventeenth-century French collectors of ancient manuscripts was Colbert, the practical-minded Minister of Finance who so continually emphasized the importance of commerce, finance and hard work and who so consistently criticized the nobles at Versailles for their idle hobbies. In fact Colbert became such an avid collector of ancient manuscripts that he significantly enriched the King's Library as well as forming a very valuable personal collection and he accomplished this by means of despatching special expeditions to the Levant with all expenses paid, for the purpose of finding and purchasing ancient manuscripts. The first expedition sent by Colbert was composed of several scholars who left France in 1668 and toured the Levant for nearly six years, collecting many valuable manuscripts and medallions. A second expedition "to discover and purchase Greek and oriental manuscripts" was headed by a German Dominican monk, Père Wansleben who toured Cyprus, Syria, Egypt, the islands of the Greek Archipelago, Asia Minor and Constantinople for a period of four years. Before leaving Paris, Père Wansleben was furnished by Colbert, at the King's expense, with the following items:

A complete suit, a coat and some underwear
A wig
Spy glasses
A quadrant and a compass
A sun dial
Seals of the King, the Queen and the Dauphine
Detailed instructions on how to recognize old manuscripts
Standards for judging the condition of old manuscripts
Instructions on how to bargain the price
A list of the most eagerly sought authors and subjects
Pocket money of all nations

Not long after the death of Colbert, the Abbé Jean Paul Bignon received the appointment as Director of the King's Library and he was determined that the royal collection of ancient manuscripts should contain at least as many valuable works as were to be found in the personal collections of the King's ministers. While inquiring about the best way to accomplish this plan, Abbé Bignon learned that the former Turkish Ambassador to France, Zaïd Aga, had received the appointment as Director of the Seraglio Library in

Constantinople and furthermore was opening a new printing shop in the Ottoman capital. He therefore wrote to Zaïd Aga ostensibly to request a copy of all books published by the new printing shop for the King's Library but for the real purpose of obtaining a catalogue of all the Greek and Latin manuscripts present in the Seraglio Library. The actual contents of the Seraglio Library had never been made known to the non-Moslem world and Abbé Bignon, like others before him, believed that the Library might well contain manuscripts of inestimable value, perhaps even some items from the libraries of the Byzantine Emperors.

Zaïd Aga replied to Abbé Bignon that he would be delighted to send complimentary copies of all books which his printing shop brought out to the King's Library but that unfortunately he could not remit a catalogue of the Greek and Latin manuscripts in the Seraglio Library because no such catalogue existed. Furthermore there was no one on the library staff at that time who was sufficiently proficient in Greek and Latin to compile such a catalogue. He suggested that if the Abbé Bignon wished to send a French scholar to Constantinople to prepare a catalogue of these Greek and Latin manuscripts, he would secure the necessary permits for his entry to the Library.

Since no Christian had even been permitted by the Turkish authorities to inspect the contents of the Seraglio Library, Zaïd Aga's reply was received in France with great excitement. Abbé Bignon immediately requested the Comte de Maurepas, the King's Minister, to finance an expedition of French scholars to Constantinople to make a catalogue of the manuscripts existing in the Seraglio Library and urged that this be done with the utmost promptitude as the authorities "in that part of the world are prone to the swift changing of their minds". He sounded the following warning:

We must keep this information in the most profound secrecy lest the English hear about it and secure permission for themselves to enter this library of Constantinople, where they would undoubtedly do an irreparable harm to religion by suppressing or falsifying that which they found in manuscripts which did not agree with their religious errors.

The Comte de Maurepas agreed with Abbé Bignon and two priests from the Académie des Inscriptions et Belle-Lettres left

France in September, 1728, for the purpose of compiling a catalogue of the Greek and Latin manuscripts in the Seraglio Library in Constantinople. The elder of these two priests, the Abbé Sevin, was a professor of Greek and the younger, the Abbé Fourmont, a professor of Syriac and interpreter of Chinese, Tartar and Indian. It was anticipated that their work in the Library would be completed within six months and it was arranged that they would be fed and lodged at the residence of the new Ambassador, the Marquis de Villeneuve, with whom they were travelling to Constantinople. They were amply provided with clothing and money so that "they could conduct themselves in a manner which would not bring dishonour to the Ambassador", and given, in addition:

A timepiece, absolutely necessary in order to be able to tell the distance which one has passed.
A perspective mirror, in order to take from afar the plan of antiquities when they are found, without arousing the suspicion of the Turks.
A magnifying glass
An abacus
Writing tablets
Oiled paper and India ink.

Constantinople was in the grip of a serious outbreak of plague when these two French priests arrived there in December, 1728, and they were not permitted either to see Zaïd Aga or to enter the Seraglio Library. While they waited for the epidemic to subside they visited the English Ambassador whom to their horror they found very well informed about the purpose of their mission. The Ambassador assured them that Zaïd Aga had no intention of permitting them to examine the Seraglio collection of Greek and Latin manuscripts. Furthermore, he said, they could abandon any hopes they might cherish of finding any old manuscripts in Constantinople because the Prince of Walachia had just visited there to buy up all the remaining old manuscripts. The two French priests were greatly distressed by this interview and by the way the English Ambassador had received them. They immediately sent a report of this meeting to the Comte de Maurepas, describing the English chaplain who had also been present as: "a mediocre connoisseur of ancient works who could hardly speak with them because he was overcome by the charms of a young Greek girl who caused him frequent distractions."

After a few weeks had passed with no word from Zaïd Aga, Abbé Sevin and Abbé Fourmont began to fear that the English Ambassador had been correct in his pronouncement that the Turkish authorities had no intention of permitting them to enter the Seraglio Library. They therefore decided to occupy themselves with an intensive search for old manuscripts so that if all else failed, their trip to Constantinople would in some way be justified. There was a rumour in Constantinople that the English Ambassador had sent a man to the Greek island of Chios in order to buy some manuscripts which were to be found in a monastery there and the two abbots wondered if it would not be wise for them to investigate this story. They finally decided that the Abbé Fourmont should proceed to Chios to see if he could obtain some of these manuscripts from this monastery while the Abbé Sevin remained in Constantinople to press the issue of obtaining permission to enter the Seraglio Library. Abbé Fourmont left Constantinople in February, 1729, on a small coastal boat bound for Chios.

He wrote to the Abbé Sevin from Chios that he had experienced a harrowing voyage of four weeks duration, for they had been beset with such violent storms that they were constantly forced to put into coves along the desolate Turkish coast, and that he encountered on Chios "a terrible outbreak of plague, to complete my happiness". When he finally managed to visit the monastery, which could be reached only by what he described as "the most atrocious road full of precipices and falling rocks because of the violent torrents of rain", he failed to accomplish anything. According to his report to the Abbé Sevin, the monks first provided him with walnuts, dried raisins, almonds, honey and a good strong wine—and no manuscripts—but when he placed two coins on the table before them, they agreed to let him inspect their library. Their manuscripts, however, turned out to be Greek Orthodox religious texts rather than ancient works, "the dreams of scorched brains", as the Abbé Fourmont described them.

He also visited several other monasteries on Chios but found no manuscripts of interest in any of them. By this time the epidemic of plague had grown worse, "to the point that all Chios trembled, and all the houses were shut, and the lazar house was full, and the people spoke only of the sick and the dead."

Abbé Fourmont had travelled to Chios in the company of Gaspay, the French Consul in Athens, a man possessed with a terror of contracting the plague. Gaspay, in his anxiety to leave Chios, suggested to the Abbé Fourmont that he had positive information about the existence of many exceedingly precious ancient manuscripts in the monasteries of Athens and Abbé Fourmont finally agreed to go with him to Athens to see these manuscripts. He found no valuable ancient manuscripts in the monasteries of Athens but, while exploring the once famous ancient city, the Abbé Fourmont got involved in another project which enthralled him far more than his fruitless search for ancient manuscripts. He had brought with him from France a copy of a book written by a French physician, Dr. Spon, and an English traveller, George Wheler, about their voyage to Greece and Constantinople, in which they quoted the texts of all the ancient inscriptions which they came across on their travels. While wandering around Athens, the Abbé Fourmont noticed that there were a number of ancient inscriptions in this city which Spon and Wheler had failed to remark and he assigned himself the task of recording them. In fact he spent all his time frantically searching among the ruins of Athens for inscriptions with a group of Turkish labourers whom he employed to shift the ruins in order to investigate what lay beneath them, for he had now become passionately interested in seeking out ancient inscriptions.

As was so often the case with men who became involved in a search for objects of the past, the Abbé Fourmont's enthusiasm for ancient inscriptions eventually passed all bounds of reasonable behaviour and grew into an insatiable mania. He decided that the Almighty had sent him to Greece for the purpose of discovering all the inscriptions remaining in this ancient land—despite the fact that he was by training a scholar of Chinese, Tartar and Indian but not of Greek. Undismayed by this anomaly and convinced of the supreme importance of his mission, he set out on a tour of Greece in search of ancient inscriptions. He travelled through southern Greece for almost two years and in his frenzy he completely forgot about his assignment to catalogue the manuscripts of the Seraglio Library in Constantinople and ignored the question of searching for and purchasing ancient manuscripts.

The Abbé Fourmont's great enthusiasm for copying old inscriptions was not shared by his superiors who were not pleased by his disregard of the assignments for which he had been sent to the

Levant at the King's expense. The Abbé Sevin became so distressed by the Abbé Fourmont's refusal to comply with his instructions to return to Constantinople that he informed the Comte de Maurepas, the King's Minister, of the situation. The Comte de Maurepas did not hesitate to write to the Abbé Fourmont:

> Although this work to which you are applying yourself may be useful, it seems to me that you have forgotten the main purpose of your mission, which *must* be the search for manuscripts. The King most certainly did not intend that the money which was given you to purchase ancient manuscripts be used for another purpose . . .
>
> The travels which you are continuing throughout Greece only for the purpose of looking for inscriptions is resulting in an expense which His Majesty has no intention of making . . .
>
> The King hopes that as soon as you receive this letter you will go to visit the monasteries about which you have been told, where there may be manuscripts, and then you will return immediately to Constantinople.

The Abbé Fourmont did not pay the slightest attention to these communications from the Abbé Sevin and the Comte de Maurepas to which he replied that, "God has blessed my work and I must continue it", and requested more money "because I am ashamed for France to be seen in my ragged costume".

The Abbé Sevin stayed on in Constantinople until the spring of 1730 awaiting the promised permission to enter the Seraglio Library and for the Abbé Fourmont's return. When he finally came to the conclusion that neither of these events was in the least likely to occur, the Abbé Sevin returned to France, leaving his recalcitrant companion to wander alone through Greece on his self-appointed mission.

In fact by this time the Abbé Fourmont had embarked on a wildly demented course of behaviour. Outside the city of Patras in the Peloponnese he had come across a Byzantine castle which had been constructed with stones taken from ancient structures. He observed that some of the stones used in the walls of this castle were ancient inscribed marbles and suspecting that there might be other valuable inscriptions embedded in the structure of the castle and thus hidden from sight, he decided to find out if this was true. According to his own account he was "half-crazed with a fever contracted from the

wines which the Greeks had poisoned", when he hired some workmen and instructed them to demolish the castle. This demolition,
although it yielded no additional inscriptions, provided the Abbé
Fourmont with his first taste of the "joys of destruction" and
launched him on his incredible career of demolishing all sorts of
ancient Greek monuments in the Peloponnese which he accomplished with such ferocity and thoroughness that it was later said
of him: "Never since the invasions of the Goths and the
Vandals did Greece have such a formidable enemy as the Abbé
Fourmont "

The Abbé Fourmont spent more than a year bludgeoning the
ancient ruins of the Peloponnese in a frenzy of elated excitement
and it is apparent from his many letters to the Abbé Sevin, the
Comte de Maurepas and others in Paris that he derived great satisfaction from the very act of demolition. His bizarre behaviour was
certainly not due solely to a desire to uncover ancient inscriptions
hidden among the ruins for in fact he uncovered few inscriptions,
not one of which turned out to be of significant importance. In
his letters he positively boasted of his demolitions. In Patras he
wrote:

Despite the bad quality of the water, in spite of the fever they have
given me . . . I have completed the perfect destruction of this castle.

Of Modon he wrote:

I have torn down a castle which had three square towers and a wall
thirty feet high. It took fifteen workers nineteen days to destroy this
castle, but I finally succeeded. . . .

Of Argos:

It was one of my greatest expeditions, and it mas not accomplished
without murmurs from the people of the countryside, but I put myself
above these little things.

Of Hermione:

Every castle, every citadel and every old tower has been razed to
the ground.
6

Of Phliasia:

> I have done it . . . not only destroyed it . . . but demolished it from
> the top to the bottom. In all this great village, there is no longer one
> stone which rests on top of another.

In one letter to the Abbé Bignon, Director of the King's Library,
the Abbé Fourmont described his "work" in the Peloponnese:

> I have looked for ancient cities in this country, and I have found
> and destroyed some of them, including Hermione, Trezene, Tyrins,
> half of the citadel of Argos, Phliasia and Phinios . . .
> I do not remember having read in the accounts of travellers who
> have preceded me that they have ever dared to tear down castles and
> other buildings . . .
> Although I am not the first traveller in these lands I am, I believe,
> the first destroyer . . .
> Our mission to Constantinople had so many hopes placed in it that
> I must do this thing which is really startling . . .
> I do not permit myself to think in a small way, I must always think
> big.

At the beginning of 1730 the Abbé Fourmont arrived in Sparta
and turned the full fury of his destructive urge on the remains of
this ancient city, once the great rival of Athens. Abbé Fourmont had
spent the winter months travelling through Mania in the South-
eastern Peloponnese and felt that he had been very badly treated by
the inhabitants there whom he judged to be the direct descendants
of the ancient Spartans. All the Maniotes, he wrote, are:

> a very bad people . . . a people completely barbarous, without know-
> ledge of anything . . . warlike . . . without honour . . . brigands . . .
> murderers . . . wild dogs . . . engaged only in brigandage, murder and
> carnage.

As a consequence of this lack of hospitality shown him by the
Maniotes, the Abbé Fourmont decided to punish these people whom
he considered to be the descendants of the Spartans by demolishing
Sparta. He explained his decision in a letter to the Comte de
Maurepas:

> I do not wish that there remains anything of a city built by the
> fathers of this riff-raff . . .

For what good, you may say to me, Your Excellency, to throw oneself so furiously on a village and reduce it to the point of being unrecognizable, because of the sins of its children? I have the honour to reply that Sparta was too old, that she tried to keep her secrets from me, that she was too cold to me. No other traveller dared to lay their hands on her—the Venetians, once masters of this country, respected her . . .

For what I do I have won the admiration of the Turks . . . the Greeks shake with rage, the Jews are astonished, and I am content.

This demolition of Sparta was the highpoint of the Abbé Fourmont's extraordinary and frenzied career. He remained in Sparta for several months engaged in this furious destruction and described his accomplishments in many letters:

For thirty days I have had thirty and sometimes forty or sixty workers tearing down and exterminating Sparta. . . .

The blows that they give, the noise that the towers make when they crash to the ground, and the sound of the broken stones rolling down to the village below and to the banks of the Eurotas, can be heard not only in Laconia and all along this river, but also in all the rest of the Peloponnese and beyond . . .

I have destroyed the Temple of Apollon Amyclaeon even down to the foundation stones . . .

Imagine, if you can, what joy I have now, for Sparta is one of the biggest cities of antiquity . . .

Wherever I have workers to make demolitions, I am the first and most ardent at work . . .

If in turning over these walls and these temples, if in not permitting one stone to stand on the other in the tiniest of its ruins, Sparta becomes unknown to man, it is I who have at least made it famous, and that is something . . .

It is by this way that I will make my voyage to the Peloponnese famous and this will benefit both France and myself.

The superiors of the Abbé Fourmont were alarmed by his incoherent reports of demolition which struck them as being ill-suited to a man of God and they decided to force him to return to France. In June, 1730, the Comte de Maurepas wrote to the Marquis de Villeneuve, the French Ambassador in Constantinople, of this decision:

I see with pleasure that you think as I do that it would be useless to continue the researches to which Abbé Fourmont has attached himself, and I am very glad to learn that you have also from your part told him to leave for France.

The Abbé Fourmont, however, was still busy in Sparta and quite unwilling to stop his work. The Marquis de Villeneuve pressed his demand that he cease in yet another letter of late July: "You could not do better, if this letter finds you still in the Peloponnese, to profit from the very first opportunity that presents itself to go to Marseilles."

This last order was accompanied by a drastic reduction in the Abbé Fourmont's funds and this did make an impression on the frenzied priest who was very hurt by this action. As he wrote to a friend: "I am astonished that they reduced me to five or six hundred francs. One treats a domestic for whom one has affection with more respect."

Under these circumstances he had no choice but to comply, although he put off his departure as long as he could. His exuberant elation during the demolitions at Sparta was followed by an emotional collapse and he wrote to the Marquis de Villeneuve:

> I cannot go immediately to France because I have no strength. I must retire a few months in a monastery close to Nauplion to rest a bit from my longest fatigues which have become so insupportable that I can no longer eat, and the wine of this country is poisoned with resin and plaster, and they have only a poor bread in the country and the monasteries which I cannot digest.

While recuperating in a monastery near Nauplion, the Abbé Fourmont sent a final plea to his superiors:

> I could do so much more if you would let me. If I could do to Tegea and to Antigone and to Nemea and to one or two other villages that which I have done at Hermione, Troezene and Sparta, there would be no need to ever send anyone to Greece again, because there would no longer be anything to see.

But he remonstrated in vain for he was not permitted to return to his demolitions. Depressed and deflated, the Abbé Fourmont arrived in Paris at the end of 1730 bearing by his own account two thousand and six hundred new inscriptions which he intended to make public immediately. However it was not until after the Abbé Fourmont's death that his nephew published a few of these inscriptions which were of little historical value.

In the end the Abbé Fourmont did not manage to catalogue the ancient Greek and Latin manuscripts of the Seraglio Library, or to locate and purchase rare manuscripts, or even to copy valuable ancient inscriptions. The question remains as to whether he actually in fact did accomplish the destructions of which he boasted. It is difficult to reach any conclusion on this point. The Abbé Fourmont's familiarity with Greece was so slight and the medieval nomenclature of Greek villages so confused, that it is impossible to identify positively most of the places which he claimed to have found and obliterated—with the exception of Sparta. Since there is little doubt that the Abbé Fourmont was quite mad, it is a matter of choice whether to accept his ravings as fact or fancy. It is true that there are remarkably few ancient remains to be found in Sparta today but there is no real proof that this is the result of the Abbé Fourmont's demolitions as the ancient historian Thucydides described Sparta as having no costly buildings or sanctuaries. On the other hand Pausanias, in the second century A.D., described many ruins in Sparta which have since disappeared.

Some English scholars proposed an interesting explanation of the Abbé Fourmont's behaviour by announcing that he had invented his stories of demolitions in order to cover up the fact that he was not actually copying ancient inscriptions but forging them. They cited as proof the fact that most of the inscriptions published by Fourmont's nephew were of very dubious content and most probably forged and dismissed the Abbé Fourmont as a "bombastic and impudent fraud".

French scholars were horrified by this aspersion on the moral character of a French priest and stated categorically that the Abbé Fourmont was neither a forger nor a fraud. Furthermore they added that he had not actually destroyed ancient monuments, but that, as it was well known to all his contemporaries, the Abbé Fourmont had a weakness for drink. The sad fact was that all of his letters had been written "with the joy of the juice of the grape" and were therefore merely drunken ravings, for the Abbé Fourmont "had sacrificed to Bacchus Limneate when he let fall his signature on the bottom of these despatches".

Chapter VI

THE DILETTANTI

ONLY a few members of the English aristocracy concerned themselves with the search for ancient Greek remains in the Ottoman Empire during the eighteenth century and collecting ancient sculpture remained in England, as it was in Europe, a hobby of the wealthy upper classes. A man required both money and leisure to venture to the distant Turkish territories and to ship heavy and delicate sculptures back to his homeland.

Those who went to the very considerable trouble and expense of collecting ancient Greek sculpture did so because the possession of this ancient art still served, as it had in the days of Sulla, as a means of vaunting an individual's cultural pretensions and power. It was this intense desire for cultural pretension that led to the foundation of the national museums and art collections during the eighteenth century. The British Museum, the Hermitage, the Vatican Museum and the Louvre were opened during this period and a few decades later, the Glyptothek Museum in Munich was founded. These national museums gradually became the repositories for many of the collections of ancient statuary, inscriptions, manuscripts and paintings which had been gathered by wealthy individuals and there eventually grew up a strong sentiment that it was the privilege and duty of a gentleman to glorify his nation by adding to its national collection of art. This feeling is clearly expressed in the diary of a typical traveller of this period:

I also dreamed and hoped of having the happiness of offering to my country some little gift, but when I passed to Rhodes, the weather did not permit me to realize these hopes that I had made, and I could not return also Spolis Orientis Onustus.

Once this sentiment was firmly established, the collections of ancient statuary, busts, architectural details, pottery and coins to be found in these national museums were increased both by donation and purchase, although there continued to be collectors who preferred to display their "discoveries" in the gardens and salons of their ancestral mansions. Fortunately most of these private collections eventually ended up in museums where their contents were protected from the appalling damage and loss which had occurred on such an enormous scale to similar collections during the reign of the Stuarts.

The British Museum originated in the unusual and diverse interests of Dr. Hans Sloane who was by profession a physician of such wide repute that he became President of the Royal College of Physicians and of the Royal Society. Dr. Sloane was also a widely travelled man of enormously varied enthusiasms, a great naturalist and a born collector. Early in his medical career he went to Jamaica where he collected many of the private journals of the Caribbean buccaneers as well as eight hundred different plant species and this voyage served to make him an inveterate collector. When he died in 1752 he willed his immense collection to the British nation on payment of a stipulated sum of £20,000 to his heirs. Sloane's legacy to his country included:

> 50,000 books and manuscripts
> 1,555 fishes and their parts
> 1,172 birds and their parts, nests, eggs, etc.
> 521 vipers, serpents, etc.
> 5,439 insects
> 12,506 vegetables, including seeds, roots, etc.
> 1,125 antiquities, including ancient coins.

A public lottery of £300,000 was authorized by the British Government in order to purchase Sloane's collections and found a museum. This was the beginning of a great national collection which was opened to the public as the British Museum in Sloane's house in Bloomsbury in January, 1759. At the start only a small and select public were permitted to view the collection, according to *A Guide Book to the General Contents of the British Museum* published in 1761:

> Fifteen persons are allowed to view it in one Company, the Time allotted is two Hours; and when any Number not exceeding fifteen are inclined to see it, they must send a List of their Christian and Sirnames, Additions, and Places of Abode, to the Porter's Lodge, in order to their being entered in the Book; in a few Days the respective Tickets will be made out, specifying the Day and Hour in which they are to come, which, on being sent for, are delivered. . . .

The collections of the British Museum were enlarged from various sources soon after its foundation. Among those who contributed to the Museum in its early days were Sir William Hamilton who sold the so-called "Hamilton vase" and other pieces to the Museum in 1772; Charles Townley who donated his collection, mostly comprised of Roman sculptures, in 1805; William Hamilton who arranged for the Museum to acquire many valuable Egyptian antiquities—including the Rosetta Stone—after the surrender of the French army in Egypt in 1801; and Charles Cockerell who discovered the Phygalian frieze of the Temple of Bassae and helped the Museum to procure it. All of these men were members of the Dilettanti Society.

The Dilettanti Society was founded in the early eighteenth century by a group of young Englishmen who wanted to "encourage at home a taste for those objects which had contributed so much to their entertainment abroad". These young aristocrats wished their society—they never referred to it as a "club"—to be very exclusive and stipulated that in order to become a member a man must not only be of suitable family but must also have travelled in Italy. Even as early as 1734, when the Society was started, a gentleman completed his formal education by broadening his character and polishing his manners in a Grand Tour of the Continent, usually taken in the company of a "man of mature age" such as a minister of the Church or a tutor from a university. The Dilettanti soon found it impractical, however, to limit their membership requirements to applicants who had travelled in Italy as an insufficient number of suitable young men had visited Italy during their Grand Tour.

They first attempted to broaden this limitation by adopting a resolution that: "It is of the opinion of the Society that Avignon is in Italy, and that no other town in France is in Italy." However this also proved to be unsatisfactory and they abolished the restriction in 1750 and thereafter only required of prospective members that they should have travelled outside of Great Britain, "preferably to Italy or upon some other classic ground". The purpose of this emphasis on travel to Italy was to try to ensure that all members were endowed with a "taste for classical lands", but it would be a mistake to conclude that the original Dilettanti were serious patrons of classical art. In fact they were neither scholars, historians nor artists and the "objects" for which they specifically wanted to encourage a taste in England seem to have been principally food and wine. From its foundation and for many years afterwards the Dilettanti Society was primarily a successful dining and drinking club. The founders, of whom there were forty-six, were mostly young men in their twenties, many of whom were best known for their exploits with wine, women and song. One of the most active founders was Sir Francis Dashwood who, at twenty-five, had already "earned an ill name in history for profanity and profligacy". Dashwood's Grand Tour in Europe had given him an international reputation as an adventurer and there was little which he did not attempt in the various countries and courts which he visited. In Russia, for instance, he masqueraded as King Charles II and tried to become the lover of the Tsarina. Later he was deported from Italy for "outrages on religion and morality" and on his return to England Dashwood was one of the leaders of the "blasphemous and indecent orgies of Black Magic" which were held at Medmenham Abbey. Such was the character of the man who was one of the leading members of the Dilettanti Society during its early years.

The other founding members had interesting reputations, although none acquired quite so much of a gaudy notoriety as Dashwood. There was the Earl of Middlesex who spent most of his life and his family fortunes backing unsuccessful opera companies; Simon Harcourt whose uneventful career came to an untimely end when he fell into a well in his own garden at Courtenay; Sewallis Shirley who specialized in "consuming affairs of gallantry" with many of England's most prominent ladies; and Sir Hugh Smithson whose claim to fame lay in fathering an illegitimate son who later went to America and founded the Smithsonian Institute in Washington D.C. There was also the Earl of Sandwich who gave his name to a group of islands and a "familiar article of diet", and who was known in his own day for "the scandal caused by his conduct in private life" which included the sensational murder of his mistress and association with Dashwood in the orgies at Medmenham; the Duke of Kingston who was "less remembered on his own account than on that of his wife, the beautiful and bigamous Elizabeth"; William Berkeley who obtained the governership of Virginia where his misrule caused a rebellion and the burning of Jamestown, the first English settlement in America; and Lord Deskfourd whose "gravity and good understanding had no better end than melancholy and suicide". Other members, not quite so flamboyant, eventually became quite respectable. The official historian of the Society, while admitting that the early meetings were "convivial and perhaps uproarious", emphasized that most of the founders were men of education and distinction who later filled positions of real importance in the history of their country as statesmen, soldiers, diplomats, divines and merchant princes. The reviewer of the Dilettanti *Official History* which was privately published in the Victorian age, was not quite so kind in his estimate of the founders. In his words:

> These were times of what would now be considered very licentious merriment and very unscrupulous fun—times when men of independent means and high rank addicted themselves to pleasure and gave vent to their full animal spirits with a frankness that would now be deemed not only vulgar but indecorous, while they evinced an earnestness about objects now thought frivolous.

Although the foundation of the Dilettanti Society roughly coincided with the birth of the modern industrial and commercial age, it was several decades before the rising merchant classes, with their new power and wealth, seriously encroached on the social privileges of the old aristocracy and before the Dilettanti Society was faced with the problem of admitting applicants of non-aristocratic origins. The Society remained, with a few exceptions, exclusively aristocratic for over a century.

The early members of the Society seem to have thoroughly enjoyed themselves. Carefully and with great pomp these young gentlemen endowed their Society with an elaborate set of rules, regulations and paraphernalia. Their fortnightly dinners were held at different taverns on alternate Sunday afternoons and ended in the early evening. There was a standing rule of the Society that the President called for the bill at seven o'clock and that "No one be so disrespectful as to go away before the Bill is called for, without leave Publickly asked from and obtained of the President".

There was a fine of one guinea for the breach of this rule and there were a variety of other fines to which members were subject. A Dilettanti was always assessed a considerable sum, for instance, if his income was increased, the amount of fine being calculated on a complicated scale according to whether the increase accrued by inheritance, legacy, marriage or preferment. In addition, a careless member had to pay the Society for any number of infringements such as failing to attend a meeting if he neglected to send an excuse beforehand, drinking to another member during the Time of Dinner (Hob and Nobbing this was called), producing upon the Table a Dish of Tea or Coffee, calling the respectable Society by the disrespectful name of Club, or making a motion which nobody agreed to second. With so many restrictions a member needed to be wealthy and the numerous fines succeeded in raising funds for the Society.

At the very beginning the Society decided to appoint a variety of officers whose duties and costumes were elaborately specified. Holding of these offices automatically rotated from one member to the next and was obligatory, although in a few instances a member was permitted to decline to serve on the payment of a considerable fine. First and foremost there was the President, clad in a very elaborate scarlet toga which he was obliged to put on before the meeting began and could remove only when he descended from the official mahogany presidential chair. This costume was so ornate that they appointed another official, the Painter of the Society, to arrange its folds and apparently he was not always attentive to his duties, for there is in the record books of the Society in 1780 the following notice:

That Mr. Steward be desired to undertake to have the folds of the Toga newly arrang'd which have been derang'd by the ill Taste of the Painter with whom it had been instructed.

At a slightly later date there was a great fuss when somebody stole this Presidential Toga and a notice appeared in the books:

Resolved that secreting the Toga belonging to the Society is a high crime of misdemeanour. That all such as shall be convicted as being concerned in secreting the said Toga shall be considered as guilty of high crimes and misdemeanours. That a committee be appointed to inquire into the mode in which the Toga of this Society has been secreted and to draw up Articles of Impeachment against all such delinquents as shall be suspected of being principals or accessories in secreting the same.

Other officers of the Society included a Secretary to keep the records dressed in a costume "according to the dress of Machiavelli, the celebrated Florentine secretary" and a Very High Steward whose duties involved "the inspection of the economy of the Society at their several meetings" and who, for this purpose, carried a "short Baton of Command" and wore "a small Bacchus bestriding a Tun" around his neck on a silver chain. An Archmaster of the Ceremonies was appointed for the "more decent introduction" of new members and other ceremonial purposes and his costume was equally elaborate—a long fully pleated crimson taffeta robe with a scarlet belt and a crimson tassel, a rich scarlet "Hungarian cap" decorated with fur and a long Spanish toledo sword. The Earl of Sandwich was the first Archmaster of the Ceremonies but he treated his position and costume with such levity that he was quickly suspended from office for contempt of the Society. This was the same man who was praised by his father's chaplain in the following terms: "The prominent feature which marks his character is the reverence which he pays to authority, with entire submission to discipline."

The Society also accumulated a number of official possessions which were gradually added to over the years. There were red morocco volumes of Minutes and vellum bound books of Committee Reports, a silver inkstand, a public seal in the shape of Medusa's head and a silver box for keeping records which was called "Bacchus Tomb". The latter became elaborately engraved as the result of a Society resolution, noted in the minutes of 1767, that: "As Bacchus backside appears bare, there should be some covering provided for."

The Society also owned an increasingly large collection of portraits as a result of the strict requirement that every member present the Society with his formal portrait. The early members took this regulation very seriously and went to great expense to sit for enormous oil paintings of themselves. Among the better examples of these early portraits were the Earl of Sandwich depicted as a Mohammedan heretic, Lord Holdernesse as an Italian gardener, Lord Galway as a Roman Catholic Cardinal, Lord Ledespencer as an ill-behaved Franciscan monk, Sir James Grey as a Venetian gondolier, Lord Blessington as a Spanish minstrel, Lord Bessborough as a Turk, and the Duke of Dorset and Lord Barrington as Roman generals.

Curiously enough it was the existence of this growing collection of unusual membership portraits which led the Society to become involved in the serious study of ancient remains. It became increasingly desirable for the Society to have its own building where this collection of portraits could be permanently hung in a dining hall suitable for the regular meetings. The members found it most unsatisfactory to rent tavern dining halls for the purpose of hanging these portraits during their fortnightly dinners, even though the taverns which they used were friendly and accommodating, and they concluded that the only way they could ensure themselves a suitable permanent gallery was to build one. Within a few years after taking this decision they collected a substantial building fund from various enforced and voluntary contributions from their members and in 1747 the Society purchased a plot of land in Cavendish Square, London. They cleared the ground, planted eight elm and six horsechestnut trees and dug the foundations for the building, but for some reason the building was never completed and the Society sold the land in 1759 at a considerable profit. The proposed building scheme was brought up several times in the years that followed but it never came to anything and the Dilettanti continued to hold their meetings and hang their portraits in various assorted London taverns. After the sale of their land in Cavendish Square, the Society had a capital of many thousands of pounds which they eventually expended on a series of publications concerning classical Greek art and architecture.

There was at this time a growing demand in England for publications concerning classical art and architecture which contained accurate drawings of Greek sculpture as well as detailed measurements and descriptions of the ancient buildings which had survived in Greece and Asia Minor. Although Greek language, literature and philosophy had long since been the basis of education in England, relatively little detailed information existed on the art and architecture of ancient Greece and partly for this reason, Greek art was generally considered effeminate and inferior to its massive and better known Roman counterpart. The Turkish occupation of Greece and Asia Minor had discouraged most students of art and architecture from travel and exploration in these far-distant lands and it was commonly believed in artistic circles that all worth-while Greek monuments and sculpture had long since been destroyed. Of the few English collectors of ancient sculpture who had ventured into the depths of the Ottoman Empire the majority were singularly devoid of artistic appreciation and they, with rare exceptions, exhibited their "treasures from the Levant" only to their aristocratic friends. The attitude of these early collectors and especially of the agents whom they employed to collect for them was acquisitive rather than inquiring. They deliberately concealed any knowledge which they possessed about the location of ancient ruins in order to prevent others from locating the sites and removing their contents.

There were some early travellers, however, who expressed a real interest in the beauty of ancient ruins and described in enthusiastic terms the antiquities which they had seen in the course of their travels in the Levant. At the turn of the seventeenth century a French physician, Dr. Spon, and an English surveyor, George Wheler, travelled together through Greece and the Levant and published an extensive and immensely popular description of their voyages. At about the same time Edmund Chishull, an Englishman who had served for a number of years as chaplain to the Turkey Company factory at Smyrna, published an account of his travels in Asia Minor. These two books proved without a doubt that a great deal of exceedingly valuable Greek art and architecture had survived in Greece and Asia Minor and kindled the interest of English artists and architects.

In 1751 two young English artists who had been studying in Rome—James Stuart, son of a seaman and Nicolas Revett, of an old Suffolk family—set out to make drawings and measurements of the ancient monuments which Spon and Wheler had described as remaining in Athens. On their way to Greece they stopped off in Venice where they made the acquaintance of Sir James Grey, one of the most active members of the Dilettanti Society at that time and through his influence they were elected members. Stuart was the first member who had not been "drawn from those men who by rank or wealth figure as social leaders" but contrary to the fears of some members, his election was an exception which set a precedent that was not followed for many years to come. It did indicate, however, that the tone of the Society was changing from that of a mere drinking club into an organization which was more seriously interested in the study of the arts of antiquity.

Stuart and Revett remained in Athens until 1754 when they left during a severe outbreak of plague without having completed all the drawings and measurements which they had planned. On their return to England they became active members of the Dilettanti Society and ultimately persuaded the Society to give them financial assistance so that they could publish the drawings which they had made in Athens. The Society provided them with a generous sum drawn from their Building Fund capital and this was the first of a series of ventures by the Society of Dilettanti "for the intention of promoting interest and knowledge in England concerning classical art". As a result of these ventures, which were financed by their inactive Building Fund, the Dilettanti came to regard themselves as the greatest patrons of Greek art and architecture in the British Isles.

The first volume of Stuart and Revett's *The Antiquities of Athens* was published under the auspices of the Dilettanti Society in 1762 and was an immediate success. It was an attractive and expensive volume with drawings printed from finely engraved copper plates. Within months "Grecian Gusto" became the great fashion of architects in England and both Stuart and Revett abandoned the study of art for the practice of architecture and were very much in demand as designers of town and country houses in the classical style. This popular application of Greek architecture was often a most unfortunate choice for buildings in the damp northern climate of Britain and the Society of Dilettanti came to regret the popularity of their protégés. When the Society decided that it would like to continue as sponsors of other works on classical art, they insisted that they would only do this under conditions in which they could maintain a strict control over the men and the works involved. This was clearly stipulated in 1764, when the Society decided to spend a further sum from their Building Fund to finance an expedition to explore the ancient ruins of Asia Minor and make drawings of the worth-while classical remains of this area which they planned to publish in another work designed to "promote Public Taste and do Honour to the Society". They hired three men under contract for this expedition—Nicolas Revett, W. Pars and, as senior member, Richard Chandler, who had a reputation as a scholar of ancient Greek at Magdalen College—and these men were provided with funds and specific instructions. They were ordered to proceed directly to Smyrna where they should remain for at least twelve months:

> Making excursions to the several remains of antiquity in the neighbourhood . . . procuring the exactest plans and measures possible of the buildings . . . making accurate drawings of the bas-reliefs and ornaments, and taking such views as judged proper, copying all the inscriptions met with, and remarking every circumstance which could contribute towards giving the best idea of the ancient and present state of those places.

They were also instructed to keep careful journals of everyday occurrences and observations "representing things exactly in the light as they strike you", and these journals as well as all their drawings were to become the property of the Society which was free to use them as it pleased.

When this expedition returned to England after two years in Asia Minor, the Society expressed its praise for their "Gratefull and Proper Behaviour" and in 1769 published the first volume of these new drawings which were entitled *Ionian Antiquities*. The Dilettanti Society had every intention of bringing out the subsequent volumes of this work in rapid succession, along with the rest of Stuart and Revett's drawings of Athenian antiquities but for some reason this project became indefinitely delayed. Their publications only came out in intervals of twenty years and volume IV of *The Antiquities of Athens* was issued fifty years after the publication of volume I, while volume IV of *Ionian Antiquities* appeared one hundred and twelve years after this expedition took place. Needless to say a great many other books concerning ancient Greek art and architecture were printed in England during this long interval, so that the Dilettanti volumes did not serve the "unique function of making known the state of classical remains to the nation" as they had intended. The

VEDUTA DEL CAST: D'ACROPOLIS DALLA PARTE DI TRAMONTANA

Contemporary drawing of the explosion of the Turkish arsenal in the Parthenon at the time of Morosini's expedition.

A view of Athens that appeared in Spon and Wheler's *A Journey into Greece*.

Two Dilettanti Society paintings: (*left*) The Earl of Sandwich depicted as a Mahomedan heretic, and (*right*) Lord Galway as a Roman Catholic Cardinal.

Dilettanti also financed the publication of several other smaller
volumes on Greek architecture and another expedition to Greece
in 1814 for the purpose of making drawings.

Some of the Society's publications, however, were not in such good
taste. Towards the end of the eighteenth century Sir William Hamilton (whose wife was Lord Nelson's Lady Hamilton and whose
collection of antiquities was purchased by the British Museum in
1772) wrote a letter to a fellow Dilettanti describing his search for
antiquities around Naples. In this letter Sir William told of his
discovery in one small Italian village of:

> A curious ritual still surviving in which the ancient phallic worship
> of the Romans is maintained in all its primitive simplicity in combina-
> tion with and under the shadow of the rites paid at the shrine of the
> two martyrs St. Cosmo and St. Damian.

This description interested the Dilettanti to such an extent that
in 1786 they published a slender volume entitled *The Priapeia* which
contained Sir William Hamilton's letter:

> Concerning the great toes of the Holy Martyrs St. Cosmos and
> Damian with such illustrations as considered proper, causing the
> drawings annexed to be engraved "for the use of the members of the
> Society".

Appended to Sir William Hamilton's letter and drawings in *The
Priapeia* was a treatise by Richard Payne Knight entitled *A Dis-
course on the Worship of Priapus and its Connexion with the Mystic
Theology of the Ancients* which was described by one critic as "a
fantastic farrago of mystico-symbolical revelation and groundless
hypotheses".

The Society did not immediately realize that the publication of
The Priapeia was, as one member later expressed it, "a most unfortunate error in judgment", and at the time of publication they
even held a special ceremony in which the Archmaster, dressed in
his crimson taffeta robe and with all his insignia, delivered the
official gratitude of the Society to Richard Payne Knight for the
"able and elegant manner in which he investigated the interesting
and difficult subject of this invaluable work". About eighty copies of
The Priapeia had been distributed, including copies to the Prince of

Wales, the Royal Society and the Royal Academy, before the Society realized its error and attempted to recall these volumes of *The Priapeia* which have remained, as a consequence, one of the most keenly sought items by rare book collectors up to the present time.

A second unfortunate publication by the Dilettanti Society was a volume entitled *Specimens of Ancient Sculpture Preserved in the Several Collections of Great Britain* which they brought out as a treatise describing the best pieces of ancient Greek sculpture present in the British Isles at that time. Unfortunately the authors of this volume—Richard Payne Knight of "Priapeia" fame and Charles Townley the collector—had no feeling for unbiased scholarship and categorically stated in the name of the Society that the most valuable Greek art in all of England happened to be those pieces which were to be found in their personal collections of ancient sculpture. Regrettably the other members of the Dilettanti Society backed them in this preposterous statement and concurred when Payne Knight and Townley pronounced the Parthenon marbles which Lord Elgin brought to England as worthless fakes not to be compared with their own ancient marbles as described in *Specimens*. The reputation of the Society of Dilettanti suffered grievously from this condemnation of the Parthenon marbles.

By the early nineteenth century the Society was no longer the same exclusive, raucous dining and drinking club that it had been at the time of its foundation, a hundred years earlier. England itself had changed and the sons of a leisurely aristocracy no longer held a monopoly of wealth or patronage of the arts. While at the turn of the century there were still a majority of young Earls and Dukes among the membership of the Society—and an occasional colourful figure such as John Charles Crowle, the barrister, who was once ordered to appear and kneel at the bar of the House of Commons for having spoken ill of the House and, on rising, wiped his knees and remarked that it was the dirtiest place he had ever been in—there was a steadily increasing proportion of more serious members, such as the actor David Garrick, the painters Sir Joshua Reynolds and Benjamin West, the politician Sir Robert Peel, the banker Thomas Hope and the naturalist John Hawkins. By the end of the century there were even a few foreign members including the Italian sculptor Baron Marochetti and the Greek Ambassador Johannes Gennadius, although by this time the Society was definitely on the wane. In the days of its prime it had been felt necessary to limit membership to seventy persons but by 1850 there were less than fifty Dilettanti and many of these were honorary, inactive members. The young Englishmen of the late nineteenth century were no longer interested in belonging to the Society. Meetings became occasional and membership continued to dwindle away in the decades that followed, although the Society had survived until the present day.

The Society was most adversely affected by the disposal, after Waterloo, of Napoleon's fantastic collection of artistic spoils. Like Constantine the Great, Napoleon had been consumed by a passion for demonstrating his greatness and glory by adorning his capital with works of art and had despatched "art commissars" with all his conquering armies to select works of contemporary and ancient art "worthy of the Emperor". These commissars confiscated great quantities of paintings and sculpture from the private collections and public museums which they found in the lands overrun by Napoleon's armies, and their confiscations included not only vast numbers of valuable paintings but also hundreds of ancient sculptures which they secured principally from the museums of Italy. In some cases the Emperor's demands for artistic spoils were incorporated into the body of his treaties, as, for instance, in the truce of Bologna, where it was specifically stated that:

> The Pope will deliver to the French Republic 100 pictures, busts, vases or statues, of the choice of the commissars who are sent to Rome, among which objects are notably comprised the bust in bronze of Junius Brutus and that in marble of Marcus Brutus, both at the Capitolini, and 500 manuscripts which the commissars shall choose.

The ancient sculptures which Napoleon's commissars confiscated from Italy included many valuable works from the Belvedere and Capitolini Museums as well as items from several important private collections, such as those of the Duke of Braschi and Cardinal Albani. They acquired some five hundred and seventeen ancient sculptures in Italy and packed these into two hundred and eighty-eight cases which remained on the docks of Naples for many months awaiting shipment to Paris. Transportation was finally arranged, at a cost of 174,000 francs, on a well-armed frigate to Marseilles, and at Marseilles these sculptures were loaded onto ten barges which proceeded up the rivers and canals of France to Paris. A holiday was

decreed in the French capital to celebrate the arrival of these artistic
spoils from Italy and the sculptures were unloaded, unpacked and
placed on chariots which were drawn in triumphal procession
through the streets of Paris. Included in this shipment were the
bronze horses of St. Mark's Cathedral which the Venetians had
pillaged from Constantinople in 1204, "The Apollo of Belvedere",
"The Melpomene", "The Venus of Capitolini", "The Mercury of
Belvedere", "The Laocoon", "The Dying Gladiator", and "The
Thorn Extractor", as well as many other valuable sculptures. At the
end of the day the chariots were arranged in a circle in the Champs
de Mars and the commissars officially presented these artistic
trophies to the Emperor in a ceremony "of great solemnity". A few
months later the Louvre Museum, with a colossal bust of the
Emperor over the door, was opened to the public to display these
ancient sculptures along with many paintings gathered from the
defeated countries of Europe. These magnificent collections in the
Louvre were increased after every campaign and in 1807 Napoleon
celebrated the first anniversary of the Battle of Jena with an international exhibition of the "artistic trophies of the Grande Armée".

The repatriation of these pillaged works of art after Napoleon's
final defeat was an exceedingly complicated affair which lasted for
several years and in the end most but not all of these sculptures and
paintings were returned to their previous owners. But although
Napoleon's fantastic collection was short-lived, the effect of his
pillaging was lasting, for it became necessary for the experts who
gathered in Paris after the victory to set a monetary value on those
items which were retained in the Louvre in order to settle the question of "fair compensation". In this way ancient sculpture acquired
a cash market value. From this time on ancient statues in both
bronze and marble, ancient busts and even inscribed marbles were
bought and sold by private individuals and governments on the basis
of their "going market value". It soon followed that the collecting
and selling of ancient sculpture—not to mention the production and
selling of fakes—became a lucrative business and the amateurs of
the Dilettanti Society could not hope to compete successfully with
the shrewd businessmen who dominated the field of collecting by
the mid-nineteenth century.

Nor could the later Dilettanti compete with the professional
archaeologists when the "discovery of classical remains and the

judging and publicizing of classical art and architecture" passed into their hands during the second half of the nineteenth century. The Society did not have the means to engage in specialized and expensive archaeological expeditions with its Building Fund exhausted by the many and costly publications and with a dwindling membership which was unresponsive to demands on its purse. Although it was requested to give financial aid, the Society could only verbally support the excavations in Ephesus and Cyprus and the founding of the British School of Archaeology in Athens.

Finally, the Society could not withstand the sobering effect of Queen Victoria on England, during whose reign it ceased to flourish as a boisterous dining and drinking club. The Victorian pall effectively dampened the Rabelasian tastes of the descendants of such profligates as Sir Francis Dashwood and the irresponsible Earl of Sandwich.

Chapter VII

MARBLES FOR A SCOTTISH MANSION

IT WAS primarily a result of fantastic good fortune that Lord Elgin, a man with little artistic appreciation or interest in classical history, managed to remove all the decorative sculptures from the Parthenon in Athens. He did so with the intention of using these ancient marbles to decorate the mansion which he was building in Scotland and was sufficiently naïve—and egotistical—to believe that no one would question his right to confiscate whatever he wanted, for his own purposes.

This seventh Earl of Elgin and eleventh Earl of Kincardine was born in 1766 and succeeded to the title in his early childhood. After attending Harrow, Westminster and St. Andrew's he purchased an army commission and eventually progressed through the purchase system to the rank of Major-General. However Elgin was not interested in the army and embarked on a diplomatic career in 1790 by serving briefly as British Envoy to Brussels. It was on his return from his second diplomatic assignment as Envoy Extraordinary at Berlin in 1795 that he decided he ought to marry in order to ensure an heir. He selected an appropriately wealthy young lady and promised her the wedding gift of a magnificent new mansion in Scotland for which he commissioned Thomas Harrison, a young architect, to draw up the plans. The fashion for buildings constructed on the lines of classical monuments was still prevalent in England at this time and Harrison wanted to design the new mansion —which Elgin intended to call "Broom Hall"—in this mode. He had studied architecture in Rome where he had developed a great passion for classical buildings and had already designed one public building in England in the style of an ancient temple. Harrison eloquently described the beauty and advantages of the classical style to his Scottish patron who was more sensitive to the dictates of fashion than to the attractions of an architectural style. Elgin was easily persuaded to accept a design which would assure him the role of a forerunner of the English mode in Scotland.

Shortly after this decision was taken Elgin was appointed Ambassador at Constantinople and decided to leave promptly to take up his new post. It was a far more important diplomatic assignment than any he had previously held, for England hoped to profit from the reaction of the Ottoman government to Napoleon's invasion of Egypt, then part of the Ottoman Empire. Elgin accordingly completed the arrangements for his marriage and prepared for a long absence from England. His wedding present could not be completed before leaving for Constantinople but Elgin promised his bride that Broom Hall would be ready and waiting for them on their return. He contacted Harrison to give him last-minute instructions and found the young architect in a state of great excitement over his employer's appointment as Ambassador to Constantinople. Harrison insisted that Elgin should take advantage of this "magnificent appointment" by including architects and draftsmen on his staff whose occupation would be to make drawings of the ancient monuments which still remained in Greece and Asia Minor. He explained that the data to be found in Stuart and Revett's *The Antiquities of Athens*, which had been published by the Dilettanti Society, was incomplete and there were still a great many ancient structures in Athens alone which had not been measured and drawn. He pointed out that Lord Elgin would be doing his country a great service if he brought back new and invaluable knowledge of Greek architecture to England.

Elgin was interested in this suggestion but not convinced that it was worth his while to go to all the trouble and expense of hiring architects and draftsmen to take with him to Turkey. Harrison suggested that the British Government might be willing to pay the cost of such an expedition and pointed out that Elgin would also be able to use these architects to get the exact measurements and proportions of original Greek temples and that such information could be used in the building of Broom Hall. In this manner Lord Elgin's mansion would be the first building in Great Britain which was in fact an exact duplicate of a classical Greek building. Furthermore, Harrison added, he would be able to decorate Broom Hall and its gardens with unique copies of ancient Greek sculpture as there was a great deal of ancient sculpture in Greece and especially in Athens which had never before been copied. He urged Elgin to take a moulder with him in order to make copies of ancient sculptures.

This vision of a unique and magnificent Broom Hall convinced Elgin who then applied to the British Government for a party of eminent English architects, draftsmen and moulders to accompany his mission to Constantinople. The request was refused but Elgin had made up his mind and approached the young English painter J. M. W. Turner whom he offered a good salary upon the condition that he would give possession of all drawings and plans which he made in Greece. Turner, who was already so successful as an artist that he had just been elected an Associate of the Royal Academy at the age of twenty-two, refused Elgin's offer and the Scottish lord interviewed several other architects and painters who demanded what he considered to be excessive salaries. He then decided that he might be able to hire European architects and draftsmen at much cheaper rates.

Elgin left England in the summer of 1799 with his bride and personal secretary and went directly to Sicily to visit Sir William Hamilton. Sir William, the author of "The Priapeia" letter which had caused such distress for the Society of the Dilettanti, had served as British Envoy to the Kingdom of Naples for many years where his interest in antiquities had led him to collect a fine assortment of Greek vases, terracottas and bronze and gold ornaments—unfortunately this poor man was ultimately famous not for his diplomatic achievements, which were considerable, nor for his collection of antiquities which formed an important addition to the British Museum to whom he sold it in 1772, but simply as the husband of Lord Nelson's Lady Hamilton.

One reason for Elgin's visit to Sir William was to request the elder stateman's advice about hiring European architects and draftsmen. Sir William introduced him to a Neapolitan painter, Giovanni Battista Lusieri whom Elgin hired as a painter at a moderate salary and on the understanding that he was "to employ his time and his art under the orders of His Excellency, being completely understood that all the works which he would do during this trip would belong to His Excellency".

Once the contract with Lusieri was signed, Elgin and his wife went on to Constantinople, leaving his private secretary and Lusieri to hire the necessary draftsmen and moulders. His secretary, William Richard Hamilton—no relation to Sir William—was a young and competent Scotsman who later had a distinguished career as Undersecretary of State, British Minister at Naples and Trustee of the British Museum.

Hamilton and Lusieri proceeded to Naples where they were witnesses to Napoleon's plunder of the art treasures of Italy and were incensed by the sight of many of the best ancient sculptures from the Belvedere Court lying about the docks of Naples waiting to be packed and shipped to Paris. (Hamilton never forgot this experience and after the peace of 1815 he was one of the more militant members of the British commission sent to Paris to arrange the repatriation of these pillaged art works.) Hamilton and Lusieri spent the winter in Naples and hired Feodor Ivanovitch, a Tartar figure painter from Astrakhan who had studied art in Germany and Italy; two architects—Vincenzo Balestra, a hunchback, and Sebastian Ittar; and two Italian moulders, Bernadino Ledus and Vincenzo Rosati. This artistic commission left Naples in the spring of 1800 with Lusieri in command, having been supplied by Hamilton with the necessary provisions and tools of their trades and twenty-two paragraphs of incredibly detailed and ambitious orders from Elgin. They were instructed to go directly to Athens to "carefully and minutely measure every ancient monument . . . make rough and finished architectural drawings of all buildings . . . make moulds of all the sculptures adorning them, including all bas-reliefs". In addition, these artists were instructed to "assiduously search for any buried ruins in Athens", as well as to "measure and delineate all remains which can be discovered in the several other parts of Greece."

In their spare time they were instructed to "make landscape drawings of Athens, of the Greek mainland, and of all the Greek islands". Lord Elgin was very thorough in his plans and did not anticipate that his artists would encounter any difficulties in the execution of his orders.

The resident British Consul in Athens at this time was a Greek named Logotheti who was astonished by the arrival of Elgin's artists. When they showed him their instructions, he stated categorically that it would be impossible for them to do these things, since all of the important monuments of Athens, including the Parthenon, the Erechtheum and the Propylae, were to be found on the Acropolis which then served as a Turkish fortress. The Disdar who was in command of the fortress refused to permit any foreigners to enter the citadel. Nevertheless Lusieri and Logotheti visited the Disdar in his headquarters in the Propylae and managed to bribe him with lavish gifts of tea and sugar so that he agreed to permit Elgin's artists to enter the fortress of the Acropolis on payment of five guineas per day. At the end of one week Lusieri returned to the Disdar with more tea and sugar and requested his permission to erect scaffolding around the ancient monuments so that they could make the necessary measurements and make casts of the decorative sculpture. The Disdar refused this request, pointing out to them that there were a great many Turkish dwellings on the Acropolis at this time and if the artists erected scaffolding they would be in a position to look down into the Turkish courtyards where Turkish women lived. It was axiomatic that no Turk ever permitted another man—and especially a Christian—to look upon his women. The Disdar was adamant on this point. Under these circumstances there was nothing the artists could do but measure and copy those sections of the monuments which were accessible at ground level and for more than one year they worked under these conditions, paying their daily five-guinea entrance fee.

In the spring of 1801 Dr. Philip Hunt, the British Embassy Chaplain who spent much more of his time and energies travelling around Greece in search of antiquities than in ministering to his small flock in Constantinople, passed through Athens where he talked to Lusieri. They agreed that the artists must find some means to study the upper sections of the monuments, especially the frieze of the Parthenon, and Dr. Hunt suggested that the only solution was to get permission to erect scaffolding from a higher Ottoman authority in Constantinople. An insatiable collector, Dr. Hunt also conceived the idea of removing some souvenirs of antiquities from the Acropolis. He sent a memorandum to Elgin from Athens stating that:

Dr. Hunt recommends that a *Firman* should be procured from the Porte [the Ottoman government in Constantinople was officially entitled the Sublime Porte] addressed to the Disdar, or Governor of the Citadel, stating that the artists are in the service of the British Ambassador Extraordinary and that they are to have not only permission, but protection in the following objects:

(1) To enter freely within the walls of the citadel, and to draw and model with plaster the ancient temples there.

(2) To erect scaffolding and to dig where they may wish to discover the ancient foundations.

(3) The liberty to take away any sculptures or inscriptions which do not interfere with the works or walls of the citadel.

When this memorandum reached Elgin he had already started collecting ancient sculpture around Constantinople and his collection then included several statues and a marble throne. He wrote Lusieri that he would use all his influence to procure the necessary *firman* for erecting scaffolding and it is apparent from this letter that Elgin had by this time conceived the idea of decorating Broom Hall with original ancient sculptures rather than with copies:

Balestra has with him several drawings of my house in Scotland, and some plans of the site on which it is intended to build . . . the plans for my house in Scotland should be known to you. The building is a subject that occupies me greatly, and offers me the means of placing, in a useful, distinguished and agreeable way, the various things that you may perhaps be able to procure for me . . . the Hall is intended to be adorned with columns, the cellars underneath are vaulted expressly for this. . . . In either case I should wish to collect as much marble as possible. I have other places in my house which need it, and besides, one can easily multiply ornaments of beautiful marble without overdoing it, and nothing, truly is so beautiful and also independent of changes in fashion. . . .

You do not need any prompting from me to know the value that is attached to a sculptured marble, or historic piece. . . .

The statement which appeared in a prominent English magazine at a later date that the "Elgin marbles were acquired for England primarily by her great hero, Lord Nelson" is an exaggeration, but there is no doubt that the Ottoman government was predisposed to favour the English Ambassador's request as a result of the British victories over the French in Egypt. Nor is there any question that the *firman* was granted to Elgin in his capacity as British Ambassador rather than as a private citizen, so that it could well be argued that what he took from Greece as a result of this *firman* legally belonged to the nation in whose name he acted, rather than to himself, personally. The *firman* which was granted by the Ottoman authorities in the summer of 1801 was delivered to Lusieri by the wandering chaplain, Dr. Hunt. It was addressed to the Disdar of the Acropolis and stated:

> It is hereby signified to you that our sincere Friend His Excellency Lord Elgin, Ambassador Extraordinary from the Court of England to the Porte of Happiness, has represented to us that . . . in particular the ministers or officers of state, philosophers, primates and other individuals of England have a remarkable taste for the drawings, or figures, or sculptures remaining ever since the time of the said Greeks. . . .
>
> His Excellency, the said Ambassador, has therefore engaged five English painters, now dwelling in Athens, to examine and view, and also to copy the figures remaining there. . . .
>
> That as long as the said painters shall be employed in going in and out of the said citadel of Athens which is the place of their occupations, and in fixing scaffolding round the ancient Temple of the Idols there, or in modelling with chalk or gypsum the said ornaments and visible figures thereon, or in measuring the fragments and vestiges of other ruined edifices, or in excavating, when they find it necessary, the foundations, in search of inscriptions among the rubbish, that no interruption may be given them. . . .
>
> That no one may meddle with the scaffolding or implements they may require in their works, and that *when they wish to take away any pieces of stone with old inscriptions or figures thereon, that no opposition be made thereto.* . . .
>
> That is the explicit desire and engagement of this Sublime Court endowed with all eminent qualities, to favour such requests as the above-mentioned, in conformity with what is due to the friendship, sincerity, alliance, and good will subsisting ab antiquo between the Sublime and ever durable Ottoman Court and that of England.

While the Disdar of the Acropolis hastened off to warn the Turkish women, Elgin's artists went promptly to work erecting scaffolding, and as soon as the scaffolding around the Parthenon was complete, they started to dismantle the frieze. It is impossible to say who gave the final order to remove the sculptures of the Parthenon rather than merely to measure and mould them as was originally planned. There is no doubt that Dr. Hunt had some hand in this decision, for his greed for antiquities knew no bounds and few scruples. He wrote to Elgin from Athens that summer that:

> The Caryatids which support the Erechtheum are items of great value and beauty and if your Lordship would come here in a large Man of War that beautiful model of ancient art, the Erechtheum, might be transported wholly to England.

Dr. Hunt also suggested removing the entire palace of Mycenae to England, but reluctantly came to the conclusion that it was "too gigantic and too distant from the sea to give any hopes of being able to obtain it".

It was Lusieri who directed the operations for the removal of the Parthenon sculptures and Elgin himself visited Athens only once, in the spring of 1802, when he saw the antiquities of the Acropolis for the first time. The removal was a huge undertaking and Lusieri employed more than three hundred workmen for more than a year taking down and packing the frieze and architectural ornaments of this famous ancient temple. Elgin insisted that the job be completed quickly, before the French were reinstated in the favour of the Turkish government. "Every moment is very precious in securing our acquisitions, for there are already rumours that French frigates might soon be permitted to enter the Aegean Sea," he wrote.

There is little evidence that Elgin's fears of French interference were justified.

What Elgin actually took from the Parthenon were seventeen figures from the pediments, fifteen metopes and fifty-six slabs— two hundred and forty-seven feet—of the frieze. The frieze slabs and pediment statues were removed without doing any appreciable damage to the building but the metopes could not be detached until the cornices above them were destroyed. In addition to the Parthenon marbles, Lusieri also collected for his employer one Caryatid column from the Erechtheum, four slabs from the frieze of the Temple of Victory, the statue of Dionysus from the monument of Thrasyllus and plaster casts of the Theseum, as well as thirteen marble heads, thirty-four odd pieces of marble sculpture, several

hundred vases, eight altars, thirteen sepulchral pillars, fifty-one
casts and moulds and sixty-six slabs with inscriptions. All of these
items were packed into more than two hundred cases and shipped
to England gradually over a period of years. In most cases shipments
were made without charge on English men-of-war which were
ordered to stop at Piraeus to pick up the Ambassador's plunder.
There was, however, one shipwreck. *The Mentor*, a brig purchased
by Elgin for the purpose of transporting his antiquities, was caught
in a storm off the southern coast of the Peloponnese and sank,
taking her cargo of seventeen cases of Elgin marbles to rest in
twelve fathoms of water. These cases were eventually recovered by
divers but only after four years and at considerable cost.

There were several Englishmen who visited Athens during the
removal of the Parthenon marbles and they were extremely critical
of the entire operation, although jealousy was often a factor in-
fluencing their disapproval. One traveller wrote to friends in England
that he had discovered a fragment of a metope in a corner of the
Acropolis but could not take it away:

> Owing to the embargo then laid upon everything of this kind by our
> Ambassador and the absolute prohibition against moving anything,
> except into his storehouse. The Ambassador has secured every rich
> morsel of sculpture that was to be found.

Another English traveller reported that he had the:

> Inexpressible mortification to see the Parthenon dismantling. It is
> painful to reflect that these trophies of human genius, which had
> resisted the silent decay of time during a period of more than twenty-
> two centuries, which had escaped the destructive fury of the Icono-
> clasts, the considerable rapacity of the Venetians and the barbarous
> violence of the Mohamedans, should at last have been doomed to
> experience the devastating outrage which will never cease to be
> deplored.

The most outspoken and influential critic of Elgin's removal was
the romantic exile, Lord Byron. On the rock of the Acropolis Byron
carved his succinct *"Quod non fecerunt Gothi, fecerunt Scoti"* ("What
the Goths spared, the Scots have destroyed") and he wrote three
caustic poems on the subject. At least one of these poems, "The

Curse of Minerva", was widely circulated in England, with verses such as:

> Daughter of Jove! In Britain's injur'd name,
> A true-born Briton may the deed disclaim,
> Frown not on England—England owns him not;
> Athena! No—the plunderer was a Scot.
>
> First on the head of him who did the deed
> My curse shall light, on him and all his seed.
> Without the spark of intellectual fire,
> Be all his sons as senseless as their sire.

Elgin was unconcerned with this criticism of his removal of the Parthenon marbles when he left Constantinople at the beginning of 1803. On his way to England he stopped off in Rome to request the Italian sculptor Canova to restore and renovate these sculptures but Canova refused, declaring that "they were the work of the ablest artists the world has ever seen and it would be a sacrilege for me, or any man, to presume to touch them with a chisel".

This statement greatly impressed Elgin with the value of the antiquities which he had gathered to decorate Broom Hall and he was congratulating himself on his good luck when a misfortune befell him. While travelling through France he was arrested in accordance with Napoleon's decree ordering the detention of all Englishmen between the ages of eighteen and sixty as prisoners of war. He was confined in France for more than three years, until the summer of 1806 when he was allowed to return to England on parole.

While Elgin was forcibly detained in France, his wife and children went on to England and Lusieri stayed in Athens to arrange the shipment of the marbles. (Lusieri remained in Athens until 1813, often hampered in his work by the reinstated French Consul, Fauvel, who once managed to delay the removal of the marbles from the Acropolis by hiding the wheels of the only suitable cart in Athens.) Cases of the so-called Elgin marbles began to arrive at the English docks in 1805 and eventually filled a number of warehouses. These cases addressed to Lord Elgin became a topic of conversation in English salons where opinions were loudly expressed on the value of the collection long before the cases were opened and the marbles displayed. Richard Payne Knight, self-styled art critic of the Dilettanti Society, created a sensation by announcing that the Elgin marbles were worthless second-rate sculptures which had been added to the Parthenon during Roman times, citing as proof the comment of the early travellers, Spon and Wheler, that one of the figures on the frieze resembled the Roman Emperor Hadrian. The principal reason for Payne Knight's condemnation of the Parthenon marbles—a condemnation which was echoed by other collectors— was their fear that Elgin's collection might turn out to be superior to their own.

When Elgin finally arrived in England in 1806 he was confronted not only by a public controversy over the value of his marbles and the propriety of his removal of them from the Parthenon but also with a domestic crisis. His wife announced that she no longer cared for his company and would have nothing to do with him or his wedding present, Broom Hall. Under these circumstances Elgin decided to stay in London and not to move the sculptures to Scotland. He brought the marbles first to the house of the Duchess of Portland and then to the residence of the Duke of Richmond, although it was several years before the whole collection arrived in England. When war broke out between England and Turkey in 1807, Fauvel, the active French Consul in Athens, seized eighty cases of Elgin's marbles which Lusieri had left behind in his flight from Athens but he was unable to arrange their shipment to France before peace was signed and Lusieri returned to claim them. The complete collection of the Parthenon marbles finally reached England by 1808 and was then installed in a large shed at the corner of Park Lane and Piccadilly which Elgin had built for this purpose.

This Park Lane shed served as a private museum to which a few selected visitors were invited to view the sculptures. Elgin exhibited his collection in order to prove that the Parthenon marbles were not second-rate art and that he had, in fact, the finest collection of ancient Greek sculptures in the British Isles. He had become convinced of their value not merely by Canova's pronouncement on their artistic merit but also by the fact that several times during the course of his arrest the French government had proffered his release on condition that he donate these marbles to France. In addition, he hoped that the publicity received by exhibiting these marbles would increase their market value, for he was already considering

A sketch by W. Pars of the Acropolis as it appeared in Lord Elgin's time.

Two of the figures forming the frieze of the Temple of Aphaea in Aegina
after its restoration by Thorwaldsen.

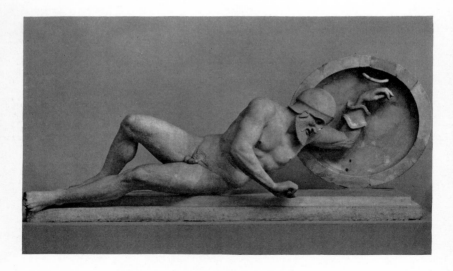

the possibility of selling the collection as he was feeling the pinch of financial stress. His marriage to his wealthy wife had been dissolved by Act of Parliament and his subsequent involvement and re-marriage to a woman of lesser financial resources had forced him to consider this possibility. He had already determined to give up the property in Park Lane and felt that he could not afford to build a suitable and permanent accommodation for the collection elsewhere. He no longer wanted, or felt it advisable, to take the widely publi-cized collection to Scotland.

Exhibiting the marbles to a select public produced the effect which Elgin desired and several critics and artists were outspoken in their praise, including the painter Benjamin Haydon who was exceedingly impressed and eloquent: "I felt as if a divine truth had blazed inwardly upon my mind, and I knew that they (the marbles) would at last rouse the art of Europe from its slumber of darkness."

Quick to follow in rapturous description of the Elgin marbles were Benjamin West, President of the Royal Academy, and Henry Fuseli, Keeper of the Royal Academy. Keats was so moved by the beauty of these sculptures that he composed a sonnet entitled "On Seeing the Elgin Marbles". In retaliation, Byron published another barb:

> Let Aberdeen and Elgin still pursue
> The shade of fame through regions of Virtu;
> Waste useless thousands on their Phidian freaks,
> Misshapen monuments and maimed antiques,
> And make their grand salons a general mart,
> For all the mutilated blocks of art.

On the strength of this publicity Elgin offered his collection of marbles to the Paymaster-General of the British Government for £62,440. The Government made no formal reply to Elgin's offer but it was unofficially intimated to him that the most the Govern-ment would be prepared to pay for his collection was £30,000. Enraged by this response Elgin refused to discuss the price and closed the Park Lane museum. The marbles were moved in the summer of 1811 to a shed in the yard of Burlington House and their owner returned truculently to Scotland, having written to Lusieri to put his accounts in order and bring all work in Athens to a close.

In 1816 Elgin renewed his offer of the collection to the British Government. His timing was then more opportune, for during the

8

interim several European collectors had shown a considerable interest in the marbles. One of these prospective buyers was Crown Prince Ludwig of Bavaria whose passion was collecting ancient statues, having them badly restored and displaying them in the Glyptothek Museum in Munich which he had constructed for this purpose. Prince Ludwig was physically unattractive, "his face so covered with pimples that his red beard grew sparse and patchy" and his manners were not those of a gentleman by English standards. He had outraged the English by outbidding the representatives of the British Museum and securing for himself the marbles from the frieze of the Temple of Aegina which an Englishman had discovered and as a consequence there was considerable alarm when Elgin invited Ludwig to London to see his collection. It was reported that Ludwig expressed great enthusiasm for the marbles and that he made a handsome offer for the entire collection. Elgin declined this offer but Ludwig deposited a large sum for the purchase with his bankers in England in case Elgin should change his mind.

It was also at this period that a great number of "art experts" had been gathered in Paris to arrange the repatriation of the hoard of works of art which Napoleon had amassed from his conquests. Elgin took advantage of this gathering to request the considered opinions of some of these "experts" on the value of the Parthenon marbles. The Italian sculptor Canova wrote a tribute which Elgin had published privately. It read, in part:

> Oh that I had but to begin again! To unlearn all that I had learned—
> I now at last see what ought to form the real school of sculpture.
> Allow me, my Lord, to express to you the lively sentiments of pleasure which I feel from having seen in London the inestimable antique marbles brought by your Lordship from Greece. . . . I am persuaded that all artists and amateurs must gratefully acknowledge their high obligation to Your Lordship for having brought these memorable and stupendous sculptures into our neighbourhood.

Elgin also paid the expenses for a trip to England by the highly esteemed artist Visconti, who praised the Parthenon marbles and delivered two laudatory addresses on them to the Academy of Paris. The Parthenon marbles became the fashion, as shown in a contemporary advertisement in *The Times*:

To the nobility, Gentry and Fashionable World. Ross's newly invented GRECIAN VOLUTE HEAD-DRESS, formed from the true marble models, brought into this country from the Acropolis of Athens by Lord Elgin. Rivals any hitherto invented.

On the strength of this popular acclaim and encouraged by his former secretary William Hamilton who was then serving as Under Secretary for Foreign Affairs, Elgin offered his collection to the British Government in 1816 for the revised figure of £74,240 which he arrived at by an analysis of what the marbles had cost him, including interest, itemized as:

Cost of obtaining and removing collection from Athens	£28,000
Loss and recovery of the *Mentor* (ship that was shipwrecked)	£5,000
Interest on this sum	£23,240
Expenses in England	£6,000
Lusieri's salary	£12,000
	£74,240

On receipt of this offer a special Committee of the House of Commons was appointed to decide:

Whether it be expedient that the collection mentioned in the Earl of Elgin's petition should be purchased on behalf of the public and if so, what price it may be reasonable to allow for same.

The committee sat for eight days, having been carefully instructed to:

Recall the gravity of the subject they were about to consider and how highly the cultivation of the Fine Arts has contributed to the reputation, character and dignity of every government by which they have been encouraged, and how intimately they are connected with the advancement of everything valuable in science, literature and philosophy.

They first considered the authority by which the collection was acquired and the circumstances under which that authority was granted and found that Elgin had full authority from the Turkish Government for his activities and that he had acted in a private capacity. It was conceded, however, that only an Ambassador could have obtained such extensive powers. The committee then considered "the merit of the marbles as works of sculpture and the importance of making them public property for the purpose of promoting the study of the Fine Arts in Great Britain." They were reminded by William Hamilton, Under Secretary for Foreign Affairs, of the hope that:

> Prodigal as Nature is in the perfection of the human figure in this country, animating as are the instances of patriotism, heroic actions, and private virtues deserving commeration, sculpture may soon be raised in England to rival the ablest productions of the best times in Greece.

The committee then listened gravely to the opinions of an impressive array of English artists and art critics on the subject of the value of the Parthenon marbles. Nollekens, Flaxman, Westmacott, Chantrey, Rossi, Lawrence, Williams and West concurred in rating the marbles "in the very first class of ancient art", some placing them a little superior to and others a little inferior to well-known ancient sculptures such as "The Apollo Belvedere", "The Laocoon" and "The Torso of the Belvedere". A dissentient opinion was expressed by Richard Payne Knight who still stubbornly maintained that these marbles were Roman copies. (According to a report later prepared by the British Museum, it was "very much to the committee's credit that it discounted Payne Knight's pompous bigotry".)

On the basis of these opinions of the artistic merit of the Parthenon sculptures, the committee decided on a bid for these marbles based on the current market value of comparable statues such as "The Apollo Belvedere" and "The Laocoon", rather than on Elgin's expenses. In June of 1816 the British Government offered Elgin £35,000 for his collection.

Elgin was certainly not happy with this offer and the report of the committee which he found "pervaded by manifest coldness and ill will" but he accepted it. He had long since ceased to covet these ancient statues to adorn Broom Hall and had, in fact, never been deeply moved by the artistic merits of the sculptures which he had taken from Athens. There is no doubt that the amassing of this collection involved him in an enormous expense, the only result of which had been public obloquy and general vexation and he was finally pleased to be shot of the whole enterprise at the figure offered by the Government. In this way the Parthenon marbles passed into the keeping of the British Museum.

Chapter VIII

MARBLES FOR CAMBRIDGE

─────────────────────────────

LORD ELGIN'S acquisition of the Parthenon marbles was the envy of many an English traveller and in their jealousy these less success-ful collectors deplored the opportunities given to their ambassador, a man whom they considered totally unable to appreciate the value of ancient sculpture. One of the most outspoken of these envious critics was Edward Daniel Clarke, the Bursar of Jesus College, Cambridge, who was inspired with a real passion for collecting. A large part of Clarke's life had been spent in touring England and Europe and during the course of these trips he had collected thousands of bugs and beetles, seeds and plants and all kinds of mineral samples. He had started collecting ancient coins and manu-scripts while travelling through Asia Minor and by the time he reached Athens in 1801, he had begun to covet ancient statuary. His ambition was to win distinction at Cambridge by sending the University an unrivalled stock of rare items for its libraries and museums. His visit to Athens coincided with the removal of the frieze and metopes from the Parthenon by Elgin's agents and, as he watched these operations, Clarke raged that such priceless treasures should have fallen to the "lot of a Scottish boor". He became even more determined to secure some valuable mementos of the great civilization of ancient Greece for Cambridge.

Edward Daniel Clarke was born in Sussex in 1769 to a family of clergymen whose "learning and abilities reflected, for a long series of years, the highest credit upon the literature of their country". As a child Clarke showed no inclination to follow the example of his serious and scholarly forefathers and the best that could be said of him at this time was that he "exhibited from his infancy the same talent for playful conversation and narrative which ever afterward distinguished him in the various and extensive circles through which he moved". When his parents despaired of teaching him at home, he was sent to a nearby grammar school whose headmaster frequently complained that he was sorely deficient in application and excelled only in jumping, swimming and running. He was subsequently sent to Jesus College, Cambridge, where his career was undistinguished by scholarly accomplishments and his continued habits of "indolence and real trifling" caused "considerable alarm" to his family. In his third year at the University Clarke won acclaim by constructing an elaborately decorated balloon, so large that it occupied the entire height of the college hall where it was suspended during construction. When the balloon was scheduled for ascension from the college lawn with a kitten as its passenger, a "vast concourse" of spectators crowded on the college grounds to applaud its successful launching. It was remarked, however, that the construction of this balloon had required all of Clarke's efforts during an entire important term "in which most of his contemporaries were employed in assiduous preparation for their approaching disputations in the schools".

Clarke eventually took his B.A. degree and lacking any desire to continue his studies or to take up any profession, he accepted a position as tutor to the nephew of the Duke of Dorset. He persuaded the Duke that his nephew would greatly benefit from travel and accompanied his pupil on an extended tour of the British Isles in 1791. They gathered a great number of plants and stones during the course of this trip and Clarke came to the conclusion that travelling and collecting were the great joys of his life. "I am doomed to be a wanderer", he wrote to his widowed mother who still entertained hopes that her son would take holy orders and settle down. But the prospect of retiring to a country parish was abhorrent to Clarke and when the Duke of Dorset's nephew entered the army, he procured a similar assignment for himself as tutor to Lord Berwick on a two-year tour of France, Germany, Switzerland, Italy and Spain. An enthusiastic tourist, Clarke kept voluminous diaries and wrote innumerable letters home to his mother and college friends which contained such items as "a very lively account of the liquefaction of St. Januarius' blood at Naples". He continued to collect mineralogical and botanical specimens on this trip but did not subscribe to the fashion current in Italy at this time for collecting ancient sculpture. As he explained to his mother:

> The Romans surpass belief in faking ancient legs, arms and noses. The shop of an antiquarian here reminds me of an almanack I have seen in England where one finds a list of hips, thighs, toes, fingers, etc., adapted for every day of the week. Indeed Rome has been so long exhausted of every valuable relic, that it has become necessary to institute a manufactory for the fabrication of such rubbish as half the English nation come in search of every year.

After several other assignments as tutor to young noblemen, Clarke returned to his mother's house in Sussex in 1798 to ruminate about his future while "enjoying shooting and other country pursuits". When his name was put down for the local militia, the prospect of entering the army filled him with such horror that he applied for a position at Cambridge. He wrote to a friend:

> My going to College for a short time I am afraid will now be absolutely necessary, for they have entered my name to be ballotted for as a supplementary militia-man. Tell the Master I will be bursar, shoe-black, or gip, to avoid marching amongst a mob of undrilled recruits . . . Seriously, I will beg of you to request the Master to appoint me Bursar without delay, that I may go to Lewes and tell the justices I am exempted by a College office.

Clarke secured the position of Bursar at Jesus College and had not been long in residence when he met a wealthy young man, John Martin Cripps, who wanted to be tutored at College and then accompanied on a tour of the Continent. As only northern Europe was then open to English travellers, Clarke planned a trip with Cripps to Norway, Sweden and as much of Russia as they could cover during the summer vacation. They were joined by William Otter and another Cambridge cleric, Thomas Robert Malthus, whose recent work, *An Essay on Population*, had stirred up such a torrent of violent controversy that he wished to absent himself from England for a while. They left England in May of 1799 on a trip which was expected to last for six or seven weeks but Clarke and

Cripps did not return to England until November of 1802, after having travelled abroad for three and a half years.

Cripps proved to be an ideal travelling companion as he was both "generous of his means" and so "embued with a singular attachment and devotion to his tutor" that he was disposed to agree with every plan which Clarke put forward. Malthus and Otter left them in Sweden and returned to England as they were unwilling to participate in Clarke's scheme for launching a balloon in Tornéa, the capital of Lapland. Clarke complained that Malthus and Otter "lacked sufficient enterprise" and proceeded with his pupil to Lapland where they successfully launched an eighteen-foot balloon, an event which "attracted all the natives in droves to see the Englishmen and their wonder of wonders".

After the spectacular ascent of their balloon in Lapland, Clarke and Cripps went on to St. Petersburg where they were most disfavourably impressed by the Russian nobility and government. They considered the Tzar insane and wrote home that they had never seen "a system of administration more offensive in the eyes of God or man". One of the things which irritated them most were the official regulations concerning the attire of Englishmen:

> Englishmen are compelled to wear a dress regulated by the police; and as every officer had a different notion of the mode of observing these regulations, we were constantly liable to be interrupted in the streets and public places and treated with impertinence. The dress consisted of a cocked hat, or, for want of one, a round hat pinned up at three corners, a long cue, a single-breasted coat and waistcoat, knee buckles instead of strings, and buckles in the shoes. Orders were given to arrest any person seen in pantaloons.

They left St. Petersburg and proceeded on to Moscow in midwinter, carrying large quantities of frozen game and fish as provisions for the trip. They found Moscow no more to their taste for it seemed to them a conglomeration of huts, gardens, pig-sties, brick walls, churches, dung-hills, palaces, timber-yards, warehouses and "a refuse, as it were, of materials sufficient to stock an empire with miserable towns and miserable villages". They found all Russians, rich and poor, servile to their superiors, haughty and cruel to their dependants and an "ignorant, superstitious, cunning, brutal, barbarous, dirty and mean people". They described the rooms where they stayed as so filthy that an Englishman would hesitate to use them as a kennel for his dogs:

> The dirt on the floor may be removed only with an iron hoe or a shovel. These places are entirely destitute of beds. They consist of bare walls, with two or three old stuffed chairs, ragged, rickety, and full of vermin. The walls themselves are still more disgusting, as the Russians load them with the most abominable filth.

They stayed for a few weeks in Moscow in order to observe the celebration of a Russian Easter and were shocked with what they saw, writing home that "nothing could rival the debauchery, superstition, licentiousness and parade" which they had observed in Moscow. The Russians, they reported, indulged in every kind of excess at Easter-time and "rolled about drunk the whole week, as if rioting, debauchery, extravagance, gambling, drinking and fornication" were as much of a religious observation as starving had been during Lent.

Thoroughly disillusioned with central Russia, Clarke and Cripps headed southwards towards the Crimea, travelling in the company of several dogs and four large marmots, the latter being left behind after they had eaten away the lining of their carriage. They were beset with difficulties on this trip—"bad air, bad water, bad food, bad climate and bad people"—as well as by reptiles, vermin "unknown to an Englishman which it is not permitted even to name" and so many mosquitoes that they were forced to bind their heads in handkerchiefs. Despite the fact that he contracted malaria during this journey to the Crimea, Clarke collected some eight hundred specimens of Russian minerals as well as an equally impressive number of plant specimens. He also made a daily record of temperature with the thermometer which Malthus had given him for this purpose and kept an extensive diary.

Eventually they arrived in Constantinople and after sight-seeing in the Turkish capital for a few weeks, joined Lord Elgin's secretary, William Hamilton, on a boat laden with stores for the English armies in Egypt. They arrived in Egypt shortly after the surrender of Alexandria and became greatly interested in the "various Antiquities and miscellaneous items of Natural History" which the scientific commission of the French army had collected during their stay in

Egypt and were now, by the terms of the surrender, due to be turned over to the English authorities. Just before their arrival, the French General, Menou, had refused to comply with the order to surrender these collections and had threatened to meet the English general in a duel over them. Menou's reply to the English was quite rude:

> You may tell your Commander-in-Chief that he has as much right to make this demand as a highwayman has to ask for my purse! He has a cannon in each of my ears and another in my mouth; let him take what pleases him. I have a few embroidered saddles and a tolerable stock of shirts, perhaps he may fancy some of these!

According to Clarke, he and Cripps—along with Elgin's secretary, Hamilton—were the men responsible for forcing General Menou to surrender these valuable collections to the English. Among the items which Clarke claimed to have personally recovered from General Menou at this time were the so-called "Sarcophagus of Alexander the Great" which he found in the hold of the French hospital ship *La Cause*, "half filled with filth and covered with the rags of the sick people on board", and the Rosetta Stone. The latter was considered by the French as one of their most valuable discoveries in Egypt as it bore not only an inscription in hieroglyphs but a translation of this inscription into ancient Greek and Coptic, thereby providing the first real key to the deciphering of the ancient Egyptian language. Clarke recorded in his diary that "pointers would not range better for game than we have done for these antiquities" and described locating the Rosetta Stone "in a warehouse with General Menou's personal baggage, covered with mats". However Hamilton's account of the acquisition of the Rosetta Stone does not agree with Clarke's story.

Clarke and Cripps eventually left Egypt in an old Turkish ship bound for Syria. They briefly toured the Holy Land but found it difficult to work themselves up into a state of ecstasy by the sanctity of Jerusalem. "When a traveller is exposed to the burning beams of an Eastern sun", Clarke wrote to his friends at Cambridge, "mounted on a sorry mule dislocating his very loins, fatigued and breathing hot pestilential vapours, he will feel little disposition to moralize." From Syria they proceeded northwards to visit the Greek ruins of Asia Minor which completely enthralled them. The sight of the many ancient cities and temples with their great quantity of ancient statuary in the vicinity of Smyrna gave them the idea of collecting ancient sculpture. They had previously limited themselves to amassing mineralogical and botanical specimens and an occasional ancient coin but now a new possibility presented itself. Clarke wrote to his friend, Otter, at Cambridge:

> We are here knee-deep in antiquities and have broken our skins over moralizing marbles that have held converse only with toads and lizards for ages till our arrival.

and he was moved to declaim:

> At this instant I have before my eyes such a range of historic territory as would draw tears down the cheeks of apathy. Do you not see the little fleet of the Argonauts creeping along close to the shore, the crews in canoes, surveying the objects round with a mixture of exhultation, wonder and curiosity?

Clarke's own "mixture of exhultation, wonder and curiosity" led him to propose to Cripps that they should try to acquire a collection of ancient sculpture for the University, as it was only fitting and right that Cambridge should have a collection at least as brilliant as that which Oxford possessed as a result of the gifts of Ashmole and Arundel. Cripps agreed to finance this project and they immediately applied to the Turkish authorities for permission to remove an ancient Greek tomb which they had found in a village near Smyrna, being used as a public wash-basin. In the end they were forced to abandon this scheme as the authorities refused to grant them the necessary permission. Clarke was bitterly disappointed in this failure and wrote to his mother that it would have given him "inestimable satisfaction" to have sent this tomb to Cambridge "where it might have inspired some enterprising mind to rescue from oblivion the rest of these inestimable relics, which are daily falling a sacrifice to time and to ignorant barbarians". Their plans for acquiring other works of ancient statuary in Asia Minor also failed, due to the attitude of the "obdurant Turkish authorities" and the technical difficulties of removing, packing and shipping heavy sculptures back to England. They finally decided to "try their luck" on the mainland of Greece. They stopped at a number of Aegean islands *en route* to the mainland and discovered a valuable library of ancient manuscripts in a monastery on the island of Patmos. They found these manuscripts in a "scandalous condition of neglect" as neither the Superior of the Monastery nor his assistants were sufficiently literate to read them and bribed the monks to part with a considerable number of them. They ultimately arrived in Athens "with great transports of joy", delighted to reach this relatively civilized town after their travels through the wilds of Asia Minor where they had been constantly exposed to "danger, fatigue, disease, filth, treachery, thirst, hunger, storms, rocks and assassins" as well as "lice all over your body, lice in your head, fleas, bugs, cock-roaches, rats, all disputing even to your teeth for a crust of mouldy biscuit full of maggots".

They greatly admired the ancient ruins of Athens, "compared with which the puny efforts of modern art are but the labours of children", and were immensely pleased to discover that Athens was then "open to collectors". The recent English victories in Egypt had predisposed the local Turkish authorities to accede to requests by English travellers for permission to undertake excavations and for the removal of any ancient Greek antiquities which they made in the course of these explorations. The most obvious example of this new Turkish attitude was the *firman* granted Lord Elgin to dismantle the Parthenon but there were also other Englishmen in Athens at this time who had secured permission to search for ancient ruins in other parts of the city. As Clarke later wrote to his mother:

> The business of making excavations of the Grecian tombs was then beginning in the neighbourhood of Athens and it has since abundantly rewarded the taste of those travellers under whose patronage such labours have been carried on . . . Among English travellers, the Earl of Aberdeen is particularly distinguished for his liberality in encouraging works of this kind.

Clarke and Cripps were quick to follow the example of these travellers and set out to scour Athens for ancient treasures. As soon as they publicly declared their interest in ancient mementos, they were approached by a steady stream of local peasants and small shop-keepers who sold them more than a thousand gold, silver and copper coins and several ancient vases. However they hesitated to buy the fragments of ancient sculpture which these dealers offered them at high prices. Athens was at this time a poverty-stricken village whose fifteen thousand inhabitants barely subsisted on their exports of honey and oil and whose sole industry, outside of marginal farming, was the production of bad religious paintings of saints and virgins. Clarke noted this situation in his diary. "Nothing can be more wretchedly supplied than Athens with the most common articles of use or convenience," he wrote. "It is not possible to procure the most ordinary domestic utensils, nor a single article of curriery." It was a natural consequence of this extremely debased economy that the shrewder Athenians were quick to seize any opportunity for taking money from wealthy and gullible foreigners. As soon as they realized this fact, Clarke and Cripps decided that they would only be cheated by the Athenians and refused to buy any ancient statuary from them.

They therefore searched the city carefully on their own and found two ancient sculptures which they seized—a marble statue of Pan and a torso of a small marble statue from a grotto which they believed to be a representation of Apollo. But they found little else, for in fact the greater part of the ruins of ancient Athens were located on the Acropolis which Elgin's agents had declared "out of bounds" to unauthorized collectors. Despite the strict enforcement of this rule, Clarke and Cripps managed to steal a small fragment of one of the metopes from the Parthenon off the Acropolis but foolishly boasted of this accomplishment and thereby incurred the wrath of the resident English Consul, Logotheti. When Logotheti threatened to report them to Lord Elgin, Clarke announced that "Athens will sustain more damage in being visited by travellers *calling themselves persons of taste*, than when it was forgotten by the world and entirely abandoned to its barbarian possessors" and openly criticized the "lamentable operations" which Elgin's men were then carrying on "to the utter ruin of the finest works of ancient Greece". The consequence of this incident was that Clarke and Cripps were forbidden further entrance to the Acropolis.

They then decided to undertake the excavation of several ancient wells which they had found on the outskirts of the city. Logotheti made it as difficult as possible for them to obtain the equipment and personnel necessary for such an operation and it was only by luck that Clarke was able to secure a few shovels and to hire several Albanian peasants as labourers. These excavations yielded thirty-seven objects, including terracotta vessels, lamps, pitchers and bottles of various sizes and forms. Clarke wrote to his friend Otter that they secured these only by tremendous effort:

> We had to fight through the intrigues of a herd of rascally Greeks, the obstacles arising from a thousand causes, from expense, from bad air, from want of every necessary machinery, and last, and greatest, from consular chicanery and diplomatic jealousy.

They also organized an expedition to the peak of nearby Mt. Hymettus to make excavations but found no suitable site for this purpose on the mountain. However they availed themselves of this opportunity to carve their names on a granite rock on the peak (as Byron later carved his name on one of the columns of the Temple at Sounion). As Clarke explained in his diary:

> The desire of having a memorial of the visit one has paid to any memorable spot seems to be so natural that however the practice may have been derided, the most eminent travellers, in common with the most insignificant, have left their names in some conspicuous situation: those of Wheler and Spon have been observed upon the walls of the Temple of Theseus; that of Shaw remains in the Franciscan Convent at Jerusalem, that of Pococke at Thebes in Upper Egypt and that of Hasselquist upon the principal pyramid of Memphis. Upon the summit of Hymettus no such inscriptions appeared, but the naked surface of the limestone seemed to be so well calculated for their preservation, that we felt a reluctance to return without carving our names, as indelibly as our time would allow, upon the top of the mountain.

Shortly after their return from Mt. Hymettus an incident occurred which seriously affected their reception by the Turkish authorities. Clarke decided that the time was ripe for a visit to the public baths of Athens as he had lately determined to follow "a practice to bathe frequently for the preservation of my health". He therefore arrived at the public baths early one morning but on entering found himself in the midst of a crowd of Turkish women from the harem of the Turkish Disdar, "many of whom were unveiled in every sense of the term". He was "struck dumb and mute" by the spectacle of these bathing ladies and only gradually became aware of a "general and frightful shriek" around him. Eventually several black female slaves ran up to him and held napkins in front of his eyes while they drove him backwards towards the entrance. Clarke then rushed to his lodgings and told Cripps of his unfortunate adventure. They both agreed that they should leave Athens immediately, for if the ladies reported the incident there was no doubt that Clarke would be instantly tortured and put to death. Such a fate was decreed for any who had gazed on as much as the face of a Turkish woman from the harem. They therefore hastily threw their belongings together, left the antiquities which they had collected with a friend who promised to send them on to Cambridge and embarked on a tour of the Peloponnese.

This tour lasted several months and they leisurely visited such ancient sites as the stadium at Epidauros and the palaces of Mycenae and Tiryns. They continued their search for worth-while ancient sculpture but found only a few items which they considered suffi-ciently interesting to warrant their shipment to Cambridge. The Turkish authorities whom they met in the larger towns of the Peloponnese were generally friendly and extended them hospitality, including "muddy coffee, unsophisticated by any ingredient which could add to its nutritive qualities", although the governor of Corinth left no doubt that he considered their search for ancient mementos as undignified. As Clarke noted in his diary:

> "English Gentlemen, Effendis, indeed!" he said to us in a con-descending tone. "Is it like an Effendi to be seen picking up pieces of broken pots and groping among heaps of rubbish?"

However they recovered several ancient vases from the rubbish of Corinth before deciding that it was safe for them to return to Athens. *En route* they visited the site of the ancient city of Eleusis, situated about twenty-eight miles to the west of Athens, and were delighted to find it literally covered with ruins. "At every ancient wall and at every ancient tomb in Eleusis where the traveller is induced to halt and view the noble objects by which he is sur-rounded," Clarke recorded, "a crowd of interesting events rush into his mind and so completely occupy it that even fatigue and fever, from which he is seldom free, are for a moment forgotten." They examined these ruins with great enthusiasm, especially those of the Sanctuary where the ancient Athenians celebrated the Eleusinian

Mysteries. Furthermore, they found a mutilated colossal statue of white Pentelic marble near the Sanctuary which they considered to be that of the Goddess Ceres "appearing in colossal majesty among the mouldering vestiges of her once splendid Temple". In point of fact the statue could hardly have presented an appearance of "colossal majesty" to them as they found it on the side of the road, buried as high as the neck in a heap of dung. The inhabitants of the small village which was then situated among the ruins of Eleusis regarded this statue with a high degree of superstitious veneration and, attributing the fertility of their land to its presence, covered it with the manure which they intended for their fields.

Clarke and Cripps made up their minds that they must have this statue of the Goddess for Cambridge although they realized that this would not be easy, as there had been several other attempts to remove it which had failed. The peasants of Eleusis claimed that on every occasion when this statue was moved, it invariably "returned to its former station by a miraculous flight, like the virgin of Loretto". They believed that the loss of this statue would surely be followed by no less a calamity than the failure of their annual harvest. Clarke wrote to Otter that:

> At the very mention of moving it, they regarded me as one who would bring the moon from her orbit. What would become of their corn, they said, if the old lady with her basket was removed?

It was evident to them that they would have to cope not only with the technical problem of transporting this heavy sculpture to the sea but also with the intense attachment of the Eleusinian peasants to "their lady". But Clarke and Cripps did not doubt that the "two demi-semi travellers from Jesus College, Cambridge, could whip it off in a trice".

As a first step they visited the priest of the village of Eleusis to discuss the matter with him and requested him to use his influence to persuade the peasants to give up the statue. The priest informed them that they could only pursue their plan by obtaining a *firman* giving them permission to remove the statue from the Disdar of Athens to whom, as lord of the manor, all property of this description belonged. Fortunately their interpreter was a kinsman of the Disdar and he promised to exert his influence on their behalf. They

9

proceeded on to Athens, assuming that the Disdar had never been informed of Clarke's appearance in the harem bath.

The Disdar apparently had not heard of the episode of the bath and listened sympathetically to their request for the statue of Ceres. After considerable deliberation he acceded to their demand—on the express condition that they would obtain for him the small English telescope which belonged to Lusieri, the Italian artist in charge of Elgin's mission. This request for the telescope appeared to Clarke a "very serious obstacle" as it would therefore be necessary to divulge their plan for removing the statue to Lusieri, "a person indeed in whom we could confide, but who was at the moment actually employed in collecting every thing of this kind for our Ambassador". As Elgin had prohibited the removal of any article of ancient sculpture on the part of his countrymen, it was a delicate situation, particularly as Clarke feared that the Disdar might mention the question to his dreaded enemy, Logotheti, the "intriguing English Consul" who paid the Disdar a daily visit.

These fears proved to be unjustified, however, for when they mentioned the request to Lusieri:

> Our generous friend, disdaining every unworthy consideration, not only resigned his telescope upon our promise of sending him another from England, but very kindly undertook to present it himself to the Disdar and persuaded the latter to observe silence with regard to the Consul.

When Clarke returned to England, he sent Lusieri "a very fine new telescope by Ramsden".

Once they had obtained the necessary *firman* from the Disdar they considered the difficult problem of shipping their treasure to England. In the end they decided to apply to the despised English Consul, Logotheti, for use of the ferry-boat which regularly ran between Salamis and the mainland as this seemed to them the only feasible means of conveying the heavy statue to Piraeus. They feared that their request would arouse Logotheti's suspicions but "after many questions we succeeded in lulling his suspicions; or, if he had any notion of our intention, he believed that the removal of the statue . . . would baffle every exertion that we could make."

They then returned to Eleusis after unsuccessfully searching

Athens for a cart, blocks, pulleys or even a saw. However they procured a rope, several long poles, an axe and a six-inch saw from the
natives of Eleusis and with these few tools were able to construct a
triangular frame onto which they placed the two-ton Goddess. A
crisis occurred just as they had gathered some hundred and fifty
peasants to haul the frame to the shore when an ox came up to the
statue and, after butting with its horns for some time against the
marble, ran off with considerable speed, bellowing, into the plain
of Eleusis. The peasants considered this as a significant omen and
refused to start work. Clarke and Cripps tried in vain to persuade
them with hours of oratory and, when that failed, with generous
baksheesh. They had almost despaired of success when the priest
of Eleusis put on his canonical vestments "as for a ceremony of
high mass" and, approaching the statue, gave the first blow with a
pickaxe in front of the frame so that the peasants "might be convinced that no calamity would befall them". The peasants were thus
persuaded and proceeded to haul the statue to the beach. The ferry-
boat was not able to get sufficiently close to shore to take on its
special cargo but fortunately they successfully loaded the statue
on to a passing ship bound for Smyrna.

The statue eventually arrived safely in Smyrna despite the pre-
diction of the Eleusinian peasants of the certain wreck of any ship
which stole "their lady". It was transferred in Smyrna onto a
merchantman, the *Princessa*, which later stopped at Piraeus to take
on the antiquities which Clarke and Cripps had gathered in Athens
as well as their collections of mineralogical and botanical specimens
and ancient coins. The *Princessa* then set sail for England where she
was wrecked off the Sussex coast, near Beachy Head, not far from
the Cripps' estate. Cripps's father managed to organize a salvage
of most of the cargo, including the statue of Ceres, although many
of the plants and seeds were lost. The Goddess and the rest of the
antiquities were sent along with what remained of the other collections to Cambridge. On 1st July, 1803, the statue of Ceres was
"securely placed upon a pedestal, with all due form and honours,
in the most conspicuous part of the vestibule of the Public Library
of Cambridge" and the names of Clarke and Cripps were inscribed
upon the base "by the desire of the University". Eventually this
statue, along with the other ancient sculptures which they had sent
to Cambridge, were moved into the basement of the Fitzwilliam

Museum where they remain to this day. The statue from Eleusis is no longer believed to represent the Goddess Ceres but is now referred to as a "Kistophorus" from the mystic "kisti" which surmounts the head of the figure. The entire collection must have been quite considerable as in the course of their travels, Clarke had shipped seventy-six cases of ancient souvenirs to Cambridge and Cripps more than eighty.

Clarke and Cripps finally ended their wanderings and returned to England in November, 1802, to be awarded the honorary degrees of LL.D. and M.A., respectively. Clarke married shortly after his return and resigned himself to a settled residence at Jesus College as Professor of Mineralogy. He remained at Cambridge until his death in 1822 and devoted the energies of his declining years to a series of lectures on mineralogy and to an intensive study of the "Gas Blow Pipe". He published the diary of his trip with Cripps in six immense quarto volumes and then, pressed by the exigencies of a family of seven children, sold most of the ancient manuscripts from the island of Patmos to the Bodleian Library at Oxford for £1,000 and his collection of Greek coins to Richard Payne Knight for 100 guineas. At his death a monument was erected in Jesus College Chapel, at the expense of his fellow colleagues, "in the hope that it would serve to stimulate the youth of that society in the paths of enterprise and science."

Chapter IX

SO MUCH FOR ART

NAPOLEON'S pillage of ancient statuary and paintings from the museums and private collections of Europe incited many Englishmen to become involved in a frenzy of collecting activity. On the whole they were remarkably successful and during the first two decades of the nineteenth century Englishmen succeeded in removing the sculptured friezes and architectural decorations from three of the most important ancient temples to be found in Greece. Lord Elgin became famous for his stripping of the Parthenon marbles, but Charles Cockerell, the Englishman who discovered and removed the decorative sculptures of the Temple of Aegina and the Temple of Bassae, has been virtually forgotten.

Charles Robert Cockerell was born in April, 1788, the second son of Samuel Pepys Cockerell, a man of considerable means who held a good position as architect for the East India Company. Young Charles attended Westminster until he was sixteen when he left to study architecture in his father's office and after two years of working as a draftsman he was sent by his father on a tour of the West of England and Wales in order to study the architecture of those areas. After this trip he entered the office of Mr. Robert Smirke to continue his studies until he came of age when his father decided that he should tour the Continent in order to complete his architectural education. Most of Europe was closed to Englishmen in 1809 due to the Napoleonic Wars but it was decided that Cockerell would greatly benefit from a visit to the architectural sites of Greece and Turkey. His father discussed this plan with the Under Secretary for Foreign Affairs, William Hamilton, who had recently returned from an extensive tour through Greece and Turkey in his capacity as private secretary to Lord Elgin, and Hamilton, a long time friend of the Cockerells, offered to send young Charles as a King's Messenger with despatches for the British fleet at Cadiz, Malta and Constantinople. The offer was gratefully accepted.

Charles Cockerell left England in 1810 on a small ship which he described as containing "ten guns, thirty-five men, one sheep, two pigs and several fowls".

On their way to Malta they sighted two privateers which they feared to be French, and while the small crew prepared for action, Cockerell tied his despatches to a cannon shot in order to sink them in case of capture. The emergency never materialized as the privateers turned out to be English and Cockerell experienced no other adventure during his voyage to Constantinople. In this he was disappointed, for he was eager for excitement and had expected at least a storm if not "an attack by cruel Maniote pirates" when they rounded Cape Matapan in accordance with the ancient Greek warning: "Let him who is to sail round Matapan, take a last farewell of his relatives."

In fact Cockerell barely missed an adventure, for the ship on which he travelled to Constantinople was captured and sunk by the French on its return voyage.

Cockerell was thrilled by the exotic appearance of Constantinople where he met and caroused with Lord Byron and his friend, John Hobhouse. This trio toured the sights of the ancient city and went to see the dancing and howling dervishes, the Turkish baths, the Djerid where young Turks fought with javelins on horseback, and the Sultan's visit to a mosque. Cockerell wrote enthusiastic letters home describing his dangerous life in this Eastern capital:

> There are still janissaries who wear a singular cap, from the centre of which springs a tree of feathers which, rising to a certain height, fall again like a weeping willow and occupy an enormous space, but these janissaries are dangerous men.

An even greater danger was the plague and Cockerell took all possible precautions against contracting it, even to the extent of scenting himself abundantly. His fear of plague appears to have become an obsession and he wrote home:

> On one occasion I noticed that my servant was pale and I feared that he might have succumbed to plague. At arm's length I escorted him home and I sent him to bed and then changed my garments from top to toe and smoked for several hours.

Cockerell paid his respects to Lord Canning, the British Ambassador in Constantinople, whom he found "too grand". There is no record of Canning's impression of Cockerell but it would seem probable that he was a burden to the Ambassador who, as a senior Foreign Office official, had been sent to the Turkish Court in a most crucial period of history for the purpose of countering Napoleon's plans to develop his interests in the Near East. Cockerell wrote to his father that shortly after his arrival in Constantinople he had outfitted himself with a brace of pistols, a broadsword and a musket, and had accompanied Lord Canning on an official audience with the Caimacan, "because I thought it was my duty as an Englishman to attend the Ambassador to the audience."

Shortly after this audience Lord Canning provided Cockerell with a passport so that he could travel to other parts of the Turkish Empire. This passport, which described Cockerell as being of medium stature, with a triangular face, black and shining eyes, a thin nose and a vermilion mouth and must have pleased the young man's vanity for it added that he had "a marble forehead and in total, as resembling Apollo".

Cockerell was fond of comparing himself to the ancient Greek gods and heroes and when he visited the tomb of Patroclus, he recorded in his diary that he "took off his clothes, and, in imitation of Achilles, ran three times around it, naked".

After visiting the sites of Constantinople and coming to the conclusion that all Turkish architecture was worthless, Cockerell decided to go to Greece which at that time was controlled by several Turkish pashas. He set off for Athens with the Skye terrier which he had brought with him from England and travelled in the company of another young English architect, J. Foster, of Liverpool. They arrived in Athens in December of 1810 and immediately became involved with the gay and dissipated group that had gathered around

Lord Byron. Members of this Athenian coterie included Baron Haller von Hallerstein ("a studious and accomplished artist, about fourteen years my senior, and a gentleman by birth and nature"), who was travelling on a very small allowance from his patron, Prince Ludwig of Bavaria, and Linckh, another painter from Germany. There was also a Danish architect, the Chevalier Peter Oluf Bronstedt and his brother-in-law, Mr. Koes. There were two other Englishmen besides Byron, Hobhouse, Cockerell and Foster, and this coterie permitted itself to be associated with Lusieri, Elgin's Italian agent and Fauvel, the French Consul. Cockerell and Foster took a house together on the slopes of the ancient Acropolis and they spent the winter in Athens, visiting and drawing antiquities by day and drinking the local resin-flavoured wines by night. In the spring Lord Byron decided to leave Athens for Malta and, with its doyen about to depart, the coterie began to disband. Cockerell and some others came to the conclusion that they wanted to tour Greece and in particular the Peloponnese but that first they would visit the nearby island of Aegina, in the Saronikos Bay, to see the antiquities there before going on to the Peloponnese. On the eve of his twenty-third birthday in April, 1811, Cockerell boarded a caique bound for Aegina together with Foster, Baron Haller and Linckh, and as they were leaving Piraeus harbour that evening they passed the ship which was taking Lord Byron to Malta. This ship was loaded with a cargo of Parthenon marbles and although he was exceedingly outspoken in his criticism of Elgin for removing these Parthenon marbles, Byron did not hesitate to travel with Elgin's loot when it suited his convenience. Cockerell wrote to his father that: "As we passed under the stern of Lord Byron's ship, we sang a favourite song of his."

The inevitable party resulted and the four young men boarded Byron's ship where they consumed bottles and bottles of port while sitting on top of the Elgin marbles. Eventually Cockerell and his friends scrambled back into their caique and were transported in a drunken stupor to the island of Aegina. Cockerell observed that, "It was a dangerous voyage, for these seas are infested with pirates and one of their favourite haunts is Sounion which we had to pass."

They reached Aegina by morning and slowly ascended to the Temple of "Zeus Panhellenius" (it was later decided by archeologists that this temple was not in fact dedicated to Zeus but to the

Goddess Aphaea). They pitched their tents on top of the hill and installed their servants, as well as the Turkish janissary whom they had employed as their guard, in a cave at the north-eastern side of the site. The temple was remarkably well preserved and since there was a crop of barley growing on the soil covering the temple floor, the whole site had a pleasantly rustic appearance. This quartet of young adventurers stayed on Aegina for twenty days while they made drawings of the temple. They hired peasants from a nearby village to serve as labourers for their excavations and these villagers also provided them with provisions. They cut wild thyme for fuel, bought small kids from the shepherds, shot partridges which they found in abundance around the site of the temple and thoroughly enjoyed themselves. As Cockerell wrote home:

> When the work was over for the day there was a grand roasting of kids and partridge over a blazing fire with an accompaniment of native music, singing and dancing.

A great stroke of luck befell them on the second day after their arrival on Aegina. One of the peasant labourers whom they had employed to excavate in the field of barley in order to uncover the platform of the temple reported that he had come across "a piece of marble". This discovery greatly impressed them since the temple itself was constructed entirely of limestone and they all ceased their various occupations in order to supervise the excavation of this "piece of marble" which turned out to be an undamaged head of a helmeted warrior. Cockerell recorded this discovery in his diary:

> It lay with the face turned upwards and as the perfect features came out by degrees you can imagine nothing like the state of rapture and excitement to which we were wrought.

They immediately realized that they had found what must have been one of the decorative sculptures of the temple. Since there was every possibility that they might find other such sculptures buried in this spot, they rushed off to the village and hired several dozen peasants to excavate the entire barley field. These excavations yielded them sixteen torsos, thirteen heads and a quantity of legs, arms and other fragments, all buried about three feet beneath the surface of the ground. These sculptures, carved from Parian marble, had formed part of the frieze of the temple.

The news of these remarkable discoveries quickly spread through the island and soon they found themselves surrounded by a large audience which alarmed them. As Cockerell noted:

> It was not to be expected that we should be allowed to carry away what we had found without opposition. However much people may neglect their possessions, as soon as they see them coveted by others, they begin to value them.

When a group of the island dignitaries, including the Turkish Pasha who controlled the Archipelago, visited their camp to inquire what they intended to do with the marbles, Cockerell and his friends became very worried and decided that they should try to remove the sculptures from Aegina as quickly as possible. They judged that they had excavated the greater part of the frieze since the previous two days of digging had yielded nothing of value and felt that it was far better to be sure of removing what they had already found, than to risk losing it all for the sake of a few more fragments. They therefore hired a caique and loaded the sculptures on to it during the night and sent them off to Athens with Foster and Linckh while Cockerell and Baron Haller remained on the site of the temple the following day apparently continuing the excavations in order to divert the suspicions of the Turks. As soon as they heard that the sculptures had safely arrived in Athens, Cockerell and Baron Haller paid off the labourers, gave the Pasha of the Islands a sum of forty guineas for "digging rights" and left Aegina to join the others in Athens where they celebrated their good fortune with festivities that lasted for several days and nights. According to Cockerell, the other members of Bryon's coterie were "dying with jealousy" over their discovery of these sculptures, to the extent that one youth 'literally made himself quite ill with fretting". And the French Consul, Fauvel, "was also a good deal disappointed; but he is too good a fellow to let envy affect his actions".

The discoverers of the frieze from the Temple of Aegina rented a large building in Athens to house their sculptures and to sort them out. Poets, painters, architects and their friends, including the disappointed Fauvel, were eager to lend a helping hand in fitting together arms and legs with the appropriate torsos and in selecting the correct head for the whole, while others mixed up plaster to cement the statues back together again. As Cockerell reported in a letter:

> We are now hard at work joining the broken pieces. Some of the figures are already restored and have a magnificent effect. We conduct all our affairs with respect to these marbles in the utmost secrecy, for fear the Turk should either reclaim them or put difficulties in the way of our exporting them.

They all agreed that the sculptures should not be parcelled out in individual portions and that the frieze at all cost should be kept together as a whole. Since the discoverers were of different nationalities, however, there arose the problem as to the final disposition of the frieze. Cockerell, Foster, Baron Haller and Linckh solemnly signed a contract of honour that no one of them would take measures to sell the sculptures, or to divide the total find, without the consent of the other three, which thus permitted them to find a potential buyer, with a clear conscience. Cockerell wrote to both his father and Lord Canning, the Ambassador in Constantinople to ask their advice, while Baron Haller wrote to his patron, Prince Ludwig of Bavaria and Foster and Linckh wrote to their friends in England and Germany.

In the meantime the French Consul, Fauvel, had already notified the French Government about the discovery of these sculptures on Aegina and he was the first person to receive an authorization for their purchase. Other offers for the frieze of the Temple of Aegina reached Athens in rapid succession and by far the highest was that of Prince Ludwig who offered six thousand pounds sterling calculated on the basis of the current market prices for ancient statues in Rome and Baron Haller was authorized to raise this bid to eight thousand pounds sterling if necessary.

Despite the fact that they had agreed to sell these sculptures to the highest bidder, Cockerell and Foster could not bear the thought of the frieze of the Temple of Aegina going to Bavaria. In a moment of dramatic self-sacrifice and national pride, abetted perhaps by the effects of resin-flavoured wine, these two Englishmen pledged to "give up their shares to England" without financial reward. Shortly after making this noble resolve they met two wealthy English

travellers who were persuaded to offer Baron Haller and Linckh
two thousand pounds sterling for their half share of the sculptures
with the object of donating the frieze to the British Museum. Linckh
was uncertain whether to accept this offer but Baron Haller refused
on the grounds that he could not honourably fail to help his patron,
Prince Ludwig, to obtain the collection. Under these circumstances
the four discoverers found themselves faced with a dilemma. After
great discussion they decided that the only fair solution was to offer
the entire frieze for sale at a public auction on some neutral ground.

It was mid-July when they made this decision and they felt that
they had completed the piecing together and restoration of the
sculptures to the best of their ability. They selected the island of
Zante, then under English control, as the "nearest place of security"
for the auction to be held and turned their attention to the problem
of how to smuggle the sculptures out of Greece without being discovered by the Turkish authorities. It seemed unwise to attempt to
load the sculptures onto a boat in Piraeus harbour where Turkish
officials checked the cargoes of all departing vessels and they came
to the conclusion that they could not hope to successfully smuggle
the frieze out of Greece without some assistance. In the end they
asked Gropius, the Austrian Vice-Consul in Athens, to help them.
They all knew and trusted Gropius who, since he had a Greek
mother, was able not only to speak Greek fluently but knew how to
deal with Greeks. Within a matter of days Gropius arranged for a
caique to transport the sculptures from Porto Germanos, a small
fishing village on the Gulf of Corinth, not far from Athens. As soon
as Gropius informed them of this plan they carefully packed the
sculptures and, loading them onto a caravan of horses and mules,
set out late one night in July to cover the forty miles across the
mountains to Porto Germanos. They arrived the following morning
without having experienced any mishap and found the caique awaiting them. The sculptures were safely loaded and all four young men
accompanied their "treasures" on their journey to Zante. When the
caique stopped in Patras for provisions they were met by the
Chevalier Bronstedt, a former member of Byron's Athenian coterie,
who was so impressed by their successful kidnapping of these
"excellent sculptures" that he arranged for a "grand salute of pistols"
when they sailed from Patras. They arrived safely in Zante and unloaded their sculptures and the auction for the frieze of the Temple

of Aegina was set for the first of November, 1812, at Zante. An announcement to this effect was inserted in the newspapers of every country of Europe, including England, and by common consent, Gropius was appointed to act as agent for the sale.

There seemed to be no reason for Cockerell and his friends to wait on Zante for more than a year and a half until the auction was held and they decided to go off on their long-delayed tour of the Peloponnese. In August Cockerell, Gropius, Baron Haller, Foster and Linckh crossed over from Zante to Pyrgos and walked to Olympia where they stayed several days although they were not enthusiastic about the ruins which they saw there. After Olympia they went to Andritsaina, having in mind to visit the Temple of Apollo Epikourios which had been built by the Phygalians at Bassae. This temple, designed by Ictinos, one of the architects of the Parthenon, had been discovered in this remote area of the Peloponnese by a French traveller in 1765 and was reputed to be a magnificent specimen of Doric style architecture. The peasants in Andritsaina warned them against visiting "The Columns" as the temple was commonly called, as there was a "band of fierce robbers who lived amongst the ruins", but despite this warning the five young travellers proceeded on to Bassae. They found the temple breathtakingly beautiful in its architectural proportions and dramatic setting on the edge of a plateau surrounded by ravines. They camped on the site for ten days, living on mutton and bread, harassed by wolves which hunted near their camp at night but undisturbed by any "band of fierce robbers". Once again they hired local peasants to do excavations on the site but these Peloponnesian peasants were apparently unsatisfactory as labourers. Cockerell reported peevishly in his diary that "they were so stupid that I was obliged to be always with them and in doing this I tore my hand and got exceedingly fatigued".

Cockerell, however, was very pleased with this visit to Bassae and made a number of measurements and drawings of the temple. He had already conceived the idea of publishing a book containing his drawings and measurements of the Temples of Aegina and Bassae when he returned to England, thus furthering his architectural reputation.

Their excavations yielded them no treasures and they were preparing to leave Bassae one morning when Cockerell noticed a fox emerging from a mass of fallen blocks which were situated in the interior of the temple. He went over to investigate and made an exciting discovery which he described in a letter to his father:

> I went in carefully lest there be another fox, and on scraping away the accumulations where the fox had its lair, I saw by the light which came down a crack among the stones, a bas-relief.

He made a rough sketch of this bas-relief which he then covered over again and returned to report his discovery to his friends who were agreed that this bas-relief must be a section of the frieze of the temple and that there might well be other sections of the frieze to be found in the same spot. However by this time the peasant labourers had been paid off as a wealthy landowner from the nearby village had arrived to complain of their digging on the site, which he claimed to be his land. They were therefore afraid to recommence their excavations as this landowner would undoubtedly create a great fuss and might even attempt to seize any discoveries which they made. After a whole day of discussions they decided that it was best for them to leave Bassae as planned and return the following spring with some "decent workmen" and an official authorization from some higher Turkish authority to excavate the site. They all promised that in the meantime they would not inform anybody about the bas-relief which Cockerell had found.

After visiting some other ruins in the Peloponnese, Cockerell returned to Athens where he was horrified to find a letter from his father stating that he had persuaded His Royal Highness the Prince Regent to give six thousand pounds sterling for the Aegina sculptures and that a British man-of-war was on its way to Piraeus to pick up the frieze. There was nothing Cockerell could do but wait for the warship, the *Pauline*, to arrive. He boarded the *Pauline* in Piraeus harbour and explained to the captain that the marbles had already been shipped to Zante where they were to be sold by public auction in a year's time. The captain of the *Pauline* was "very indignant" and it took Cockerell several hours to soothe him. When he had somewhat recovered from his rage Captain Percival commented that they had selected a poor place of security for their auction, since there was a grave danger of Zante being at any time attacked by the French. Cockerell was very much frightened by this information and he finally persuaded the captain to proceed to Zante and move the sculptures to Malta for greater security.

Cockerell and his friend Foster then decided to leave Athens to visit the island of Crete, and after a month there they crossed over to the Turkish mainland to inspect the Greek ruins of Asia Minor. In Smyrna Foster "fell hopelessly in love with a Levantine girl" and refused to leave, so that Cockerell was forced to continue his exploration of the sites of Asia Minor on his own. He hired a caique to transport him along the coast and met with "many adventures—brigands . . . shooting . . . fighting . . . plague". Eventually he took to "dressing in a Turkish costume to avoid being noticed". Ultimately he came across an English ship which took him to Malta where he was laid up with an attack of bilious fever.

Cockerell had wandered through Asia Minor for more than a year and during this interval his friends returned to Bassae as planned. Gropius had managed to secure permission to excavate the site of the temple from both the Turkish authorities in Constantinople and the local Turkish Pasha of the Peloponnese, and had assured the latter's co-operation by promising him half of any treasures which they might discover in the course of their excavations. Gropius, Baron Haller, Linckh, the Chevalier Bronstedt, a Livonian Baron named Otto Magnus von Stackelberg and Mr. Leigh, an English traveller, proceeded to Andritsaina in July of 1812 with a party of more than one hundred workmen and a plentiful supply of equipment and provisions. They erected huts close to the site at Bassae and hired local shepherds to entertain them in the evenings with "Arcadian music".

These excavations at Bassae were a great success. They dug up the entire site of the temple over a period of three months and discovered twenty-three slabs of the frieze as well as a number of metopes. Although Cockerell was not present, it was understood that he was to be a "participator in any sculpture that should be disinterred" since he had discovered the original bas-relief. Furthermore it was determined, even before these excavations commenced, that all their discoveries at Bassae would be put up for public auction at Zante, together with the Aegina sculptures.

Veli Pasha, the Turkish Governor of the Peloponnese, frequently visited the excavations and refused to believe that the broken pieces of marble which they were collecting were in fact the "treasures" for which they were seeking and it was with great difficulty that they convinced him that they were not concealing other treasures of gold and precious stones. They were highly amused when Veli Pasha examined one of the sculptures which they had uncovered and mistook the round shields of the warriors for tortoises, commenting that "as such they were rather well done". They ceased to be amused, however, when the excavations were brought to a close and they were faced with the problem of Gropius' promise to Veli Pasha of half of their finds. They were angrily debating what to do about this promise when they learned that Veli Pasha was about to be superseded in command. Without a moment's delay they hastened to his residence to offer him four hundred guineas for his share of the treasures and permission to remove the sculptures from the Peloponnese. Veli Pasha gratefully accepted their offer and they managed with difficulty to transport the sculptures over the mountains to the sea where they were loaded on a caique for Zante. All of the sculptures were safely on board ship except for one Corinthian column when the replacement Pasha suddenly arrived on the beach with a troop of soldiers to stop them. The caique immediately hoisted anchor and set sail for Zante and the Turks "were so enraged that they hacked to pieces the Corinthian column which was standing half in and half out of the water".

These sculptures which had formed a large part of the decorative sculpture of the Temple of Bassae—and were commonly referred to as the Phygalian marbles—arrived in Zante in September, 1812. Since the date set for the auction of the Aegina frieze was then less than two months off, it was decided to sell the Phygalian marbles at a separate auction which was set for 1814, and a notice to this effect was sent to continental newspapers.

Another reason for this second and separate auction was the fact that the Aegina sculptures had some months earlier reached Malta in the *Pauline*. As the day for the auction drew near, bidders, including a representative of the French government and Martin Wagner, a sculptor representing Prince Ludwig of Bavaria, began to arrive on Zante, unaware that the Aegina sculptures had been moved. The British Museum sent Taylor Coombe, Keeper of the Greek and Roman Antiquities of the Museum, as their representative at the auction, but when Coombe reached Malta and found the sculptures there, he was given to understand that the place of the auction had also been shifted to Malta. Coombe was therefore absent from the sale as Gropius, either by accident or by design, conducted the sale at Zante in the absence of the sculptures and the frieze of the Temple of Aegina was sold to Martin Wagner, acting in the name of Prince Ludwig, for six thousand pounds. Ludwig subsequently had these sculptures drastically restored by the fashionable Danish sculptor Thorwaldsen and constructed a national museum in Munich—the Glyptothek—to exhibit them along with the rest of his collection. (It was partly as a result of Ludwig's passionate interest in collecting ancient Greek sculpture that his second son, Otto, was offered the throne of the newly independent Greek nation twenty years later.)

The sale of the Aegina sculptures to Prince Ludwig horrified Cockerell when he heard of it on his "sickbed of bilious fever" in Malta and he hastened, still feverish, to Zante where he tried unsuccessfully to upset the transaction. Reluctantly Cockerell acknowledged that Ludwig's purchase was final but he was determined that there would be nothing underhanded at the next auction of the Phygalian marbles from Bassae. He realized only too well that it was he who had arranged the transport of the Aegina sculptures from Zante to Malta and that he was therefore responsible for the failure of the British Museum to obtain them. He sent a letter of apology and explanation to his father, adding that "Gropius after his failure has been dismissed as our agent and I personally will be present at the Phygalian marbles' sale to be sure that these marbles, at least, go to England."

The British press echoed Cockerell's indignation over the sale of the Aegina sculptures. The *Edinburgh Review* wrote:

We cannot conceal our mortification at the unfortunate errors by which our country was deprived of the possession of the very interesting statues of the Temple of Aegina.

While waiting for the Phygalian auction which was scheduled for May, 1814, Cockerell occupied himself by wandering through Greece, sometimes in the company of the other young architects and sometimes alone. Occasionally one of this group experienced some of the "dangerous adventures" which Cockerell longed for. The Chevalier Bronstedt was attacked by a band of eight robbers

10

near Sparta, robbed of all his wealth and left for dead, and Baron Otto Magnus von Stackelberg was captured by pirates when crossing the Gulf of Volos and ultimately ransomed by Baron Haller von Hallerstein for the large sum of five hundred guineas. Baron Haller subsequently died of pneumonia while making excavations in the Vale of Tempe in Greece, and Cockerell's closest friend, Foster, married his Smyrna love "much against his family's wishes" and took his bride back to England. When he was not travelling, Cockerell spent his time in Athens preparing his drawings for his book on the Temples of Aegina and Bassae. He returned to Zante in the spring of 1184 for the Phygalian marbles' auction and with great satisfaction witnessed the sale of these sculptures for fifteen thousand pounds to General Campbell, Commandant of the Ionian Islands, who was acting on behalf of the English Prince Regent. He remained on Zante to oversee the packing of these sculptures that were destined for the British Museum and then prepared to go to Italy to visit Rome and Florence which were finally accessible to English travellers after the defeat of Napoleon. Before leaving Greece for the last time he went to Athens to gather up his belongings and bid farewell to his friends. The Turkish Disdar who was acting as Commandant of the citadel on the Acropolis decided to make Cockerell a gift as a parting gesture. Cockerell described this gift in a letter:

> As he knew that I was very fond of old sculptured stones he asked me if I would like to bring a cart to the base of the Acropolis at a certain hour of the night. I accordingly arranged this. As I drew near the Acropolis there was a shout from above to look out, and without further warning the block which formed one of the few remaining pieces of the southern frieze of the Parthenon was bowled down the cliff. My men successfully caught it and put it in the cart and it was taken to Piraeus and loaded that same night onto my ship.

Cockerell finally returned to England in 1817. His tour of the Continent, which his father had planned to take no more than one year, had been extended to cover seven years. At the end Cockerell was forced to abandon his dreams of "travel and adventure" and to apply himself to the mundane practice of architecture in his father's office in England. He had intended to publish his drawings of the Temples of Aegina and Bassae as soon as he returned but his book was not completed until forty-three years later, in 1860. By then it was too late to create any excitement for Baron Otto Magnus von Stackelberg had long since published a book on his travels in Greece in which he claimed to have discovered the first bas-relief at Bassae, and Martin Wagner had published a book of drawings on the Phygalian marbles from Bassae which he had made while waiting on Zante for the Aegina sculptures' auction. The Chevalier Bronstedt had also published a book using many of Cockerell's sketches of the temples and many of Cockerell's letters from Greece had already appeared in a book written by a friend, T. Hughes. Cockerell, in fact, was betrayed by all his friends and received little credit in his lifetime or after for his discoveries.

Chapter X

THE AEGEAN TREASURES OF THE LOUVRE

On a large-scale map the Aegean Sea appears to be cluttered with islands but the greater number of these are no more than jagged rocks rising abruptly out of the sea and only a few are large enough or have sufficient soil to support any kind of a population. The modern island peoples are a hybrid of many races—Greek, Albanian, Venetian, French, Lombard and Turk,—who succeed in eking out no more than a bare existence from a sea that provides few fish and still fewer sponges and from an infertile soil with insufficient rain to nourish it. Their tiny white-washed villages reflect the Aegean sun with a dazzling brightness and appear to have the beauty of a picture postcard in their stark setting of a landscape on which grows little more than wild thyme and sage and an occasional wind-swept pine. In reality the life of these unfortunate islanders is far from beautiful as they struggle to survive under the most adverse circumstances.

Many of the islands of the Aegean, such as Andros, Melos, Cos, Naxos and Santorini, have been inhabited from high antiquity and at least two of them, Delos and Samothrace, are known to have served in ancient times as important holy sanctuaries. Because of their strategic location on the trade routes of the Eastern Mediterranean, the later history of these islands was one of conquest and rule by a series of various merchant peoples. Their harbours frequently sheltered vessels from the violent seas to which the Aegean is prone and early travellers were quick to note their extensive ancient ruins. Adventurous collectors of ancient statuary began to investigate these Aegean islands during the Renaissance and they were often extremely successful in their search. The famed "Marmor Parium" which Lord Arundel's agent secured on Paros is but one of the many valuable ancient works found on these islands at an early date. But it was during the nineteenth century that two Aegean islands, Melos and Samothrace, provided French collectors with two unusual sculptures which are still considered as among the most priceless treasures of the Louvre: the Venus de Milo and the Winged Victory of Samothrace.

The islands of the Aegean are commonly classified in groups, one of the best known being the Cyclades, so called because they form a rough circle around the ancient sanctuary island of Delos. The island of Melos is the most westerly member of this group and, like most of the Cyclades, it is virtually only a peak whose steep and irregular slopes are interspersed with a few small cultivable valleys. Until quite recently Melos was relatively prosperous due to the fact that it possessed an excellent, deep and sheltered harbour on its northern coast. In ancient times this harbour, in which ships were safe from the prevailing summer and winter winds, served as a port for the many boats which traded between Greece and Asia Minor. While there is no evidence of any sizeable ancient city having ever existed on Melos, the island, curiously enough, must have served at one time as an important graveyard, probably for all the Cyclades, as its hills are perforated with ancient catacombs.

Melos profited from her excellent harbour until very modern times and the island served for several centuries as the base for the Cyclades pilots as well as the principal Aegean port where both commercial and naval foreign ships called to receive their orders and to pick up provisions. Both the British and French governments established consular agencies on Melos at an early date, and enterprising islanders made an excellent living by providing for the foreign ships which regularly called at Melos until the end of the nineteenth century when the famous harbour began to silt up and the invention of wireless telegraphy made it possible for ships to receive orders at sea. A number of shrewd islanders also discovered the foreigners' passion for souvenirs of the ancient Greeks and developed a flourishing business for themselves by trading in archaeological fragments with the captains and officers of the passing ships. They paid peasants a paltry sum for the coins, vases, jewellery and occasional pieces of statuary which they had plundered from the ancient catacombs on the island and then sold these antiquities to the foreigners for a good price. At the beginning of the nineteenth century Baron Haller von Hallerstein, the friend of Charles Cockerell and Lord Byron, discovered an incomplete ancient Roman amphitheatre on Melos and the site of this amphitheatre was subsequently purchased by Prince Ludwig of Bavaria who paid excellent sums to local labourers for any ancient pieces which they found while excavating. As a result of this new market, the trade in antiquities became so brisk that findings were brought in from as far away as Athens to be sold as genuine Melos ruins.

Only a small proportion of the island population lived on the various profits arising from the port and most of the islanders barely subsisted as poor peasant farmers. Due to the scarcity of cultivable land in the few small valleys of the island, these peasants had resorted to farming the long narrow terraces which they had constructed on the rugged mountain slopes, and it was in one of these terraces that a most unusual discovery was made on Melos in the spring of 1820. A peasant named Georgos acquired a terrace situated on the slope of the hill rising from the harbour, not far from the site of the ancient Roman amphitheatre and set out to work his new field early one morning in March. He decided to remove the stump and root of an old tree which remained in one corner of the terrace before he began ploughing, and as he was digging up this root the ground on which he was standing suddenly began to crumble and give way. Georgos scrambled to one side as the soil disappeared into a concealed cellar or underground cavity of considerable depth. He peered with astonishment into the gaping hole at his feet and saw a quantity of marble sculptures. When he had removed the dirt and rubble which covered these sculptures he found that he had opened up an ancient catacomb which, like others of its kind, turned out to be a chamber of considerable size. The walls and ceiling were made of brick and masonry which had remained sufficiently intact to protect the contents—a large nude female statue broken at the waist into two pieces, several small busts and a variety of fragments, all in marble. Georgos reasoned that with luck he would be able to peddle these sculptures to some of the foreign ships for a good price. He therefore removed the upper half of the female statue and two of the small busts and took them to the cottage which served as a home for himself, his mother and his sheep. He left the lower half of the female statue and the various fragments in the catacomb which he lightly covered with soil so that others might not find and steal his treasures. When he had finished this task he considered the question of finding a buyer. He decided to consult the French consular agent as there were two French naval ships anchored in the harbour at that time whose captains or officers could conceivably be persuaded to purchase ancient sculpture.

The French consular agent was an islander named Brest who had served in this capacity for almost fifty years and claimed descent from the French knights who had participated in the conquest of Greece in 1206. Brest was sceptical when Georgos related the story of his spectacular discovery but agreed to return with him to his cottage. When he saw the sculptures Brest was greatly impressed, particularly by the appearance and size of the female figure. He instructed Georgos to return immediately to the catacomb and excavate all of its contents, bringing every piece of marble which he could find to the cottage in order that he would be able to see and judge its value. He promised to do all that he could to find a buyer and then returned to his home in Castro village to search through the many communications which he periodically received from the French Government. He ultimately found the directive which he sought, a paper from the French Consul General in Smyrna reminding him that:

> One of your duties as consular agent for France is to purchase any antiquities of value which are found on Melos . . .
> It is important to remember that the Fine Arts are also a source of prestige for the country you serve and you must always attend to acquiring any archaeological pieces of value . . . in the utmost secrecy.

Brest, however, was not endowed with any great aesthetic sensibility or experience and he had not the slightest idea whether the female statue which Georgos had found was in fact "an antiquity of value" in which the French Government would be interested. The thought of purchasing the statue with his own funds without some assurance that he would be fully reimbursed by the French authorities absolutely terrified him and he did not know what to do for the best. He finally decided to ask the captains of the French

naval ships which were anchored in the harbour to see the statue
and give him their opinion of it. Both of these captains accompanied
him the next day "in the utmost secrecy" to Georgos' cottage and
examined the two sections of the statue but they were as uncertain of
its value as Brest. However they suggested that since they were
proceeding in a few days to Smyrna, they would be able to talk
personally to the French Consul General stationed in Smyrna and
get his advice. Brest decided to wait until he heard from the Consul
General before making an offer to Georgos.

Shortly after these naval ships left for Smyrna, the French corvette S.M. *La Chevrette* called at Melos on its way to a hydrographic
exploration of the Turkish coast and the Black Sea. One of the
members of this hydrographic party on *La Chevrette* was the
naturalist Dumont d'Urville who toured the island on several occasions in the company of Matterer, a ship's officer, in order to collect
specimens of the plants growing on Melos. D'Urville and Matterer
met Brest on one of these excursions and when they expressed
interest in the story of Georgos' discovery of ancient marbles, they
were taken "in the utmost secrecy" to see them by the French
consular agent. D'Urville subsequently prepared a written report on
the female statue which he called "Venus" and presented this report
to the Marquis de Riviere, the French Ambassador in Constantinople, when *La Chevrette* called at the Ottoman capital several weeks
later. De Riviere, an aristocrat on close terms with the newly restored
French monarchy, was at this time preparing to return to his beloved
Paris after what he considered to be a four-year exile while serving
as Ambassador to the Ottoman Empire. He had already heard of
the discovery of the statue on Melos in a letter from the Consul
General in Smyrna, who in turn had been informed of the discovery
by the French naval captains whom Brest had taken to see the
statue. The Consul General had written to de Riviere that:

> The statue which has been discovered on Melos is apparently of great
> beauty and although it is in very bad condition it could undoubtedly
> be restored. . . .
> I have written you so that you can decide if you wish to acquire this
> statue for the Royal Museum. It might be good for Your Excellency
> to enrich this great repository of the arts in this way.

After talking to d'Urville, de Riviere decided to acquire this statue of Venus and to purchase it with his own money rather than with government funds as in this way he would be able to present a beautiful ancient statue as his personal gift to the King. He therefore instructed his secretary, Marcellus, then on a tour of the Greek islands, to stop at Melos and secure the statue. Marcellus arrived at Melos on 23rd May.

However eight weeks had passed since Georgos had uncovered his treasure trove of ancient marbles and he had not waited for the laborious churning of French governmental wheels. At the beginning of May Georgos sold the statue of Venus to a Greek priest for the small sum of 718 piastres. The priest had been furnished with this sum by the Turkish dragoman of the arsenal in Constantinople and, after acquiring the statue, he endeavoured to arrange its shipment to the Turkish capital. Brest, who had just received instructions from the French Consul General in Smyrna that the French Ambassador was personally interested in the statue and therefore to hold it for him, was naturally quite frantic. He sent a letter to de Riviere:

> It is impossible to describe to you all the difficulties which I have experienced with this statue which has been discovered on Melos. . . .
> I promised that I would do my best and that no one would take this statue until I had a reply from Your Excellency or the Consul General. But then this priest told the islanders that the Dragoman wanted all antiquities which were found on Melos and he bought Venus!
> This priest has been accused of embezzlement by the Archbishop and he hopes to curry favour with the Turks by securing this statue. . . .

The only action which Brest could take at this point was to try to stop the shipment of the statue from Melos until some representative of the French Government arrived to deal with the situation. On 10th May the statue of Venus was carted down to the beach where it remained while the Greek priest tried to arrange its shipment to Constantinople and while Brest tried to prevent it. Brest managed to persuade the captains of two French ships which called at Melos during this period to refuse to load the statue but unfortunately for the French consular agent a Russian brig arrived whose captain was unmoved by Brest's plight and agreed to transport the statue to Constantinople for the sum of 100 piastres. It was exactly at this moment that Marcellus, de Riviere's secretary, arrived on the French warship *Estafette*.

Marcellus' account of what then happened is so flamboyant—referring to the statue as "my pupil . . . my daughter . . . my Goddess . . . my glory . . . my Venus"—that it is hardly credible. According to the story which he later published, Marcellus had the "great unhappiness" when he came into the harbour of seeing the statue, which he immediately recognized, pass by him in a small dinghy on its way to be loaded on to the Russian brig. At the same moment the distraught Brest boarded the *Estafette* and related the sad story of Venus' sale. Marcellus reacted with despatch. He ordered the naval officers of the *Estafette* to stop the Russian brig from getting under sail "at any cost", but the wind fortunately was such that the brig could not sail and "they did not need to have recourse to violence to stop the departure".

Seeing the Russian brig safely becalmed, Marcellus then disembarked with Brest and gathered together "the more important Greeks of the island" to show them the French Ambassador's instructions for the purchase of this statue. Marcellus also "spoke to them with force of the inconvenience of their conduct and of their lack of faith in their engagement with France".

After Marcellus displayed such eloquence and forcefulness, the islanders agreed to give him the statue which was accordingly unloaded from the Russian brig and transferred to the *Estafette*. Marcellus reimbursed the furious Greek priest with the 718 piastres which he had paid Georgos for the statue as well as the 100 piastres which he had already given to the captain of the Russian brig. (Ultimately the statue cost the Marquis de Riviere an additional 7,210 piastres, paid at a later date to "several important Greeks on Melos" to reimburse them for their three months of imprisonment and fines which the outraged Turkish dragoman imposed on them when he learned that his statue had been stolen by the French.)

The statue of Venus, carefully wrapped in canvas, left with Marcellus on the *Estafette* on 26th May and its departure was well timed for, despite Brest's attempts to handle the discovery "with the utmost secrecy", the story had leaked out. On 29th May an English warship called at Melos with orders to purchase the statue and several days later a Dutch ship arrived for the same purpose. Venus sailed the Aegean and Mediterranean Seas with Marcellus for five months while the *Estafette* called at Rhodes, Cyprus, Acre and Alexandria. In September the *Estafette* anchored in the harbour of Piraeus and the statue was reassembled and exhibited one moonlit night to Baron Stroganoff, the Russian Ambassador to the Ottoman Empire, and Fauvel, the aged French consular agent in Athens, amidst "flaming torches and shouts of appreciation". Fauvel, who had suffered so acutely during Elgin's removal of the Parthenon marbles and Cockerell's discovery of the frieze of the Temple of Aegina, burst into tears when he saw the statue of Venus and later wrote to Paris:

> M. le Marquis de Riviere is giving a present to the King which cannot be equalled, according to me, by all the bribes and oriental spoilage which the English Ambassador has taken the pleasure to fill his baggage.

The statue of Venus began its final voyage to France on 10th October when it was transferred at dead of night in Smyrna from the *Estafette* to the *Lionne*. The Marquis de Riviere boarded the *Lionne* shortly thereafter and returned to France with his gift for the King. The Venus de Milo reached the Louvre at the beginning of 1821, almost a year after its disinterment on Melos.

French art critics descended like locusts to see the long-heralded statue when it arrived in Paris. The recent loss of the many ancient sculptures which Napoleon had gathered in Paris and displayed in the Louvre still distressed the French and this affected their reception of the statue from Melos. Their critical judgment of the artistic merits of the sculpture was definitely clouded by their intense desire that France, by her own right, should possess a work of antiquity of greater merit than the Parthenon marbles which the British Government had purchased from Lord Elgin to display in the British Museum. There was no longer any doubt that the Parthenon frieze was the work of the school of the famous ancient sculptor Phidias, so that the French were tempted to emphasize the superiority of their "find" by insisting that the Venus de Milo was the work of an equally famous ancient sculptor such as Praxiteles. This thesis seemed plausible, as Praxiteles was believed to be the first Greek sculptor to portray the female body naked and he was known to have produced at least one nude female statue, "The Aphrodite of Cnidus", which had never been discovered. This view of the statue of Venus was stated clearly by one of the leading French art critics of the day, Quatremere de Quincy:

> This is a work which offers us, aside from the highest idea of the imitation of feminine nature, the greatest concept of form, the happiest mixture of truth and grandeur of style, of grace and nobility. It must be from the atelier or school of Praxiteles.

In the end such an unbelievable quantity of confusion and myth came to surround this statue of the Venus de Milo that it is impossible to distinguish fact from fantasy and the total mystery about the origin of the sculpture has been the cause of much of this subsequent heated controversy and muddle. No one has ever been able to offer a logical explanation for the presence of this statue on the island of Melos, particularly since no other sculpture of importance has ever been discovered there despite a thorough subsequent excavation. Nor has any evidence ever been uncovered of an ancient city on Melos large enough to have logically produced a sculptor's workshop. For this reason it can only be assumed that the sculpture was brought to Melos for some unknown purpose, at some unknown date, presumably from some city on the Greek mainland. More than this cannot be stated with any degree of certainty.

The controversy began when the artisans of the Louvre attempted to assemble the pieces of marble with which they had been presented. Among these fragments there were two pieces of marble which appeared to have been broken from the base of the statue. One of these pieces—which had been found in the catacomb by Georgos and seen in Georgos' cottage by d'Urville—was inscribed with the name of a sculptor who was known to have lived some five to six hundred years later than Praxiteles. When the statue was first assembled in the workshops of the Louvre, these pieces of a base were fitted to the sculpture. The statue thus assembled was not displayed for public viewing as it had not yet been officially presented to the King, but an artist named Debay, who was the son of one of the sculptors involved in the restoration, made a drawing of the statue which he sent to his friend, the painter David, then living in exile in Brussels after the restoration of the monarchy. This drawing shows the statue on a base with the sculptor's name clearly visible— "Alexander, son of Menides, originally of Antioch of Meandre."

If this inscribed piece was actually part of the base of the sculpture it meant that the statue was not the work of the school of Praxiteles and was in fact the product of a period when Greek sculpture had passed its prime and become decadent. This idea greatly distressed the French art critics and in truth the style of the sculpture, judged on a purely technical basis, was more characteristic of the period of Praxiteles than of the much later date. The experts therefore decided that the broken pieces did not exactly fit the base and when the statue was officially presented to the King by the Marquis de Riviere, the section of the base in which the sculptor's name had been cut had been removed. When the question of dating this statue was reopened years later, this piece could not be found. Sometime during the nineteenth century it mysteriously vanished from the Louvre but whether by accident or by design will never be known.

The broken base was only one of the problems confronting the men who tried to reassemble this statue in Paris. For some quite inexplicable reason the statue was divided at the waist into two completely separate pieces, carved from dissimilar blocks of marble. Since Greece is a country where large blocks of marble are readily available, it was completely illogical that a sculptor should have put himself to the considerable trouble and technical inconvenience of cutting his sculpture from two separate blocks of dissimilar marble rather than one large block. There seemed no plausible explanation for this mystery and the Louvre restorers effected a joining of the two halves of the statue by means of cleats and plaster. It was a clumsy and faulty arrangement, however, and during the Franco-Prussian War of 1870 these cleats fell out when the Venus de Milo was being transferred for safe-keeping from the Louvre to the basement of a police station. It was then decided that the original fitting had been wrong and the statue was reassembled in 1871 in a slightly different manner but no more successfully, for in 1964 when the Venus de Milo was sent to Japan for exhibition, the statue once again came apart at the waist.

Having reconstructed and then taken apart the base and effected a poor joining of the torso, the restorers at the Louvre turned to the question of the arms, both of which were missing. While the statue remained in the privacy of the workshops of the Louvre, Brest, the consular agent on Melos, was instructed to organize a thorough excavation of the catacomb and adjacent area on Melos and to send all the fragments of sculpture which he found, regardless of their

size, to Paris. Brest obligingly shipped seventeen cases of fragments
to the Louvre, including a number of miscellaneous arms and hands
which he had gathered by the simple procedure of offering a small
sum to any peasant who brought him a marble hand or arm. Since
the islanders were known to have previously imported antiquities
to accommodate their profitable trade in ancient fragments with the
officers of foreign boats calling at Melos, it is quite likely that at
least some of these arms and hands which Brest gathered did not
originate on Melos.

The experts reconstructed a partial left arm from these fragments
sent to the Louvre and, according to the drawing which Debay
made of the statue, it was originally outfitted with this arm. However when the Venus de Milo was presented to the King, this
reconstructed partial left arm had been removed as it was decided
that the fragments from which it had been composed were of still
another kind of marble and of a distinctly inferior workmanship.
Restored arms were never again attached to the Venus de Milo after
its presentation to the King although several curious rumours have
persisted concerning the existence of arms at the time of the statue's
discovery on Melos. The written reports of the three men who saw
the sculpture in Georgos' cottage all agree on the existence of an
arm, a hand and an apple, but unfortunately these reports were so
vaguely written that it is impossible to determine whether or not
these arms, hand and apple were actually connected to the statue.
Brest, who was a native of Melos and for whom French was only a
second language, described the statue briefly in a somewhat confused despatch to the Consul General in Smyrna:

A peasant has found three marble statues, one of which represents
a Venus holding the Apple of Discord in her hand. It is a bit mutilated
—the arms are broken and the statue is divided into two pieces at the
waist.

The report to the Consul General in Smyrna by one of the French
naval captains whom Brest consulted at the time of the discovery is
more succinct: "A statue representing Venus receiving the Apple of
Paris has been found on Melos."

The detailed description which the naturalist Dumont d'Urville
presented to the Marquis de Riviere in Constantinople is even more
irritating in its vagueness:

The statue of Venus is in two pieces, designed to be joined at the waist by two strong tenons of iron. The peasant who discovered it was afraid of losing the fruit of his labours and removed the upper section of the statue together with the two smaller marble busts from the cave and took them to his cottage. I carefully examined all the marbles which he found and they seemed to me to be in good taste, as far as I could judge with my insufficient knowledge of art.

I measured the two sections of the statue separately and it is approximately six feet tall. It represents a nude woman whose left hand is raised and holding an apple and whose right hand holds a sash which is folded and covers the statue from the loins to the feet. However they are both mutilated and actually detached from the body. The hair is tucked up behind and held in place by a band. The face is very beautiful and well preserved except for the end of the nose, which is broken. The only foot which remains is bare.

All this seems suitable for the Venus of the Judgment of Paris, but where then are the statues of Juno, Minerva and the good shepherd? Among the fragments found at the same time there was a foot covered with a buskin and a third hand . . .

The name of the island—Melos—greatly resembles the word Milo —which means apple—and it seems to me that this coincidence may prove that this is the Venus of the Judgment of Paris.

Since the fragments which reached the Louvre were so shapeless and of such inferior marble and workmanship, it was finally decided to disregard them. The reports that the arms had been discovered in Melos were dismissed by the experts as errors of judgment on the part of witnesses who were unqualified to ascertain which fragments actually belonged to the statue. An armless Venus de Milo has always been displayed in the Louvre and students of this well-known sculpture have attempted to ascertain the original pose by minutely studying the muscular structure of the torso. Opinions on the original pose have formed a subject of great controversy and periodically drawings have appeared showing a Venus with the Apple of Paris, a Venus holding an amphora, a warlike Venus holding a shield, a coy Venus holding a mirror, an amorous Venus holding Mars, an embarrassed Venus emerging from her bath, an intent Venus arranging her hair.

Some enthusiastic students of the Venus de Milo were not content with merely studying the statue in the Louvre and actually visited the island of Melos in the hope of uncovering some new clue about

the condition of the statue when it was unearthed. The French
consular agent, Brest, who survived the discovery by several decades,
recounted a different version of the discovery every time that he was
questioned. Shortly before he died, Brest, who by then had persuaded himself that he had in fact played a very prominent role in
the unearthing of Venus, told a journalist:

> When the peasant Georgos saw the ground give way and the figure
> of a white goddess at his feet, he was terrified. He dropped his spade in
> his fright and immediately came to me, screaming that the earth was
> giving forth phantoms. I calmed him a bit and then accompanied him
> back to the field. It was I who helped him to extract Venus from her
> grave.

In 1852 a new sensation occurred when an aged and retired sea
captain, Matterer, announced that when he was a naval officer serving on *La Chevrette*, he had accompanied Dumont d'Urville to
examine the newly discovered statue at Georgos' cottage and that
he had seen the statue "with its left arm, which was raised and holding an apple, *intact and actually attached to the torso*".

Journalists and art critics rushed to interview Matterer and demanded to know why he had remained silent about this fantastically
important question for thirty years. The old captain promptly burst
into tears: "I could not speak while the great Dumont d'Urville
was still alive . . . but I saw the left arm, the left hand and the
apple . . . and I still have a very good memory . . . and God is my
witness, I do not lie."

When a sceptical journalist asked him how this arm had vanished,
Matterer offered an amazing explanation:

> When the French Ambassador's secretary Marcellus arrived in
> Melos the statue was not in a dinghy which was taking it to be loaded
> onto the Russian brig as Marcellus has claimed. Actually it was still
> lying on the beach. . . .
> When Marcellus saw the statue on the beach he ordered his crew to
> seize it and there occurred a tremendous battle between the French
> sailors—energetic, prompt at obeying, ardent in the attack—and the
> Greeks—savages, impatient with any delay, violent by nature. They
> fought wildly for Venus and even Marcellus and Brest were themselves
> swinging clubs and swords at the Greeks. . . .

VENUS VICTRIX,

*découverte dans l'Ile de Milo, au mois de Février 1820.
donnée au Roi le 1.er Mars 1821, par M.r le Marquis de Rivière.
son Ambassadeur à Constantinople.*

Drawing by Debay showing the Venus de Milo as first assembled with the name of the sculptor which was subsequently removed.

Drawing from Spon and Wheler's, *A Journey into Greece*, showing the ruins of Branchidae, visited by Charles T. Newton.

Sculpture of a lion removed by Charles T. Newton from the Castle of Budrun.

Poor Venus was transformed immediately into a living Venus, groaning and weeping hot tears as she was dragged along the beach, treated roughly, thrown about by furious men in a rage . . .

It was during this battle that the left arm of Venus was broken off and lost.

Matterer's "confession" created a great sensation when it appeared in the French press. Marcellus was dead but his brother wrote a furious reply to what he considered to be an attack on his family honour and the Louvre quickly denied the validity of this tale by a "demented sentimental old man" and made public a report prepared by the Director of Antiquities of the Museum on receipt of the statue in 1821. This report, curiously enough, could be interpreted as supporting Matterer's story, for it read, in part:

The marks of ropes with which they had tied the statue indicate that it was dragged along the beach . . . It was in this fatal trip that the shoulders and some parts of the back and the haunches were bruised . . . the marble had been damaged to the width of several fingers. . . .

Despite the improbability and lack of corroborating evidence for Matterer's story, rumours have persisted, particularly on the island of Melos, of a battle between the French sailors and Greek priests for the possession of the Venus de Milo. In 1960 an American of Greek descent organized a thorough but unsuccessful underwater exploration of the harbour of Melos for the missing arm.

The sensation of Metterer's confession had almost been forgotten when yet another tale arose about the Venus de Milo. In 1870 another retired French naval officer, Voutier, wrote to a leading French newspaper that in fact *he* had discovered the Venus de Milo. He said that:

I was then a young midshipman on a ship anchored at Melos and a great lover of art. I was walking on the island one day searching for ancient ruins when I came across a peasant leaning over a hole . . .

I guessed that this peasant had just made a discovery and I rushed over to him and persuaded him to dig carefully and to remove the statue which he was just about to break up into building stones . . .

Then I helped the peasant to move the statue to his cottage and I made sketches of it and later I went to inform the French Consul, Mr. Brest, and told him that he should purchase this statue for France.

But for me, the Venus de Milo would have been destroyed!

Along with this letter, Voutier presented to the French press a drawing which he claimed to have made of the sculpture when he first saw it. This drawing depicted the Venus de Milo without arms, standing upright and in one piece. In view of the immense difficulty and lack of success encountered by the experts of the Louvre when they attempted to join the two halves of the torso together, Voutier's claim that the statue was found intact and upright seems completely untenable. Yet, ironically, his story was widely accepted. The London *Sunday Times* in 1922 ran a long article on the centenary celebrations of the discovery of the Venus de Milo in which it was succinctly stated: "Practically nothing is known of the young midshipman Voutier, to whom the civilized world owes the preservation of the statue."

In fact practically nothing is known about the Venus de Milo (why has it been named for the Roman Goddess of Love and not for the Greek Aphrodite?) and it is most probable that the statue will never be positively identified. The intense desire of the French art critics to present this sculpture as a work of Praxiteles led them to commit so many irrevocable errors of judgment and to create such a confusion of fact and fantasy that it is no longer possible even to ascertain the facts of its discovery. The Venus de Milo suffered from being over-publicized. Ironically, the second French discovery in the Aegean, that of the statue of the Winged Victory of Samothrace, suffered from neglect. The Winged Victory was considered to be a relatively worthless sculpture at the time of its arrival at the Louvre and was virtually ignored in the Museum workshops for several decades.

In ancient times the island of Samothrace, in the Northern Aegean, was the site of a famous shrine of the mysterious Cabiri, spirits both evil and divine whose protection was sought against the perils of the sea. Today the island is sparsely inhabited by a small colony of fishermen and a few peasants who attempt to farm the valleys set between the bare granite hills and the sea. There is no harbour and the few available anchorages are very precarious because of the prevailing winds and the currents from the Dardanelles.

Barren and difficult to reach, Samothrace was rarely visited by Europeans until the mid-nineteenth century. In 1858 Alexander Conze, a German student, decided to complete his classical studies with a tour of the northern Aegean Islands. He stopped at Samothrace and noticed the presence of a few ruins of the Cabiri shrine lying at the bottom of a ravine but did not bother to attempt any excavations of them as he felt that it was too difficult a project with too little prospect of success. Four years later, in 1862, Charles François Noël Champoiseau, a young Frenchman then serving as French Consul at Adrianople, visited Samothrace. Unlike his predecessor, Champoiseau was so impressed by the ruins of the shrine of the Cabiri that he requested financial assistance from the French Government in order to undertake an excavation of the site. A government grant was made for this purpose and in 1863 Champoiseau began his excavations of the Cabiri shrine on Samothrace with a party of Greek labourers.

It was during these excavations that the Winged Victory of Samothrace was discovered. According to Champoiseau's report of the event, he was himself walking some fifty yards to the south-east of the area where his men were digging when he noticed a fragment of marble in the ground. He cleared the soil from this fragment with his hands and found it to be "the most beautifully shaped woman's breast". He then immediately ordered the workmen to excavate this spot and they uncovered, at a depth of two feet, "a statue of a goddess whose pose and whose outstretched wings immediately identified her as the Victory." Champoiseau's story must be considered somewhat fanciful and untenable as some two hundred fragments of the statue were excavated at this time, which suggests that on first sight Champoiseau could not possibly have realized the "pose" or composition of the sculpture.

The workmen continued to excavate the area of the discovery for several weeks after the discovery of the statue and uncovered twenty-six large marble blocks of unusual shape to which Champoiseau paid little regard. He had already notified M. de Moustier, the French Ambassador in Constantinople, of his discovery and the Ambassador sent a French naval vessel to Samothrace onto which the various fragments of the statue were loaded—with the exception of the large marble blocks—and sent to France. The sculpture was not received with enthusiasm at the Louvre where it was reassembled after three years, classified as a "mediocre decorative figure of a late period" and set up at the end of the Caryatid Room "in one of the darkest corners of the museum".

Despite the fact that contemporary guide-books of the Louvre gave the Winged Victory little more than a line and a half of description, there was an enthusiastic acclaim by a few critics when the sculpture was finally displayed. In 1866 the French Government decided to finance a second expedition to Samothrace and sent G. Deville, a former member of the French Archaeological School of Athens and M. Coquart, a former student of the Academy of Rome, to undertake further excavations on the island. This expedition was a complete failure. Rayet, a contemporary French art critic, lays this failure to the fact that "neither of these men had the proper spirit for such an expedition" as they "totally lacked both self-confidence and a belief in the possibility of their mission's success". In fact Deville was so weakened by the malaria which he had contracted in the Levant and Coquart so prejudiced in his aesthetic judgments, that they both failed to attach any importance to the twenty-six large marble blocks which Champoiseau had left exposed on the site. After only a few weeks of desultory spade-work, Deville and Coquart left Samothrace with empty hands.

In the meantime Conze, who had been the first archaeologist to visit the island, had worked himself up into a state of great agitation over the discovery which the French had made on the very site which he had dismissed as unpromising. Appointed professor at the University of Vienna, Conze prevailed upon the Austrian Government to finance an expedition to excavate at Samothrace. His mission consisted of two architects, Alois Hauser and George Niemann, and a photographer and an Austrian man-of-war was placed at their disposal. They arrived in Samothrace in the summer of 1873 and returned for further excavations of the shrine of the Cabiri in 1875. Although these two expeditions yielded them few statuary remains —four or five fragments of sculpture and twenty inscriptions—they were sufficient to enable the architects to draw elaborate plans of the foundations and probable architecture of the Cabiri sanctuary. These drawings and descriptions were subsequently published in Vienna in "two beautiful volumes which did great honour to M. Conze" and undoubtedly contributed to his later appointment as Director of the Berlin Museum.

The two expeditions headed by Conze also failed to attach any particular importance to the twenty-six marble blocks which Champoiseau had left on the site, although Hauser, one of the architects, did take their measurements and made sketches of them. The first suggestion that these blocks might have formed the pedestal of the statue was made when the notes and drawings of these expeditions were being assembled for publication in Vienna. M. Benndorf, who was assigned to do a chapter on the Winged Victory for this publication, became exceedingly impressed by these blocks and, after a careful study of Hauser's drawings, came to the conclusion that these blocks had formed the pedestal of the statue and that this pedestal had been in the shape of the prow of a ship. This discovery made it possible to identify positively the Winged Victory, for the sculpture when set on a pedestal shaped as the prow of a ship corresponded exactly to an image represented on coins which had been issued in 306 B.C. by Demetrios Poliorketes to commemorate his decisive naval victory off Salamis. Benndorf could therefore quite logically conclude that the statue of the Winged Victory of Samothrace was a work dedicated by Demetrios Poliorketes to honour his victory and therefore an important sculpture of early Hellenistic times.

According to the Austrians, Benndorf informed Champoiseau of his discovery but, according to the French, Champoiseau had already arrived at this conclusion by himself. There then ensued a fierce quarrel over the question of who deserved the credit for the realization that these blocks were in fact the pedestal of the Winged Victory. Art historians prefer to forget this quarrel, during the course of which a great many harsh things were said on both sides. It is sufficient to note that in 1879 Champoiseau received a grant from the French Government for the purpose of returning to Samothrace and securing the twenty-six pedestal blocks for the Louvre.

Despite the fact that the sculpture had now been identified as a valuable work of an important period in the history of Greek sculpture, the Louvre still refused to acclaim the Winged Victory. The statue was reassembled on its pedestal and then stored in a corner of one of the Museum workshops for an additional fifteen years. Then for some quite inexplicable reason their attitude changed and the Winged Victory of Samothrace was finally brought up from obscurity and placed in its present position on the Daru stairs—on the occasion of the visit of the Czar Nicholas II to the museum in 1896. It had languished, unappreciated, in the Louvre for thirty-four years.

Chapter XI

NEWTON'S LIONS

THE Greek War of Independence began in 1821, only a month after the Venus de Milo arrived at the Louvre, and continued until 1832 when Greece was recognized as an independent kingdom under the protection of Great Britain, France and Russia with the son of the insatiable collector, King Ludwig of Bavaria, as its first monarch. This struggle of the Greeks for their independence from Turkey fired the imaginations of many romantic young men of Europe who sincerely believed that the glorious republic of Pericles, Aristotle and Socrates would rise like a phoenix from the ashes of the past. More than one hundred young Englishmen rushed as volunteers to Athens, a French army invaded the Peloponnese, and a combined French, British and Russian fleet fought and destroyed the Turkish fleet at Navarino. A great many of these volunteers, including Lord Byron, lost their lives in this war.

But those who expected a rebirth of ancient Greece were quickly disappointed in the new kingdom, for in very few ways did the new nation resemble the Greece of the past. The Greeks of 1832 were a fractious and belligerently nationalistic people not at all given to discussing matters of philosophy and art while strolling in stoas dressed in free-flowing togas. On the contrary, they displayed what the Europeans considered to be an unwarranted selfishness by refusing to share the treasures of their past with their liberators. Even before the independence of Greece had been recognized, the acting Greek Government had prevented a party of Frenchmen from excavating in Olympia. It came as an incredible shock to all Europeans when one of the first laws of the Kingdom of Greece in 1832 forbade the export of ancient remains—"any works of artistic or archaeological value"—from Greece.

However the Hellenic world of Asia Minor still remained under Turkish control after this date and it was several decades before the Turkish Government in its turn promulgated a law forbidding the exportation of antiquities from Turkish territories. In point of fact the ancient Greek remains in Asia Minor, particularly in the area around Smyrna, were and still are considerably more extensive and better preserved than any ruins in Greece with the exception of those on the Acropolis of Athens. There were a few collectors and antiquarians who realized the existence of these valuable ancient remains in Asia Minor and sought to pillage them during the middle years of the nineteenth century. Among these was an Englishman, Charles T. Newton, who was employed by the British Museum to collect antiquities in Asia Minor while ostensibly serving in the British Consular Service on Lesbos.

Charles T. Newton was without a doubt one of the most dynamic and persevering collectors which any nation has ever produced. He was born in 1816, the year in which the British Government purchased Elgin's Parthenon marbles for the British Museum and at the time when Napoleon's hoard of pillaged works of art were being revalued and redistributed throughout Europe. He began his career with the British Museum in 1840 and served as a leading figure in the Museum during the half-century which witnessed the birth and growth of the trade of archaeology which grew up as a result of the Greek and Turkish laws forbidding the exportation of ancient remains. His retirement as Director of the British Museum in 1888 coincided with the establishment of the British Archaeological School in Athens where archaeologists were trained to excavate ancient ruins, examine their contents carefully on the site and then were frequently forced to rebury them. When Newton died in 1894 the era of the amateur antiquarian and collector had passed.

Newton was called in his day "an archaeological explorer" as he was both a serious scholar of classical history and a man who never hesitated to visit the most remote areas of the Levant in order to seek out ancient remains. He was an exceedingly successful collector and as a result of his ceaseless activity devoted to obtaining classical remains for the British Museum, England acquired, among other things, all that remained of two of the Seven Wonders of the Ancient World—the Mausoleum of Halicarnassus and the Temple of Artemis at Ephesus. His whole life revolved around ancient Greece, so much that it was said that he even resembled "some rather weather-worn, antique Zeus" in appearance, and he displayed an almost complete indifference to any considerations other than those involved in realizing his goal of obtaining antiquities for England. He was frequently criticized during his long and busy career for his obstinate single-mindedness, particularly on those occasions when he refused to accept restrictions and regulations in Greece and Turkey which might have obstructed him from acquiring objects which he desired and even publicly rebuked members of the British consular service for failing to assist him to circumvent these regulations. It was stated with intended kindness in one of his many obituaries: "His obsession for antiquities gave him a demeanour marked by a touch of suspicious caution and reserve which caused him sometimes to be misunderstood."

Newton received a degree in classics from Christ Church, Oxford, where he wrote and published graceful Latin verse. He joined the staff of the British Museum almost immediately after leaving Oxford to work in the Greek and Roman Department where his enthusiasm and ability was quickly recognized by his superiors. He was serving in this department when it received the important acquisition of twelve large slabs from the frieze of the Mausoleum at Halicarnassus which the British Ambassador in Constantinople, Lord Canning (who later became Lord Stratford) had removed from a castle built by the Knights of Rhodes at Budrun, in southwest Turkey. The acquisition of these portions of this frieze suggested to the Directors of the British Museum that they might be able to obtain other valuable antiquities from the territories under Turkish control and they discussed this possibility with members of the Government, who were described in a contemporary journal as "sufficiently enlightened to make the most of the opportunity".

The Government agreed to assist the Museum to send a "capable man" to Turkey and in 1852 the Museum secured the appointment of Charles T. Newton as British Vice-Consul on the Aegean island of Lesbos, then under Turkish control. Newton served in the British consular service in the Levant for a period of seven years and it was

frankly admitted from the start that the main purpose of his appointment was the discovery and acquisition of antiquities for the British
Museum. Newton himself reported:

> In receiving this appointment from the Foreign Office I was, at the
> same time, instructed to use such opportunities as presented them-
> selves for the acquisition of antiquities for the British Museum, and
> with this object I was authorized to extend my researches beyond the
> limit of my Vice-Consulship; a small annual allowance being granted
> me for travelling expenses.

Newton left England in February, 1852, and after a quick trip
through Greece, arrived in Constantinople in April. He discussed
his plans for the acquisition of ancient remains with Lord Stratford
who promised to "exert his influence to the utmost" if Newton
wished to undertake excavations which would require a *firman* of
permission from the Turkish Government. Newton then proceeded
to Mytilene where he arrived laden with his twenty-three cases of
luggage and promptly presented his credentials to the Turkish Pasha
of Lesbos, a man whom he described as "cloying sweet, with an
aristocratic aquiline nose, a restless wary eye, and a sinister mouth".

Newton was shocked by the squalor and filth of the capital of
Lesbos which he described in a letter to England:

> Mytilene is a straggling dirty village with squalid noisy crowded
> streets and open drains which serve as sewers, of which the exhalation
> which an eastern sun extracts of them, if not poisonous enough to
> produce a constant epidemic, is at any rate very disagreeable to the
> European nose.

In fact he had come to the Levant with the firm opinion that the
natives of this part of the world were a dirty, backward and totally
uncultured people and all his personal experiences in Asia Minor
seemed to him to confirm this idea. He found both the Turks and
the Greeks hopelessly degenerate and lacking in "moral fibre" especially when he compared them to the ancient Greeks, and he was
convinced that the wretched state of these modern Greeks and Turks
resulted entirely from their idleness and lack of initiative. He judged
the inhabitants of Mytilene as totally lacking in civilized instincts
and described the island as being populated by indolent men and

the clatter "of brawling termagants railing at each other in the streets, the yells of neglected squalid children, the howling of homeless dogs, the screams of half-starved cats".

Under these circumstances Newton was convinced that it was the duty of England and of every right-minded Englishman to "rescue" whatever antiquities still remained in these Levantine lands before they were further destroyed by a rabble who could neither appreciate nor understand them.

As soon as he was settled in Mytilene, Newton applied himself to the task of learning the modern Greek language which appeared to him to be distastefully "strong in discordant sounds" and to bear no resemblance to the beautiful ancient language. He spent all his spare time, when not occupied with his consular duties or lessons, combing the island of Lesbos for antiquities and found a few ancient ruins but was not always successful in acquiring them. On one occasion he came across a roofless chapel which contained an ancient inscription engraved on a large marble slab. After persuading the Turkish Aga of the district that he was not looking for hidden gold and inviting him to be present when the stone was lifted, Newton managed the secure some oxen and a cart with which he returned to the chapel. There he found the wife of the owner of the land:

Already in possession of the field of battle, seated on the stone itself, in the apse of the roofless chapel. She was a lady about forty, with very regular features, modelled after the classical type. At the sight of our sacrilegious party she became animated with the fury of an ancient Pythoness. She bowed down to the ground before the stone at least twelve times, kissing it, and crossing herself each time, then she lit a fire and burnt incense, to purify the place from our presence, and with great horror flung out of the sacred precinct some chicken bones, the remains of our yesterday's luncheon.

He was unable to stir this determined proprietress and never succeeded in acquiring this inscribed marble. On another occasion he found an ancient inscribed column set upside-down in the doorway of a Turkish mosque. He tried to right the column:

But the first stroke of the pick axe into the ground brought forth a fanatic in a green turban, who stamped and raged at us with all manner of maledictions. So I was forced to copy the inscription with my head between my knees, reading every letter upside down. I remained in this uncomfortable position for three days, during the greater part of which time I was surrounded by a dirty rabble.

Not all of Newton's vexations with the local conditions occurred as a result of his search for antiquities. At Easter he was invited by some Greek officials of the island to accompany them to the services at the Greek Orthodox Church which he agreed to do as he felt it was his duty as English Consul. To his horror he was met at the door of the church by a Greek priest who leaned forward to kiss him on both cheeks. "Our beards met, crossed bayonets and then retreated, and I could not help feeling that nature had done well in giving us this outwork as a defence against a very ancient, but rather disagreeable custom."

Newton described the whole ceremony in detail in a letter to a friend:

> There was an immense deal of very nasal and most detestable chanting—a chorus of pigs and cats could not have been worse. . . .
>
> I had so many questions to ask the priest that I stayed in the church until I was roused by a warning cry from without of "psylli, psylli"— "fleas, fleas" and looking down, saw my trousers covered with files of black monster fleas, who were storming me by escalade. I dashed down the leaders with my hands but they continued to crawl in such quantities that I should have been devoured without the assistance of the good natured peasants, who laughed excessively. They explained to me that as the whole population had been on their knees for several days in the church, it was very naturally swarming with fleas, whom even the Archangel Himself had no power to excommunicate.

He was unable to leave Lesbos during the first year of his appointment due to his consular duties and in the end he was so anxious to begin a search for antiquities on the Turkish mainland that he applied to the British Government for an assistant to take charge of the Vice-Consulship while he, himself, was absent from the island. Newton's request was granted at the beginning of 1853 when J. Blunt was sent from England to serve as his consular assistant but, just as he was completing his plans for a trip to the Turkish mainland, he received a letter from the British Consul at Rhodes requesting him to serve as temporary Consul there for a short period. He went to Rhodes in March of 1853 and remained there until the following January when he proceeded to England on leave. He found Rhodes much more to his taste than Lesbos: "The Rhodian peasant does not fatigue his guest with cumbrous hospitality; he does not poison him with rakée, clog him with sweetmeats, cram him with pilaf and sicken him with narguilehs."

Newton returned to the Levant in June of 1854 determined to begin a widespread, systematic search for antiquities in Turkey. The Crimean War had just started and he took advantage of the friendly attitude of the Turkish authorities towards representatives of the English Government at the onset of these hostilities to secure for himself permission to carry out large-scale excavations. He proceeded first to the island of Calymnos in September with a *firman* authorizing him to excavate wherever he wished on the island and equipped with the four shovels, four picks, three crowbars and special rope which he had brought with him from England for this purpose. He remained on Calymnos until the following spring excavating the site of an ancient cemetery with the aid of a few Turkish peasants, but all that he discovered in the course of these excavations were a few ancient vases and coins of little value. In the spring he abandoned his plans for further excavations on Calymnos and on leaving the island wrote to the Director of the British Museum:

At length I have finally succeeded in getting away from Calymnos where I was detained so long that I got utterly weary of such a monotonous life. You cannot imagine any isolation more complete than that of an European compelled to sojourn in such an island in winter time. It is something like living in the bottom of a well and seeing the same bit of sky every day.

He then proceeded on a brief trip of the nearby Greek islands and reluctantly came to the conclusion that there was little hope of finding any traces of the ancient temples which had existed on these islands as the Byzantine religious fanatics had apparently destroyed all of them and the ancient fragments which had survived this destruction had either been built into the walls of the Greek Orthodox monasteries or burnt for lime. All of the bronze statues which had decorated these temples had long since been melted down for their metal.

Newton also stopped to see the castle of Budrun on the south-western tip of the Turkish mainland on his way back to Lesbos. He had been anxious to visit this castle ever since his arrival in the Levant as it was from this fortress that Lord Stratford had extracted the twelve sections of the frieze of the Mausoleum of Halicarnassus which he had sent to the British Museum a decade earlier. The mausoleum itself had been completely destroyed and Newton found no traces even of its foundations in Budrun, the modern Turkish village which had been constructed on the site of ancient Halicarnassus. In its day the mausoleum—which had been built in 350 B.C. by Queen Artemisia as a tomb for her husband King Mausoleus— was a very impressive structure constructed of thirty-six massive columns which were surmounted by a roof in the shape of a pyramid which, in its turn, served as a base for a huge marble quadriga composed of sculptures of King Mausoleus and his Queen. Queen Artemisia had employed four of the most celebrated sculptors of her time—Bryaxis, Timotheus, Leochares and Scopas—to carve the frieze of this tomb and it was for this reason that it was considered to be one of the Wonders of the Ancient World. The mausoleum had been seen and admired in the second century A.D. by Pausanias, in the fourth century by Gregory of Nazianus, in the tenth century by Constantine Porphyrogennetus, in the eleventh century by the Byzantine Empress Eudocia and in the twelfth century by Eusthatius and until this time the structure had apparently remained more or less intact.

However the mausoleum had subsequently collapsed sometime between Eusthatius' visit and 1404, when the Knights of Rhodes landed at Halicarnassus, as all that they found was a pile of marble fragments. The Knights of Rhodes came to Halicarnassus for the purpose of erecting a castle and hospice there to replace their former hospice at Smyrna which had been captured and destroyed by the Mongol Chieftain, Tamerlane. Solemnly renaming the site St. Peter (Petros or Bedros in Greek, Budrun in Turkish), they used fragments from the ruined mausoleum in the construction of their castle, including the twelve sections of the frieze which Lord Stratford had discovered embedded in the walls, ramparts, bastions and under the drawbridge. They also consigned many of the marble decorations and broken sculpture of the mausoleum to a lime kiln in order to make mortar for their castle. This powerful order of the Knights of Rhodes (also called the Knights of St. John and later the

Knights of Malta) had been originally formed to serve as hospitallers for the pilgrims in Jerusalem. They felt justified in their destruction of the remains of the mausoleum as they considered this ancient structure to have been a monument to incest and sin since Queen Artemisia had been the sister of King Mausoleus. Their castle, when completed, overlooked the channels of Cos and Calymnos and was eventually captured by the Turks who used it as both a fortress and a prison.

When Newton visited the castle in 1855 the Turkish Commandant gave him permission to inspect it. He found some other fragments of the mausoleum almost as soon as he entered, which he described in a letter to the Director of the British Museum:

> On walking round the ramparts on the side overlooking the harbour, I made a sudden halt. What I saw was so surprising that I could hardly believe the evidence of my own eyes. In the embattled wall, between the embrasures, was the head and forehand of a colossal lion, in white marble, built into the masonry, and looking towards the interior of the castle. . . .
> After a careful investigation I found seven other such lions embedded in the walls of the castle! There is no doubt that they are from the Mausoleum of Halicarnassus.

He returned to Lesbos determined that he would have these lions from the castle of Budrun for the British Museum and that he would excavate at Budrun for the site of the mausoleum in the hope of finding some other valuable remains. However he was not able to return to Halicarnassus to fulfil this ambition as his consular assistant had been recalled and he was once again required to remain at the consular office until relieved. He stayed on Lesbos throughout the summer of 1855, fretting at the delay, until a new consular assistant arrived in November when he immediately left for Constantinople to consult with the Ambassador about his plans for excavations at Budrun. He greatly enjoyed this conference in Constantinople, according to an entry in his diary:

> At the first aspect of ladies and gentlemen at the Embassy I felt like Christopher Sly, and thought it was all a dream; and it was not till after several days of practice in talking English that my long-congealed ideas began to flow and my tongue became unlocked.

He described his plans to Lord Stratford who promptly applied to the Turkish authorities for a *firman* giving him permission to remove the lions from the castle as well as to undertake excavations in the town of Budrun. Newton stayed in Constantinople for several months awaiting this *firman* to be issued and occupied himself by excavating in the Hippodrome. Finally his patience was exhausted and he proceeded to Rhodes and from thence to Budrun without waiting for the *firman* to be granted. He excavated a few tombs in the countryside around Budrun but by April of 1856 he had spent all of the sum which he had been given for excavations by Lord Stratford and the *firman* still had not come through. Frustrated and discouraged, Newton was forced once again to return to Lesbos where he found awaiting him a Foreign Office despatch requesting him to proceed to Rome to evaluate the Campana collection which had recently been offered to the British Museum. He went to Rome, evaluated the collection and then proceeded to England where he discussed his plans for Budrun with the Director of the British Museum and the Secretary of State for Foreign Affairs. He suggested to them that the British Government should use all its influence to secure a *firman* from the Turkish Government authorizing the removal of these magnificent, ancient lions from the castle at Budrun and told them that the sum of £2,000 and the services of a warship for at least six months would be necessary to ensure their successful removal. He also suggested that an officer of the Royal Engineers and four sappers should accompany the expedition to direct the operations and that it would be very useful if one of the sappers could also serve as a photographer.

All of Newton's requests were met by the British Government. The Admiralty gave him a steam corvette, the *Gorgon*, with a crew of one hundred and fifty men, and the War Office gave him a Royal Engineer officer and four sappers, one of whom was a photographer, and provided him with:

> Every kind of stores and appliance which might be needed in the varied operations of such an expedition including miners picks, iron spades, crowbars, sledge hammers, wheelbarrows with wrought iron wheels, huge tackles and triangles, as well as pale ale and such creature comforts.

The Government also promised to secure him the necessary

firman as quickly as possible and Newton set off on the *Gorgon* with
great expectations. He arrived at Budrun in November, 1856, and
since the *firman* had not yet come through for the removal of the
lions from the castle, he decided to begin by making excavations for
the site of the mausoleum. They landed their extensive equipment
and set up a camp in the village of Budrun, "a town that is a specimen of Turkish indolence which, were it not for its ancient history,
would give little pleasure to the visitor. . . .It is a mystery, how with
their indolent habits, the Turks manage to sustain life."

There was an area in the centre of the village which was strewn
with several fragments of large Ionic columns made from Parian
marble. The area was inhabited by peasants and therefore divided
into many small plots of ground, each with its one or two-room
shack separated from its neighbour by a rough stone wall. Newton
noticed that there were fragments of ancient Ionic architectural
decorations embedded in the masonry of these peasant houses and
observed a pronounced irregularity in the ground levels of the
various plots. This area corresponded to the description given by the
ancient writer Vitruvius of the site of the mausoleum as being in the
centre of the town, half-way between the harbour and the heights
above, and it had been noticed and described by Donaldson, an
English traveller who had passed through Budrun early in the
century. Newton was familiar with Donaldson's description and in
a memorandum which he had prepared on the mausoleum several
years previously, he had specified this area as the probable site of the
tomb. However when Spratt and Ross, two English topographers,
subsequently visited Budrun, they rejected Donaldson's and Newton's hypothesis "with the contemptuous remark that such notions
show how useless it was for anyone to write about the topography
of a place without personally visiting it".

Despite Spratt's and Ross's contemptuous rejection of this area
as the site of the mausoleum, Newton determined to excavate there.
Having secured permission from the owner of one plot of ground to
excavate part of his land, he broke ground on the 1st of January,
1857, while the proprietor watched over his shoulder. Newton
recorded in his diary that: "The poor man caught a cold from standing too long on the wet soil and died . . . his life perhaps might
have been saved, but for the utter incapacity of his wife to prepare
nourishing food."

J. T. Wood.

Charles T. Newton.

Panorama of the Great Theatre at Ephesus, showing part of the excavations made by J. T. Wood.

The soil which they removed was full of small splinters of fine white marble and fragments of sculptured marble. After only a few days of excavations they came upon a mutilated section of a sculptured leg and later a fragment of a sculptured foot attached to a section of frieze moulding. Newton interpreted these discoveries as being conclusive proof that he was in fact excavating the site of the mausoleum and obtained permission to excavate a second plot in this same area. In the course of his excavations of this second plot he uncovered five drums of Ionic columns carved from Parian marble, a marble lion's leg and a quantity of carved marble which left no doubt in his mind that he had found the site. He then proceeded to excavate yet another plot and at a depth of twelve feet came across a pavement composed of four feet square slabs of green stone which were one foot thick and joined with iron tenons. Newton was exceedingly pleased with this discovery of what apparently was the pavement of the mausoleum and anxious to continue the excavations at this level throughout the entire site. However he was confronted with the presence of a small Turkish dwelling on the site. As he excavated closer to this dwelling he uncovered the base of an Ionic column, fragments of the bases of other columns and more sections of marble lions, as well as additional fragments of the green pavement. It was obvious that he would have to demolish this house in order to continue his excavations but the proprietors—"an old Turk with a termagant wife"—refused to sell. He was attempting to excavate close to the house, taking care not to undermine it, when "a long gaunt arm was suddenly thrust through the shutters from within and a discordant female voice screeched out some unpleasant Turkish imprecations on our heads".

Undeterred by these threats, the excavators continued their labours until the householders hurled a pot of burning cinders on to the back of one of the sappers. Newton then tried to win over the proprietor, Suleiman, "a trembling, decrepit old man who, though he had been a famous wrestler in his day, stood in bodily fear of his wife."

He finally managed to persuade Suleiman to let them excavate in his garden. However while he was working there, "a sapper standing on the edge of a trench was suddenly upset into it ignominiously by a well-aimed blow from a chopping block, hurled at his head from the window."

12

In the end he bought the house from Suleiman and his wife for twenty guineas.

He discovered no further fragments of green pavement in the excavations on the site of this house but came across a maze of subterranean galleries cut into the solid rock. The sappers greatly enjoyed the pursuit of these galleries which ran underneath the various houses and gardens of the area into which they would occasionally emerge: "Sometimes in a garden and sometimes in a courtyard, much to the terror of the elder ladies and the diversion of the younger ones."

Newton finally succeeded in buying up all of the land and houses in the area and demolished every house, wall, garden and tree on the site. In the course of the excavations he uncovered some important fragments of the mausoleum including the mutilated torso of a colossal equestrian figure and the torso of a seated male figure, as well as several slabs of the frieze, a number of slabs of green pavement and many drums and fragments of Ionic columns and capitals. However these successful excavations did not deter Newton from his passionate desire to secure the lions from Budrun castle. He was therefore horrified one day to see Turkish soldiers at work attempting to extract these lions from the castle walls and to learn that the Turkish Commandant of the castle had received orders to send them to the Minister of War in Constantinople. The *firman* authorizing Newton to take these lions had still not arrived in Budrun and there was absolutely nothing Newton could do to prevent the Turkish Commandant from removing one lion after another. He described his plight in a letter:

> It was not a pleasant sight for us to see this operation performed under our very eyes, after we had brought spars for scaffolding and all manner of means and appliances for the express purpose . . .
>
> However I gulped down my mortification as well as I could and despatched two letters, one by sea, the other by a swift overland runner, to Smyrna, to apprise Lord Stratford that the Turkish Minister of War was trying to steal a march on us . . .
>
> The extraction of my eye teeth could not give me so great a pang as the extraction of these lions by the Turks.

The Turkish Commandant enjoyed Newton's distress to such an extent that he visited the site of the mausoleum excavations in the company of several Turkish officials to comment on the minute size of the fragments which the Englishmen had found. Newton described this visit in a letter to the Director of the British Museum: "I endured his civil impertinence for about a quarter of an hour till at last my inward chafing found vent in a strong expression or two in English."

In a few weeks' time all the lions had been extracted from the walls of the castle by the Turks and Newton sadly watched them being loaded on to a caique which was anchored in the harbour. The evening before this caique was scheduled to sail Newton went to have a last look at his lions before going to bed "sick at heart". At four o'clock the following morning a midshipman from the *Gorgon* woke Newton to tell him that the *Swallow* had just arrived and the officer of the watch reported that they had brought the long-awaited *firman* from Constantinople. Newton refused to believe this and went back to sleep. At six a.m. another midshipman woke him and reported that the Captain wanted to see him immediately. Newton dressed and went to find the Captain impatiently pacing the quarter-deck. Newton was told that the *firman* had in fact arrived. He was not impressed.

"What does it matter?" he replied to the Captain. "The lions are gone."

"But they're not," the Captain shouted. "The caique is still in the harbour waiting for a fair wind."

Newton fairly leapt into the gig which had been drawn alongside the *Gorgon* and as they passed by the caique he noticed that its mooring lines were being drawn in and he became very alarmed. However the quarantine official who was on duty on the docks reassured him by stating that the caique could not sail until he signed their papers and agreed to delay this for several hours. Newton then hastened to the castle and demanded to see the Commandant. After waiting for an hour he was ushered into the Commandant's quarters and presented the *firman* authorizing him to take the lions. The Commandant puffed on his narquileh while he studied the *firman*.

"This *firman*," he said finally, "speaks about lions, but the animals which I have removed from the walls were leopards."

Newton was so enraged that he could hardly reply but in the end he succeeded in purchasing these "leopards" from the Commandant for a considerable sum. He returned to the docks and personally supervised the unloading of the lions from the caique and their loading on to the *Gorgon*.

He continued his excavations on the site of the mausoleum for several months after securing his lions and uncovered many valuable remains of the ancient tomb including sections of the colossal marble quadriga and its statues of King Mausoleus and Queen Artemisia. This quadriga had been described by Pliny as surmounting the mausoleum and Newton came to the conclusion from the location and condition in which he found these fragments that the mausoleum had been destroyed by an earthquake sometime after it had been seen by Eusthatius in the twelfth century and before the Knights of Rhodes arrived in 1404.

By the end of the summer the *Gorgon* was loaded to capacity with Newton's discoveries which were wrapped in old hammocks and bread bags and packed into two hundred and eighteen cases and numerous casks. The *Gorgon* sailed for England in September, taking the lions from the castle of Budrun, a colossal sculpture of King Mausoleus (nine feet tall and sixty-five separate fragments), sections from a colossal sculpture of Queen Artemisia, fragments of the colossal chariot and its horses, several sections from the frieze of the mausoleum, slabs from the pavement, a number of pieces from the building itself and other small fragments of sculpture. The British Government sent a second warship, the *Supply*, to Budrun to replace the *Gorgon*.

Newton brought his excavations at Budrun to a close in November of 1857 and proceeded to the nearby Branchidae (Didymi), site of the ancient Oracle of Didymi which was second only to the Oracle of Delphi. He removed several sculptures, including one of a lion, from the ruins of the Temple of Apollo at Branchidae and in December moved on to Cnidus. He decided to spend the winter in Cnidus in order to excavate the site of the Temple of Demeter and ordered a camp to be set up on the slopes of the steep cliff. They suffered considerably from the bitter north winds and from marauding packs of wolves and jackals at Cnidus but their excavations yielded them a statue of the Goddess Demeter in an almost perfect state of preservation: "Unquestionably one of the finest works of fourth-century Greek sculpture ever discovered."

They also found several smaller sculptures and a large quantity of terracotta figures, lamps and ancient glassware. In addition they removed a colossal marble lion, ten feet long, six feet high and weighing eleven tons, from a tomb near Cnidus, and it required one hundred sailors working for six days to haul this lion—the largest of Newton's lions—to the harbour and load it on to the *Supply*. This ship, in its turn, was then fully loaded with more than a hundred cases of ancient remains and sailed for England from Cnidus.

Newton wanted to continue his excavations in the Levant but could not do so without a further grant of funds from the Government, and the services of another warship which were not forthcoming. He was particularly anxious to reopen the excavations of the site of the mausoleum at Budrun as he had not found enough fragments of this ancient tomb to make it possible to construct an accurate model. (Models of the Mausoleum of Halicarnassus had been a popular exercise for English students of architecture from the time of Christopher Wren onwards and in fact Newton's discoveries served to confuse rather than to clarify.)

He wrote to the Director of the British Museum about his desire to do a more thorough exploration of the site of the mausoleum and added that he would need more equipment than he had previously been given in order to conduct a full-scale excavation. He suggested that it would therefore be necessary first to improve the harbour at Budrun in order to bring in this new equipment and proposed a means of accomplishing this:

> The harbour at Budrun would be greatly superior if the ancient moat at its entrance were restored. The demolition of the castle would furnish excellent materials for the reconstruction of this moat, and the cost of such a work would be amply compensated if this aided in solving the problem of the structure of the Mausoleum.

It seemed quite fitting and proper to him that since the Knights of Rhodes had used the remains of the mausoleum in order to construct their castle, their castle in its turn should be demolished in order to excavate the site of the mausoleum. The British Museum, however, did not share this view and Newton departed from Budrun, leaving a small mound to mark the site of the mausoleum for future travellers and leaving the castle intact. He remained in the Levant until the summer of 1859 when he left to take up his appointment as British Consul in Rome. The British Museum had acquired several hundred tons of valuable Greek antiquities as a result of Newton's seven years of ceaseless efforts in Turkey.

Chapter XII

THE TEMPLE OF ARTEMIS

CHARLES T. NEWTON left Asia Minor in 1859 without having met a fellow countryman, J. T. Wood, who was then working in Smyrna and privately excavating the ancient Greek ruins of that area. Wood was one of the first English architects sent to Turkey to work on the construction of railway stations along the Smyrna–Aidin line. Living conditions in Smyrna at this time, even for privileged Westerners, were extremely primitive and actually dangerous but in spite of this Wood stuck to his work for many years. To combat his boredom and loneliness during the long, dreary months spent coping with un-skilled Turkish workmen and trying to impose Western building standards on an Eastern people, he began to study the extensive ancient history of Asia Minor. What fascinated him above all was the story of Ephesus and its famous temple dedicated to the Goddess Artemis....

Ephesus, situated some fifty miles south of Smyrna, had once been the largest and most important city in all of Asia Minor. "This most magnificent and spacious metropolis of all Asia" as it was styled by a contemporary historian, owed its eminence in no small degree to an excellent natural harbour on the Aegean coast. Ephesus was ideally located on the trade routes of ancient times and much of the commerce between East and West passed through the port of the city, from the luxurious goods of the Persian Empire and Asia to the varied products of Greece and Egypt. For centuries during Greek and Roman times Ephesus enjoyed great prosperity and her streets teemed with busy people.

History relates that Ephesus was founded about 1000 B.C. by a group of refugees fleeing from the Dorian invasions of the Greek mainland. However legend insists that long before this date the countryside around Ephesus was peopled by Amazons, ferocious female warriors who worshipped Artemis, Goddess of the Hunt, and roamed free and untamed through woods and fields. The Ionian invaders, tradition maintains, fought and finally vanquished these indomitable Amazons and established a city which grew rapidly, so that by the time of Alexander the Great, it was already the capital of the whole of Ionia. The wealth of Ephesus derived not only from this trade but from the overlordship of what is still, agriculturally, the wealthiest part of Asia Minor. As a result of this wealth, many peoples sought to conquer Ephesus which was ruled in turn by the Greeks, the Romans and several Asian Kings, as well as by the Pharaohs of Egypt.

This prosperous cosmopolitan city was well known not only for its wealth but also for the "moral laxity" of its society and the unusual gaiety of its women. Even the relatively broad-minded ancient writers refer to Ephesus as a city where:

> People admire virtue and practice licentiousness and are continuously immersed in dissipation and sports, in shows and pantomimes and Pyrrhic dance, and where all the places resound with song and are filled with noise and debauchery.

Ephesian women, considerably more feminine than their Amazon ancestors, were celebrated for their beauty and willingness. Mark Antony was given Asia Minor as his share of the Roman world after the battle of Philippi in 41 B.C. and he found the women and pleasures of Ephesus very much to his taste, so much so that he was criticized by the Roman Senators for "having given himself up to idleness". His conduct was apparently quite scandalous:

> In Ephesus he is called not Consul of Rome but Bacchus, God of Wine, and he calls the women who dance for him, Bacchantes, and the men of their company, Fauns and Satyrs. The Anaxenores harpists, the Xuthi flute players, a dancer named Metrodorus, and a whole corps of Asiatic musicians, far surpassing those of Italy in impudence, have ingratiated themselves in his favour and have succeeded in influencing his government so that nothing goes well.

Mark Antony was deaf to these criticisms, however, for it was in Ephesus that he first met Cleopatra. It is said that he was presiding over a court during the oration of a celebrated speaker when he saw this beautiful Egyptian Queen passing through the market on her litter. He immediately rushed from the court to be introduced to Cleopatra and the orator ended his speech by remarking that "Bacchus has gone to feast with Venus".

Mark Antony left Ephesus to pursue his love and not long afterwards the fortunes of Ephesus finally declined. The principal cause of this decline was the silting up of the entrance to the harbour to a point where large ships could no longer call there. The once famous docks became stilled as trade ceased to flow through the city and Ephesus began to fade away. The population steadily decreased and the great houses of the wealthy merchants were abandoned and crumbled to ruins. The huge Odeon and Great Theatre of Ephesus became the haunt of jackals and wolves, the streets were empty and the fields unploughed, while the surrounding countryside slowly changed from a fertile plain into a pestilential marsh where even the tough Asiatic peasant could not survive. Ephesus, it was whispered, had succumbed to the curse of the Sibylline oracle:

Like as the ship by stormy billows thrown
Sinks in the vortex of the whirling wave;
So the bright emblem of Ionia's state,
Shall sink, confounded, in the mighty deep!
Then shall thy citizens, unhappy men,
Perish while still Artemis' help they claim.
With piteous cry their eyes to heaven they raise;
That heaven, whose thunders pour upon their heads!
. . . their guilty corpses lie
Exposed and bleaching on the burning sand!

The ill-fated city was condemned not only by the pagan oracles but also by the early Christians and one of its most outspoken critics was Paul of Tarsus—Saint Paul—who resided in Ephesus for several years and was imprisoned there. Later Christians agreed and considered the decline of Ephesus as a vindication of St. Paul in his indictment of the city. Through the centuries devout Christians made pilgrimages to the ruins of Ephesus in order to revel in its destruction. The comments of one nineteenth-century missionary on visiting Ephesus are typical:

> I have wandered amidst the ruins of Ephesus. Where once assembled thousands acclaiming "Great is Artemis of the Ephesians" now the eagle yells, the jackal moans . . . I know not if I ever spent a more solemn or more edifying day than that which was passed amongst the ruins of Ephesus. . . . Here, it was a natural reflection, is grandeur in its grave, power in its sepulchre, beauty consigned to the loathsome worm, earthly glory in the dust.

One reason for the Christian hatred of this prosperous city was the existence in Ephesus of the famous temple dedicated to the goddess Artemis, so grand and powerful that it was considered to be one of the Seven Wonders of the Ancient World. As true descendants of the Amazons, the Ephesians had erected a succession of temples to honour Artemis, Goddess of the Hunt, but these had all been sacked and destroyed at one time or another before the building of the fifth and last magnificent temple which was completed in 300 B.C. Pliny, the Roman historian, gives the fullest description of this last temple and he relates that it was composed of one hundred and twenty columns, all sixty feet high and all the gifts of different kings.

Some of the fame of this temple arose from the fact that it flourished not only as a centre for the worship of Artemis but also as a banking institution and while other ancient temples enjoyed the same kind of banking functions, none was as powerful as the Temple of Artemis in Ephesus. Not only did the temple own much valuable property in and around Ephesus from which it derived extensive revenues—acres of the most fertile lands, the fisheries of the Selinousian lakes and a park full of deer—but it functioned as a depository of wealth like a modern bank. Its banking function was supported by a vast wealth which the temple owned in its own right, for the columns and the great statue of the goddess were adorned with immense quantities of gold and precious stones which attested to its capital stability. The temple also maintained an elaborate system of lending, borrowing and providing credit and enjoyed a financial standing so secure that over a period of several hundred years kings and private persons confided their treasuries to its care. Their security was not only based upon the wealth which the temple possessed but also on its sacred nature which made it inviolate from pillage and assured that it would always be most carefully guarded. In addition, the Temple of Artemis at Ephesus had the right to levy and collect fines, to accept gifts and bequests and to benefit from confiscations. The decree of the fourth-century Byzantine Emperor Theodosius, which closed all the pagan temples including the Temple of Artemis at Ephesus, dealt specifically with these financial functions:

> It has pleased Us that in all places and cities whatsoever, the temples shall be henceforth shut, and access forbidden them; and that the power of remitting debts to debtors shall be denied them. . . . Moreover the governors of the provinces shall issue decrees, claiming the treasuries of the temples for the imperial exchequer, and if they neglect to do so they shall be punished in like manner.

The great statue of the goddess Artemis stood in the centre of this famous temple. Artemis had long been worshipped at Ephesus but the effect of trade and conquest on this city had been to change the character of this native goddess. Amazon legends described a lithe and beautiful Artemis, Goddess of the Hunt, whose right breast had been removed in order to better enable her to draw her bow. The Artemis who was worshipped in the days of the great temple was no longer a maiden huntress, for over the years the goddess had changed into a gaudy and voluptuous matron. Although the temple statue was destroyed in ancient times, small replicas of this statue have been found. These depict a wooden goddess completely covered with gold except for the hands, feet and head, which were left bare. The face was pitch black, apparently as a result of the ritual applications of olive oil which were made daily by loving attendants. There was a small square shrine resting on the top of the head which was said to contain a sacred object whose nature is unknown but which was probably an odd-shaped stone or a meteor. It was the torso of the statue which was remarkable for it contained several rows of huge pendulous breasts, more than forty in all, sumptuously adorned and decorated. The goddess of Ephesus had so many ornaments for her many breasts that Mistresses of the Robes were appointed from among the wealthy Ephesian families for the much-sought-after job of dressing and redressing the chest of this fabulous goddess. . . .

Such was the story of Ephesus which intrigued the bored English railway engineer some two thousand years later. Wood could visit Ephesus frequently, since it was close to Smyrna where he was based and he enjoyed wandering at his leisure through the ruins of the theatres and buildings which marked the site. The Turkish peasants became used to this familiar figure of a tall sombre Englishman in his black, stove-pipe hat poking about among the ruins. Wood simply could not bring himself to believe that no trace of the fabulous Temple of Artemis had survived in spite of the fact that not one column or stone or even a mound of earth remained to suggest where it might have stood. For centuries no visitor to the ruins of Ephesus had been able to do more than haphazardly guess at the site of the vanished temple. The expedition which the Dilettanti Society had sent to Asia Minor in 1765 had spent several months in Ephesus searching for the site of the temple and in its final report pronounced that: "We seek in vain for the temple . . . The Ephesians are now a few peasants, living in extreme wretchedness, dependence, and insensibility. The city is prostrate and the goddess gone."

Wood, however, refused to accept this disappearance and was convinced that the ruins of the temple lay buried somewhere beneath the desolate plain which stretched out below the miserable Turkish village of Ayasalouk. He made up his mind that he would find the lost temple and he was convinced that he would succeed where others had tried and failed. He began to lay systematic plans for the search and in the spring of 1863, with the assistance of the British Ambassador in Constantinople, he obtained a *firman* from the Turkish authorities which permitted him to excavate at Ephesus and to export from Turkey any antiquities which he might find in the course of his excavations.

As soon as he obtained this *firman* Wood began his excavations which were solely financed by his savings during his tedious employment with the Turkish railways. He did not feel he could afford to give up his work and lodgings in Smyrna under these circumstances, especially since he was not sure how much his search would cost him, and during the first months of the excavations he commuted three or four times a week from Smyrna to Ephesus, a distance of fifty miles. It was a staggering schedule, especially during the hot summer. It took him an hour and a half to walk from his lodgings to the railway station in Smyrna and then he endured a three-and-a-half-hour ride to Ayasalouk on the dirty, hot and primitive railway car. The site was another three miles from Ayasalouk station and this last section of the trip had to be covered either on horseback or on foot. In the end he only had six hours to spend in Ephesus before trudging back to catch the returning train for Smyrna. It was a measure of his blind enthusiasm and determination that he endured ten or twelve hours of wretched travel each time he visited the site.

The main problem which Wood faced was where to excavate. The only certain information he had, as all the ancient historians were agreed on this fact, was that the temple had been situated outside the city proper. While he could more or less delineate the city limits from a study of the existing ruins, this did not give him a great deal to go on and he felt that the logical approach to solving the problem of the temple's location was by an analytical study of all descriptions of the temple which had been made by every ancient writer and every visitor to Ephesus. He found that only the ancient writers were of any value in this respect since not one of the travellers who visited Ephesus after ancient times left a record of having seen the temple or even its ruins. Long before he started to excavate Wood studied the ancient Greek and Roman writers for mention of Ephesus but the information which he had extracted from these studies was both vague and confusing. Strabo, for instance, wrote only that the famous temple had been built on the foundations of a still older temple but gave no information as to where this older temple had been situated. Xenophon mentioned that the Selinus river ran past the temple and that there were fish and shells in this river but he neglected to say just how close the temple was to the river bank. Pliny confused the issue considerably by stating that there were two rivers with the name Selinus, adding that the temple had been constructed on marshy land in order that it would not suffer damage during the earthquakes which frequently occurred in that area. Diogenes Laertius also stated that the site was marshy and this information was verified by Vitruvius who mentioned that they were unable to use wagons to convey the shafts of columns and heavy blocks of marble to the temple because of the softness of the road. The ancient traveller Pausanias gave some information which Wood felt might be useful concerning the existence of the tomb of Androklos on the road which led from the temple to the Magnesian gate of Ephesus. Even more interesting, Wood felt, was a statement made by Philostrataus that a rich Roman had joined the temple to the city by extending the road "which descends through the Magnesian gates" with a stoa of six hundred feet in length, in order that the priests should not be kept away from the temple in rainy weather.

In theory, Wood decided, all that he needed to do was to locate the Magnesian gate, which two of the ancient writers had described as being somewhere at the city limits, locate the ruins of a six-hundred-foot stoa outside this gate and then follow this stoa along to the site of the temple itself. In practice, however, it was not quite so simple as it seemed because the entire plain of Ephesus had been silted over with immense quantities of sand and soil from the surrounding mountains. Wood could not find any remains of an ancient gate or stoa, nor the slightest indication of where these structures might have been located. His only other clue from his study of the ancient writers was the proximity of the Selinus river to the temple. However the two rivers which then ran across the plain of Ephesus could undoubtedly have changed their course over the centuries and it was impossible to judge which one of these was the true Selinus. Wood was forced to admit finally that the ancient writers were of very little help in the solution of this problem.

At this point he decided to attempt a different approach to the question and drew upon his architectural training. If, as an architect, he had been hired by the ancient Ephesians to build them a temple outside the city walls, where would he have put it? Wood carefully studied the layout and topography of the land, estimating, as best he could, the probable nature of the silting, and his eye fell on a long narrow plateau which rose several feet above the general level of the plain, between the city and the sea. He decided that as an architect he would undoubtedly have chosen the western end of this plateau as the best possible site for the temple since it combined the advantages of being convenient to the city with being clearly visible from the sea.

Wood therefore began his excavations for the temple on this plateau. He started off with a crew of five Turkish labourers who had recently been discharged from the railway whom he ordered to sink holes in the plateau, starting at the western end and then working slowly all the way along the strip. Each one of these holes was excavated to a depth of twenty feet as Wood estimated that the plain of Ephesus had been silted over by as much as twelve or fifteen feet of soil since ancient times (a guess which turned out to be quite accurate). In addition, he ordered the workmen to excavate several deep trenches across the width of the plateau in the hope of finding the Roman stoa which Philstrataus had mentioned as connecting the city with the temple. They started their excavations in May when it was already uncomfortably hot for such manual labour and the Turkish workmen objected to working at midday, which was the only hour that Wood could be present on the site. He managed to keep them digging for six weeks but in the course of these excavations found nothing except the substructures of some monuments and tombs and the thin brick walling of Roman and Byzantine buildings. These discoveries did not interest Wood in the least and he disregarded them. All that he cared about was locating the Temple of Artemis.

By the end of June it was so unbearably hot that the workmen refused to continue. Moreover Wood found that he could no longer endure the long journey to and from Smyrna and was therefore forced to suspend the excavations until the following September. During the long hot summer he came to the conclusion that his search for the temple could not possibly hope to succeed under the previous conditions of work and he took a temporary leave of absence from his job with the Turkish railways and moved his belongings to a room in the village of Ayasalouk, above Ephesus. His living accommodation was modest, as he recorded in his diary:

> This room was approached by a rickety external staircase and the entrance door opened from the terrace roof of a stable. The whole tenement was so dilapidated that it threatened to tumble down whenever I walked across the room.

(In fact, shortly after Wood moved from this tenement, it did actually collapse.)

Wood soon discovered that living in Ayasalouk was difficult. Food was scarce and frequently non-existent in the village, it continued to be uncomfortably hot and humid, and the sanitary conditions were frightful—amongst numerous other diseases, malaria and cholera were endemic. However, he reopened his excavations in September and employed a crew of twenty workmen to dig more holes and trenches along the western end of the plateau. But Wood suffered a serious accident only a few days after they had started this work when his horse fell into a dry irrigation ditch. He was confined to his bed throughout the entire month of September with a broken collar bone and other injuries while his unsupervised crew worked in a half-hearted manner.

It was October before Wood was able to visit the excavations which had not yielded one single shred of evidence to substantiate his theory that the temple had been constructed on the plateau. Discouraged, Wood ordered the men to sink trial pits at occasional intervals along all sides of the harbour and to the north of the city. All that he found in these pits were traces of Byzantine walls and immense quantities of oyster shells, indicating that the ancient Ephesians had enjoyed a far more sumptuous diet than the modern Turkish peasants in Ayasalouk. These peasants, in fact, barely subsisted by farming the Ephesian plain and were therefore extremely angry with Wood for digging holes and trenches in their lands. They finally prevailed upon the Englishman to fill in his excavations as soon as they were completed.

By Christmas of 1863 Wood had excavated seventy-five deep holes and trenches which he had subsequently filled in. The winter rains which had begun in the late fall continued until the entire plain of Ephesus became such a sea of mud that all excavations were brought to a halt. Wood was now thoroughly depressed and since all of his savings were gone, he was forced to return to his job with the railways in Smyrna in January. During the bleak winter days of almost continuous rain in Smyrna, he found himself forced to admit the folly of trying to locate the ruins of the temple, which were probably at least fifteen feet beneath the surface, by his method of excavating holes at random. Furthermore he no longer held any belief that the temple was located on the plateau which he had so thoroughly excavated.

Wood was not a man, however, who stayed discouraged for long and within a few weeks he had thought of a possible new approach to his problem. It seemed to him very likely that there must have been some sculptures or paintings decorating the public buildings of Ephesus which showed the temple in its setting. He thought that there was a good possibility that a painting depicting the landscape of Ephesus or a sculpture representing a procession from the city to the temple existed somewhere in the ruins of the two amphitheatres of Ephesus, the Great Theatre and the Odeon. He realized that the excavation of either of these amphitheatres would be a large undertaking requiring more labour, time and money than he had at his disposal but he had recently learned of the excavations at Halicarnassus and Cnidus which had been made by C. T. Newton on behalf of, and with the financial support of, the British Museum. He felt that the Museum might be interested in an excavation of these two well-known ancient Ephesian amphitheatres and therefore wrote a letter to the Directors of the Museum requesting financial aid in order to conduct a full-scale excavation of either the Odeon or the Great Theatre of Ephesus. He pointed out in his letter his experience in dealing with Turkish workmen after a decade of working on the Smyrna–Aidin railway, his fluency in the modern Turkish language, his intimate knowledge of Ephesian history and mentioned the fact that he had recently done private excavations in Ephesus. The Directors of the British Museum were persuaded by Newton, who had recently returned to the Museum where he had been appointed as Keeper of the Department of Greek and Roman Antiquities, to send Wood a grant of one hundred pounds to undertake the excavation of the Odeon.

In March, 1864, Wood began the excavation of the Odeon, the smaller of the two Roman amphitheatres in Ephesus, capable of seating some two thousand people and situated on the southern slopes of Mount Coressus outside the city limits. As he could not then afford to take a second leave of absence from his job with the Turkish railways, he hired a Greek superintendent to remain in Ephesus and to oversee the work done by some forty Turkish labourers. This arrangement proved satisfactory and the excavations proceeded rapidly as they cleared first the seats and then the stage. In the course of these excavations they discovered several ancient sculptures, a number of fragments of decorative carved marble and an inscribed marble containing the speeches of a Roman Consul to the people of Ephesus. These discoveries, which included a small statue of Erato, Muse of Erotic Poetry and Music, were loaded on to an English ship, the *Cornish Lass*, which was subsequently wrecked in a storm off the Greek island of Syra. The statue of Erato was later recovered by sponge divers but in such a damaged condition that it was never sent to London.

The excavations in the Odeon were completed in December, 1865, by which time the seats and stage had been cleared and the grant from the British Museum expended. Although Wood had uncovered no sculpture or painting in the Odeon to indicate the location of the Temple of Artemis, he still refused to admit defeat. From a hospital bed in Smyrna where he was recovering from a nearly fatal stabbing by a lunatic, he wrote again to the Directors of the British Museum requesting their financial aid in order that he might excavate next the Great Theatre of Ephesus. The Museum was pleased with his work on the Odeon which Newton had visited and approved and agreed to his new request. In February, 1866, Wood received additional funds to excavate the Great Theatre, one of the largest amphitheatres of the ancient world, capable of seating twenty-four thousand people.

Wood personally supervised these new excavations, overseeing a crew of seventy Turkish workmen, and he uncovered a considerable quantity of ancient sculpture and decorative marble from the Great Theatre which were shipped to the British Museum. However the strain of the fantastically heavy schedule which this man had imposed on himself for more than three years in this unhealthy climate became too great. Wood suffered frequent and serious attacks of malaria and eventually became so desperately ill that he was forced to return to England for five months of rest. He talked several times to Newton and the Directors of the British Museum while in England and finally persuaded them that he should spend a small portion of his yearly grant from the Museum in a search for the site of the temple. As soon as he returned to Ephesus, in late 1866, he began to excavate occasional pits outside the eastern walls of the city in the hope of locating some remains of the temple.

It was not until the end of 1867 that Wood made the first real discovery which seemed to contribute definitely towards locating the site of the temple. While clearing out a section of the Great Theatre, he came across several marble slabs which were inscribed with a series of decrees relating to a quantity of gold and silver images which a wealthy Roman, C. Vibius Salutarius, had given to the Temple of Artemis. This inscription included a long description of the procession of these images around the city of Ephesus and described in detail the location of the Magnesian and Coressian gates to the city. Wood was delighted with this inscription as he felt that he would easily be able to locate the site of these gates from the information given therein and that, once having located these gates, he would then be able to find the road from the city to the temple and thus the temple itself. A British warship, the *Terrible*, was at this time in Smyrna for the purpose of taking a shipment of his discoveries back to England and he requested the aid of the crew to remove the massive marbles bearing this inscription from their setting. As each of these marbles weighed more than four tons and were situated on top of a wall, their successful removal was a feat which Wood described in his diary:

> I feared that if the sailors of H.M.S. *Terrible* were allowed to begin the work without caution, we should have little of the inscription intact, when the stones were removed. I therefore told them that if they landed one stone bearing an inscription on the pavement at my feet without further injury to it, I would give them all round of pound of tobacco.

His conviction about the value of this so-called Salutarian Inscription was well founded as within a few months he was able to locate what he definitely felt to be the remains of both the Magnesian and Coressian gates. He was then convinced that the location of the temple was at last within sight and took most of his workmen off the excavations of the Theatre in order to excavate outside the Magnesian gate for the remains of a road leading through the gate in the direction of the temple. Wood had high hopes of easily locating the remains of the stoa mentioned by Philostrataus and tracing it from outside the gate to its end at the temple. After a few days of excavations he had determined that there were three routes leading through the Magnesian gate, one for pedestrians and two for chariots and wagons. The two vehicular paths joined to become one road a few feet beyond the gate and he excavated this road for a distance of one hundred and forty feet where it forked, one branch apparently heading around Mount Coressus towards the Turkish village of Ayasalouk and the other apparently heading for Magnesia.

He then proceeded to uncover both of these roads. He found the fork which headed for Ayasalouk to be wider than the other and its pavement, composed of large blocks of marble and limestone, was deeply worn with ruts, thus giving evidence to the fact that it must have carried heavy traffic. On the other hand the road towards Magnesia, while it showed much less wear, was lined on both sides with various tombs and monuments and it seemed possible that one of these tombs might be that of Androklos which the ancient traveller Pausanias had mentioned as being on the road to the temple.

Wood became very uneasy as the distance from the Magnesian gate increased along both of these routes and it was with infinite relief that he finally uncovered stones on the Ayasalouk road which seemed to have come from a stoa. He then paced out the six hundred feet which was given as the length of the Roman stoa connecting the city to the temple and excavated at this point, only to find that this could not have been the site of the temple. This discovery distressed him as his funds from the British Museum were exhausted and in May, 1868, he was compelled to release all his workmen and return to England. By then he was completely discouraged, for despite his discovery of the two gates to the city and the roads leading from them, he still had found no trace of the temple. Exhausted by his intermittent bouts of malaria, with his personal savings gone, Wood felt that he had finished with the Levant and vowed that he would never again submit himself to the difficult living conditions and the unrelenting strain of his search for this temple at Ephesus. But his enthusiasm returned with the recovery of his health in England and once again he approached the Directors of the British Museum for funds with which to excavate in Ephesus. Newton was convinced that he did in fact stand a chance of locating the Temple of Artemis and persuaded the Museum to give Wood another grant.

Wood returned to Ephesus in October, 1868, and immediately set to work methodically excavating the entire length of the road from the Magnesium gate to the Coressian gate to a depth of twelve feet. As he cleared this road he cut a continuous deep trench along the outer edge in the hope of finding a second road joining it, for after a careful study of the Salutarian Inscription in England, he had come to the conclusion that there must be a second road to the temple which joined the main Magnesian–Coressian road at some unknown point. But as the days and weeks passed and his small grant from the Museum dwindled away and yet he found no sign of a second road, he again became very uneasy. As he recorded in his diary: "The fear of failure now costs me many a pang."

Then, one February morning, he discovered the foundations of the tomb of Androklos on this Magnesian–Coressian road, the tomb which Pausanias had described as being on the road from the city to the temple. He then excavated very carefully in the vicinity of this tomb and located, at last, the traces of a road leading away from the Magnesian–Coressian road. This new road was more than ten feet wider than the one joining the two gates, a fact which convinced him that it was in fact the main road to the temple, and it led, curiously enough, in the direction of his lodgings in Ayasalouk. Wood now felt that it was only a matter of time and patience before he succeeded in finding the site for which he had sought for so long.

However the entire plain outside the city of Ephesus had been sown that year with barley which was already well up. Wood re-examined his treasury with a heavy heart and saw that he did not have enough funds left to recompense the Turkish landowners for the barley which would be destroyed by his excavations of this new road. He calculated that at the very best he would only be able to excavate a few hundred feet and that the chances of finding the temple within this few hundred feet were very slim. He felt utterly defeated as he stared at this field of barley and for the first time during his five years of searching, he did not know what to do. As he walked to his lodgings in Ayasalouk he passed through a grove of olive trees about half a mile distant from the Magnesian–Coressian road and he was suddenly struck with an illogical conviction that this was the site of the temple. Although there was no logical reason for his whim—except perhaps for a persistent tradition of sanctity of the Ayasalouk hill for both Christians and Moslems—Wood decided to gamble the last of his grant in excavating this olive grove. He made a plan to dig one or two trenches in between the trees and as many holes as he could afford in the surrounding area.

At this critical moment the Turkish officials notified Wood that his *firman* to excavate in Ephesus had expired and they forbade him to continue working. He therefore rushed off to Constantinople in a frenzy where he fortunately succeeded in getting his *firman* quickly renewed. As soon as he arrived back in Ephesus he ordered his workmen to excavate in the olive grove and they were immediately rewarded. In the very first trench which they dug they uncovered the remains of a thick wall built of massive blocks of stone. Wood felt positive that this was in fact the wall which had been built around the sacred limits of the Temple of Artemis but his trip to Constantinople had exhausted his funds and he didn't even have sufficient money to pay his workmen for their last day of work. In desperation he sent an urgent request to the Directors of the British Museum for more money and in reply the Museum sent him a small grant, but it was clearly intimated that this was sent "only in consideration of his having worked at this apparently hopeless enterprise for so many years".

The Museum added that unless he succeeded in actually finding the temple with this grant, there would be no further funds.

Wood was then faced with the problem of the most effective use of this final grant. He noticed that the ancient wall whose traces he had uncovered seemed to run in roughly the same direction as an existing wall. Once again on the basis of whim rather than logic, he decided that the modern stone wall marked the position of the ancient one and excavated a second trench further along it. His hunch proved to be correct and they uncovered a section of the ancient wall with two large inscribed marbles stating, both in Latin and in Greek, that this wall had been built by order of the Roman Emperor Augustus.

Haggard with the effects of malaria and the strain of his labours, Wood burst into tears when he read these inscriptions. He knew then that his search was ended, for it was an established fact that the Emperor Augustus had erected the wall enclosing the sacred grounds of the temple. After six years of excavations and an expenditure of more than two thousand pounds, the site of the famous Temple of Artemis had been located solely through the stubborn determination of this one man and the faith of his financial backers. Wood cleared away a section of the Augustan wall and returned to England to discuss the question of further excavations with the Directors of the British Museum.

He returned to Ephesus authorized by the British Museum to purchase the site of the Temple of Artemis on their behalf and to proceed to a full-scale excavation under their auspices and supervision. These excavations were carried out over a period of four years, until the spring of 1873, and came under the direction of Newton who visited Ephesus on several occasions during the course of the work. Wood laboured under conditions of incredible hardship and was afflicted not only by recurrent malaria but also with earthquakes, crime and desertion of his crew of Turkish workmen. He encountered almost insuperable difficulties with the drainage of the site and suffered an almost constant series of landslides, cave-ins and floods. He discovered the marble pavement of the temple at a depth of nearly twenty feet below the surface and, since the water-level of the plain had risen considerably over the centuries, this pavement was actually under water for a greater part of the year. (In January, 1871, for instance, he recorded that the pavement was under five feet of water.) Because of the impossibility of draining the site once the winter rains had begun, he was forced to suspend the excavations during most of the winter and to work only in the frightful summer heat.

Yet after all this tremendous effort, expense and sacrifice, Wood uncovered very few tangible remains of the temple. In fact, apart from the establishment of the site of the temple, there was very little to show for all the ten long years through which he had laboured under such dreadful conditions in the hope of a major architectural treasure. His architectural findings were so insignificant that they did not even permit a conjectured reconstruction of the building and he found no statue of the goddess nor any of the gold and precious gems with which the temple had been adorned. In the end his discoveries only amounted to a few sections of marble pavement, portions of the bases and drums of a few columns and a variety of fragments of decorative carving and these he shipped to England with great ceremony. The entire crew of a British warship paraded with fife and drum through the streets of Smyrna while these meagre remains of the Temple of Artemis were loaded for the journey to England where they were drawn by a team of twenty horses through the streets of London and up to the doors of the British Museum. Wood himself returned to England in the summer of 1873, sick and discouraged by the paucity of his find and he died in obscurity not long afterwards. Most modern encyclopedias of archaeology do not even include his name and his fantastic struggle to locate the Temple of Artemis has been largely forgotten.

The Directors of the British Museum decided to reopen the

excavations of the site of the Temple of Artemis in Ephesus at the turn of the century, when both J. T. Wood and C. T. Newton were dead. They assumed that Wood had exaggerated the difficulties of working in Ephesus and believed that new excavations might well yield them more significant remains of the temple. In 1900 the Museum therefore sent out a group of carefully chosen and well-trained archaeologists who, on arrival in Ephesus, were horrified by the site, "an immense water-logged pit choked with a tangled broke of thorns and reeds."

Despite extensive equipment which they had brought with them from England, including a huge steam-driven pump, these later archaeologists found it virtually impossible to excavate the site of the temple. They eventually discovered a few votive offerings from an earlier temple but nothing from the great Temple of Artemis and left Ephesus with great relief after only one ghastly season of what Wood had endured for more than a decade: "A continuous trial of cave-ins of sand and mud, of never-ending rain and winds, of flooding pits and trenches, and rampant disease."

Shortly after these later excavators left Ephesus, the British Museum was ordered by the Turkish Government to fill in the site of the Temple of Artemis permanently on the grounds that this bog was the cause of the repeated epidemics of malaria in this area. In Ephesus today there is nothing to be seen of the Temple of Artemis. The goddess has in fact gone from Ephesus.

Chapter XIII

THE WOODHOUSE COLLECTION

THE Aegean islands remained under Turkish control until they were turned over to the expanding Greek nation at the beginning of the twentieth century, but the Ionian islands, off the west coast of Greece, had quite a different history. They were acquired by Russia from Turkey in 1770 and in the course of the next thirty-five years passed under French control and were subsequently re-acquired by Turkey, Russia and again by France. In 1815 they came under British protection and were governed as a British Protectorate until they were given to Greece in 1864. There were a number of Englishmen resident in these islands throughout this half-century of English rule, one of whom was James Woodhouse, who lived on Corfu for more than fifty years. James Woodhouse served in the Commissariat Service of the British Protectorate and for many years held the post of Treasurer of the Ionian Islands. This position of considerable distinction and power enabled Woodhouse to indulge his passion for collecting old coins and other antiquarian titbits since the Greek peasants who occasionally came upon ancient graves while ploughing their lands were very willing to trade a few old coins for the goodwill of the government treasurer. It was principally through these gifts that Woodhouse acquired a considerable collection of which he was inordinately proud.

James Woodhouse stayed on in Corfu when he retired from government service as by then he had come to regard the island as his home. He never married but for more than half a century lived in the close company of his Italian housekeeper, Maria Constantini.

His closest blood relations were a nephew and niece living in England with whom he had quarrelled and it was only during his declining years that he corresponded with them. He lived with his loquacious Signora Maria in a small two-storey villa outside the town of Corfu and spent many hours with his collection which he kept carefully secreted away in innumerable little boxes under his bed, inside his chest of drawers, under the wash-basins, in the library, in the kitchen and, in fact, scattered all over the villa. He was a familiar figure of the small English community on Corfu and as he grew older his life had a fixed routine which everyone respected. It was his custom every day to go downtown in the morning to visit James Taylor, his lifelong friend who ran a general dealer's shop, and to sit for several hours in Taylor's reading room browsing through the English newspapers and chatting either about the deplorable state of the modern world or relating his often repeated anecdotes about how he had collected his various coins and antiquities. At noon he would return home to eat and rest, sometimes returning in the late afternoon to Taylor's reading room. His social life, however, was confined to this reading room for he disliked visitors at his villa and frequently refused to see anyone who called on him at home. His daily routine remained unaltered until he became ill in the autumn of 1865.

Although James Woodhouse talked incessantly about his collection to everyone who would listen, he never displayed the entire collection to anyone, perhaps because he was afraid of discovering that its value was not so great as he had pretended. As a result no one really knew exactly what the old man did have hidden away in the little boxes scattered around his villa but he apparently possessed a large assortment of Greek coins, a number of ancient rings, some bits of gold and silver jewellery, a few ivory carvings and glass vases, several bronze tablets and several small marble statues and reliefs, as well as other odd bits and pieces such as a large series of ancient lead and stone weights. In the early years of his collecting he had kept a register of the origin of each piece and the price, if any, which he had paid for it but this register gradually fell into disuse and was lost. The old man was immensely proud of his collection and determined that when he died it should go to the British Museum. Everyone on Corfu knew of this intention which he had repeatedly stated to his audiences in Taylor's reading room.

Charles T. Newton maintained an elaborate network of contacts in the Levant to keep him informed on all matters of interest concerning classical remains and through these contacts he eventually got wind of this proposed legacy. He stopped at Corfu in the autumn of 1863 on his way back to England after visiting Wood's excavations in Ephesus and went to see James Woodhouse who showed him a few of the coins from his collection and described in glowing terms the entire collection which he proposed to bequeath to the British Museum. Newton, who had recently received the appointment of Keeper of the Department of Greek and Roman Antiquities at the Museum, was greatly interested in acquiring this collection and in view of Woodhouse's well advanced years, he tactfully suggested that some definite steps should be taken concerning shipment of the collection to England. Newton also called in at the office of the High Commissioner, Sir Henry Storks, before leaving Corfu where he learned to his consternation that Woodhouse apparently had made no will. Newton suggested to Sir Henry that this omission should be quickly rectified. Another question of grave concern to him was the imminent termination of the British Protectorate of the Ionian islands. He asked the High Commissioner whether the Greek law forbidding the exportation of antiquities would affect the legacy of a British subject dying in Corfu after the islands were handed over to Greece. Sir Henry Storks was unable to answer this question and on his return to England Newton put the same query to the Under-Secretary of State for Foreign Affairs, Sir Austen Henry Layard, an enthusiastic collector and friend whose career had closely paralleled his own. Shortly before Newton was sent as British Vice-Consul to Mytilene, Layard, with the financial assistance of the British Museum, had explored the ruins of Assyria, Babylonia and Southern Mesopotamia. In the course of these explorations he had located and excavated the ancient city of Nineveh and was responsible for securing for the British Museum the greater part of its collection of Assyrian antiquities. When Layard and Newton discussed the problem of the Woodhouse collection on the basis of their past experiences, they decided that the safest procedure was to remove the collection from Corfu before the British Protectorate ended.

With this decision in mind Newton sent Woodhouse an autographed copy of his recently published book on his excavations at Budrun and took this opportunity to suggest that the collection be sent on immediately to London as the Trustees of the British Museum were most anxious to receive it. Woodhouse bestirred himself sufficiently to order two wooden packing-cases specially lined with tin in order to ship the collection to England, but he never got around to packing them and eventually Signora Maria used one of them in the kitchen as a mouse-proof larder. Months passed, the British Protectorate ended and Corfu came under the rule of the kingdom of Greece.

Newton again stopped at Corfu in the spring of 1865 and visited Woodhouse who assured him that a part of the collection had already been packed and was almost ready to be shipped to England. It was during this visit that Newton first met Sidney Smith Saunders, the new British Consul General for the Ionian islands and informed him of the Museum's interest in the Woodhouse collection. Saunders was a capable and conscientious diplomat nearing retirement after having served for more than forty years as British Consul in Albania and as British Consul and Judge in the English Court at Alexandria. His service had been so distinguished that on the recommendation of Sir Henry Storks, former High Commissioner in the Ionian Protectorate, Saunders had recently received his K.C.M.G. Newton emphasized to Saunders how vitally important it was that Woodhouse be persuaded to make his will so that at the moment of his obvious imminent demise, the collection could be promptly shipped to London. Saunders promised to do his best in this matter.

James Woodhouse became ill in the autumn of 1865 and it was clear to everyone that the old man was approaching his end. He could no longer make his daily trips to Taylor's reading room and Signora Maria hovered around his bedside with bowls of special broth, clucking over him in her incessant Italian. At his request most of his little boxes were brought into the bedroom so that he could spend his last hours near his collection which remained his greatest passion until the end. But still he made no will and no one, not even James Woodhouse himself, knew exactly what his collection contained.

One morning in late February Woodhouse, now very ill and feeble, asked one of his friends, a Mr. Zambelli, who was visiting him, to take away his collection and send it to England. Zambelli interpreted this decision to give away the collection as proof that the old man was actually dying and rushed to the British Consulate with the news. The staff which was present at that time sat down and jointly drew up a will in the terms of Woodhouse's frequently expressed wish to bequeath his collection to the British Museum. What they composed, unfortunately, was a legal document which was subsequently judged by English lawyers invalid as a proper will. It read, in full:

That as the trustees previously appointed by me are no longer residing at Corfu, and are consequently unable to act on my behalf, I hereby direct that this duty be discharged by Mr. James Taylor, of this place, and Mrs. Maria Constantini, quondam Antonio, who has been my companion during the last fifty years, well assured that these will faithfully discharge the duties confided to them in this respect, and I therefore revoke all other declarations and dispositions contrary to these present. And furthermore I declare that, having been engaged in numismatic pursuits during a long residence in these islands, and being desirous that the collection of coins and other antiquities so formed should be dedicated to national purposes, I request Mr. Sidney Smith Saunders, Her Majesty's Consul General here, to take charge thereof, and, when recovered from the hands of my trustees, transmit the same to the British Museum on my behalf as a tribute to the national collection, while regretting that I am unable to accompany this donation with a suitable catalogue as I could have wished, for which a competent person should be appointed.

Zambelli returned to the dying man's bedside with this document and in the presence of three witnesses James Woodhouse, who was then unable to sign his name, made a cross on the paper. It is questionable if he understood what he was doing, although these witnesses later declared that, "Though he was in great pain and nervous irritation from gangrene of the toes, he was perfectly in possession of his reason and faculties."

In truth, nobody really worried whether the old man was still *compos mentis* at the time of the signing since he had repeated his intentions so often to so many people that the legal document was regarded as no more than a necessary formality.

After the document had been "signed", Saunders ordered two policemen to guard the villa day and night, as he did not trust either the servants or Signora Maria and he was determined to protect the collection in which his Government appeared to be so vitally interested. James Woodhouse died during the night of 26th February, 1866, two days after the document was signed. At ten o'clock the following morning Saunders arrived at the villa with two members of the British Consulate staff and proceeded on a search of the house. They unlocked the iron safe and counted the considerable sum contained therein and then proceeded to pry open the old man's writing-desk. They found a number of ancient rings, silver coins and leaden stone weights wrapped up in old documents and newspapers inside this desk. They then went upstairs to the bedroom where they found the body of Woodhouse lying on the bed unattended and in its presence they broke open all the boxes under the bed and wash-stand. Most of these boxes contained coins and other ancient items but some of them contained Signora Maria's clothing and personal effects.

When Saunders and his assistants had completed their search of the villa they carried all of the boxes containing ancient coins and other bits into the library which they locked and sealed. During their investigation they found no previous will nor any inventory of the contents of the collection, nor did they find either of these documents in a subsequent search carried out on the following day. By a most unfortunate oversight they themselves failed to make an inventory of what they found in the villa. As a precaution Saunders ordered Signora Maria to move out of the villa after the funeral which she did, in tears, taking the servants with her and surrendering all the household keys to the British Consul General.

On further reflection these measures of security did not satisfy Saunders who decided to transport all the valuable objects from the villa to the British Consulate. He was himself an ardent entomologist who had no interest in antiquities, so that he had no real idea of the value of the Woodhouse collection. He suspected, however, that it must be considerable for the British Museum to have shown so much interest. Under these circumstances he felt it was better to be absolutely safe and hired a donkey cart which he took to the villa and himself supervised the loading. He took all of the objects from the sealed library which could easily be transported—the iron safe which contained one thousand eight hundred pounds in cash, all of the many boxes of coins and jewellery, the items which they had found in the desk wrapped in old newspapers, some silver dishes which they had found on the sideboard, an inscribed marble slab and several marble statuettes. All of these items were taken to the consulate.

By this time Signora Maria had sufficiently recovered from her grief to become voluble over the fact that she had been slighted. The entire Italian community on Corfu—who had always held her in great esteem for living with "an English gentleman"—insisted that it was wicked for the British Consul General to have locked her out of her own home as if she was but a common servant. To add insult to injury, the Consul General had seized some of her personal possessions and she was missing a crucifix, some silver images of saints and a vase which had contained her flowers. One of the people to whom she related her misfortunes was a lawyer, Dr. Luzi, who decided to take some action. He went to see James Taylor and pointed out that since the Signora Maria had been named by James Woodhouse as one of his trustees, the British Consul General had no right to force her to leave her home or to remove the household effects to the consulate. Dr. Luzi added that he was well aware of the fact that the British were anxious to send the old man's collection of antiquities to England but pointed out that it would be more prudent to be kinder to the Signora Maria considering the existence of a law forbidding the exportation of antiquities from all Greek territories.

Taylor, who was already distressed by Saunders's removal of Woodhouse's belongings to the consulate, was alarmed by this threat. He agreed to accompany Dr. Luzi on a visit to the consulate where Saunders greeted them in an abrupt and uncivil manner. When Taylor suggested that the property should not have been moved to the consulate without the consent of the trustees, Saunders replied that he had acted in his capacity as Consul General to protect the property of a British subject. He ended the interview by stating that he would continue to manage the affair in whatever way that he saw fit. Taylor was so upset by this discussion that he went home and took to his bed.

Saunders had no doubt that he had acted prudently in removing Woodhouse's possessions to the consulate and in fact prided himself on the manner in which he had handled the difficult affair. In addition to securing the possessions in the consulate, he had promptly notified the Foreign Office in London of the death and requested their instructions on whether to keep the collection in Corfu until someone had been sent from the Museum to prepare a catalogue of it, or whether to ship what he had secured on the first available boat to England. Furthermore he had also notified Newton of the death, as he knew that the Museum would be interested, and the two next of kin, James Woodhouse and Sarah Woodhouse Puddick, nephew and niece of the deceased. He therefore felt that there was nothing further to be done until he received instructions from the Foreign Office.

In London, as soon as they received Saunders's cable, the Foreign Office contacted the British Museum to see what they wanted done with the collection. Newton was willing to go to Corfu to fetch it but it was decided in a conference with Layard, who was still at the Foreign Office, that it would not be prudent to send out an envoy from England as this would only serve to draw the attention of the local authorities to the bequest and might conceivably cause the Greek Government to raise difficulties about the exportation of the collection from Corfu. Newton explained this decision succinctly in a statement which certainly would have shocked the governments of those countries possessing ancient remains:

> I consider that in all cases of exportation of antiquities from foreign countries, so far as my experience goes, and I have superintended the exportation of objects of great value from different countries, that it is always desirable that the exportation should take place with the utmost promptitude, for the better security of the property, and with as little publicity as possible, whether the local government has given permission or not.

With this in mind, the Foreign Office cabled Saunders to send on the collection immediately and ordered a British warship to call at Corfu to collect it. The decision was quickly implemented and less than two weeks after Woodhouse's demise, the *Enterprise* arrived at Corfu and took aboard a large sealed chest containing the collection which Saunders had listed and packed. (Since the Consul General knew little about antiquities, this list of contents was prepared by Mr. Reichardt, the Prussian clergyman of the Anglican Church in Corfu.) In due course the collection reached London and Saunders received a letter of thanks from the British Museum.

By this time the Consul General had another problem to cope

with. James Woodhouse and John Puddick, nephew and nephew-in-law of the deceased, had arrived in Corfu and called at the consulate to collect their inheritance. When Saunders requested them to produce the necessary legal documents proving their right of inheritance, the heirs insisted that they could not obtain these documents in England because the death had occurred on foreign soil and the will would therefore be probated in Corfu. Saunders then advised them that they would risk having the estate confiscated if they went to the Greek courts for a probate and suggested that he could surrender the property to them without a probate on the condition that they signed a document recognizing the donation of their uncle's collection of antiquities to the British Museum. The heirs were not pleased with this arrangement but they finally agreed to sign this document, whereupon Saunders surrendered to them the funds from the iron safe and the keys to the villa. They were shocked and enraged by the condition of their uncle's home when they entered it:

> The premises looked as if an enemy had been sacking the town. Papers were left all over the room, books, manuscripts and silver dishes on chairs, chairs on tables, a cabinet was on the floor and everything was broken open.

In fact the heirs were greatly disappointed in their inheritance, especially after the expense and trouble of their trip to Corfu, and they remained on the island for only three weeks to pack and ship what they wanted to take back to England. Among the items which they found in the house and took with them were several ancient bronze tablets and a collection of ancient rings and ear-rings and, after giving the Signora Maria a few worthless bits of furniture, they sold the remaining contents of the villa at a public auction. The heirs left Corfu in May, raging that they had been robbed by both the British Consul and the British Museum. After their departure Saunders considered that the whole delicate Woodhouse affair was finally and successfully settled.

This was not to be the case, however. Shortly after the Woodhouse collection had arrived at the British Museum, Charles T. Newton had made a very careful examination of its contents and was exceedingly disappointed in what he saw. He discovered that most of the ancient coins were of negligible value, that there were only a few pieces of worthwhile ancient jewellery and that there was virtually nothing else of value in the box which Saunders had shipped from Corfu. Furthermore, the box contained a number of items which were not even antiquities: several meteoric stones, a brass seal of Zante and a modern Chinese lamp in the form of a toad.

Newton absolutely refused to believe that what the Museum had received was in fact the entire Woodhouse collection and he privately contacted people who had known James Woodhouse and knew of his collection. As a result of this investigation, he came to the conclusion that Woodhouse had collected a "great number of ancient objects, gold ornaments among them" which were missing from Saunders's shipment. He then discussed this question with Panizzi, the Director of the British Museum, and was authorized to open an official inquiry concerning the items missing from the collection. He therefore proceeded to Corfu where he arrived at the end of June to investigate what he now considered to be the theft of goods which belonged to the British Museum.

Newton immediately paid an official call at the consulate in Corfu and presented Saunders with a document which stated that the British Museum considered a large part of the Woodhouse collection to be missing and that he had therefore been sent to conduct an inquiry on Corfu with "full power to prosecute anybody, civilly or criminally, if he thought proper".

Saunders was astonished by Newton's visit, particularly since he had received the impression from despatches sent him by both the Foreign Service and the British Museum, that they had been exceedingly pleased with the collection and with his prompt shipment of it. He was even more astounded when Newton stated that he intended to conduct this investigation on his own, without the assistance of the consulate. At this point he lost his temper and demanded to know if the Museum was insinuating that he, personally, had stolen the items from the Woodhouse collection. Newton merely replied that a valuable part of the collection was missing and that he had every intention of finding the thief.

The first person whom Newton interrogated in the course of his private investigation was James Taylor. Several years previously Woodhouse had requested Taylor to visit the British Museum in order to see the manner in which ancient coins were displayed and on this occasion Taylor had reported to his friend that he had been

14

"so badly received by the officers of the Medal Room that he could not help saying to Mr. Woodhouse on his return that it was a pity to leave his coins to an institution so difficult of access to the public".

Newton may well have been aware of Taylor's opinion of the Museum, for his attitude towards the old shopkeeper was exceedingly rude and hostile. He made it quite plain that he considered Taylor to have illegally abstracted some items from the collection and cited in particular an ancient inscribed bronze tablet. Taylor admitted having this bronze tablet in his possession but insisted that his old friend had given it to him as a personal remembrance in return for his promise to look after Signora Maria after his death, adding that Woodhouse had secretly entrusted him with a considerable sum for the care of Signora Maria. Newton refused to believe this story and presented Taylor with a document sequestering this bronze tablet, along with several pieces of marble statuary which were in Taylor's garden, for the British Museum. He also hinted that Taylor had been seen entering the Woodhouse villa in a suspicious manner on several occasions after the death. Taylor was so upset by these accusations that he became violently ill and left Corfu within a few days to seek medical care in England.

In the meantime Saunders openly accused Signora Maria of stealing valuable items from the villa while her consort lay dying. As proof of this accusation, the Consul General cited the fact that when Signora Maria had complained in May of having been robbed by her Albanian servant, the police, in their investigation, had found a number of coins hidden in a stocking in her wardrobe. In addition, this Albanian servant told Saunders that his mistress had given him two boxes on the night of Woodhouse's death which he had smuggled out of the kitchen window in order to avoid the two policemen stationed outside the front door. The Consul General then confronted Signora Maria with a search-warrant but only discovered a few worthless coins in her possession. Still convinced of her guilt, he wrote to the Director of the British Museum requesting the authority to prosecute her, suggesting that it might prove profitable to frighten the old woman "by the expediency of bringing ecclesiastical influence to bear upon her and of trying the effect of an excommunication under the ban of the Patron Saint, which has often produced marvellous results".

Newton was so enraged when he learned of Saunders's letter to the Director of the Museum that he stormed into the consulate and ordered the Consul General "to stop interfering in his business and to cease his investigations as they could only result in causing the missing items to be more cleverly concealed".

Newton then sent a letter to the Director of the Museum to the effect that he had determined to conduct the inquiry on his own as it was "neither necessary nor expedient to attempt any further co-operation with Her Majesty's Consul General".

The bad feeling between these two men was so great at this time that Saunders sent a long letter to his superiors in the Foreign Office complaining of Newton's behaviour. In this letter he carefully enumerated the efforts to which he had gone to send the collection to the Museum rather than to let it fall into the hands of either the Greek Government or the legal heirs "both of whom obviously possessing a perfectly valid right to it". He pointed out that "it was sufficiently apparent that the entire donation would have lapsed altogether had it not been for the persevering efforts made by me", adding that he had, in fact, cheated the legal heirs in order to aid the Museum, for they could rightfully have contested the document of bequest:

> Obviously urged upon the deceased in his latter moments when the content was not dictated by himself and when obviously incapable of accurately appreciating the precise meaning of terms and phrases supplied by others.

He then went on to comment on Newton:

> I have no wish to complain of the surreptitious manner in which all kinds of out-door proceedings and private examinations, studiously concealed from me, have been done in a corner, to the astonishment of the community . . . but Mr. Newton has mistaken his position here.

He ended his letter in a burst of righteous self-indignation:

> While acting in all good faith and sincerity, with conscious rectitude, in protecting and sustaining the interests of the Museum under very embarrassing circumstances . . . the only recompense reserved for my exertions, without which this bequest would have been irretrievably

lost . . . has been to find myself requited in a manner which must effectually deter others from embarking in such a course.

The whole community on Corfu was now taking sides in the dispute which came to a sudden end when Newton was required to return to England in July because of an illness in his family. He paid a last visit to the consulate before leaving and informed Saunders that his investigations on Corfu had conclusively proved that there were a number of items in the villa at the time of Woodhouse's death which had subsequently vanished and whose disappearance had not been accounted for. He added that the accusations which Saunders had made against Signora Maria were completely inconclusive, being based only on "the fabricated stories of a convicted felon". It was perfectly obvious, he continued bitterly, that Saunders had taken it upon himself to sort out the collection for the Museum even though he was totally incompetent to do so and that the proof of this fact was that he had overlooked the very valuable collection of ancient rings which he left for the heirs. His failure to make an inventory of the property in Woodhouse's villa at the time of the death was inexcusable, Newton added, and he trusted that it was only due to incompetence.

When he returned to England Newton prepared a written report for the British Museum concerning his investigations in Corfu in which he stated that there were a number of "appalling discrepancies" in Saunders's explanations and charged the Consul General with serious default of actions and character. The Museum sent a copy of this report to the Foreign Office where it was felt that a Consul General of such high standing and of such long service as Sidney Smith Saunders should be given an opportunity to reply to such accusations. A copy of Newton's report was therefore sent on to Corfu.

Saunders was incensed when he read Newton's report and he immediately sent a letter to the Foreign Office demanding that his name be cleared of such "calumnations". Since both Saunders and Newton were clamouring for a hearing on the subject, it was decided in a conference between members of the Foreign Office and the Museum to let the matter be investigated by a Select Committee of the House of Commons. The official hearing of this Select Committee was scheduled for 26th July, 1867, and Consul General Saunders and Charles T. Newton were summoned to appear.

The Select Committee was composed of seven members, including Layard. All correspondence between Saunders, the Foreign Office and the British Museum was introduced as evidence and Newton was called as the first witness. Newton repeated his accusation of incompetence and possible criminal malice against Saunders in his testimony but he presented an estimate of the contents of the Woodhouse collection which turned out to be principally based on hearsay—information gathered from interviews with illiterate and untutored peasants who had made gifts of coins to Woodhouse in the 1830s and conversations with servants who had once worked for the old man decades previously. The Committee then heard the evidence of the heirs, James Woodhouse and John Puddick, who expressed their unmitigated anger with both Saunders and Newton.

When Saunders was called to testify he was indignant with injured pride and insisted that he had in fact sent the entire collection which had existed at the time of Woodhouse's death to the Museum—with the exception of the ancient rings. He cited as proof of this the fact that James Woodhouse in 1863 had ordered only two small boxes for the purpose of shipping his collection to England. It was obvious, Saunders commented, that two such small boxes as these could only have been intended to contain a small collection. He became defiant when questioned about his failure to make an inventory, arguing that the trustees should have made an inventory if they wished one and that if he had stopped to make an inventory, the shipment of the collection would have been delayed and perhaps prevented by the Greek authorities. The Consul General ended his testimony by remarking that if he had made an inventory, the British Museum would undoubtedly have lost it.

The Select Committee then considered the opinion of the Queen's Advocate, the highest legal authority in Britain. The Queen's Advocate, after commenting that it was "rather an invidious and certainly a difficult task" to form a judicial opinion on this case, pointed out that "Woodhouse was unquestionably subject to the laws of Corfu where he was domiciled". He then went on to say that:

It was certainly questionable as to whether Saunders in his zeal to serve the British Museum should have made such a deed for the moribund Woodhouse to sign, and while it was perhaps unreasonable to expect the Museum Trustees to show much sensitiveness upon this point, it appears to me extraordinary that it should have had so little influence in the judgment they have formed upon the conduct of Mr. Saunders.

He also pointed out that:

It was highly improper to have despatched the collection to England so quickly for the purpose of evading the laws of the country and thus giving the heirs no opportunity to prevent the transmission of the goods to the Museum.

He ended his opinion:

Those who had a perfect legal right to complain were in fact the heirs and the Government of Greece. . . . it is remarkable that the British Museum should have complained.

The Select Committee then adjourned to prepare its report which carefully avoided the issues which the Queen's Advocate had brought up. The report expressed a mild rebuke of Saunders's handling of the affair:

It is extremely regretable that the Consul General had prepared a document for the dying man to sign which was so vague that even the authors did not have a clear understanding of its meaning.

and pronounced that:

Although the Consul General appeared not conscious of his errors, he did in fact commit several serious breaches of duty.
There is, however, nothing to substantiate the imputation that, in acting as he had done, he was influenced by improper motives.

The Committee's report concluded with the simple statement that it was impossible to ascertain from the evidence introduced whether in fact any items had been stolen from the Woodhouse collection after the old man's death. These findings did not satisfy either Newton, Saunders or the heirs but the British Government wished the matter ended as it was attracting an unpleasant amount of publicity. Saunders returned to his position of Consul General in Corfu after this hearing and remained there until he retired in 1870, while Newton went on to become Director of the British Museum, and the heirs continued to complain of their loss until the end of their days.

The Woodhouse Affair was a fitting swan song to the whole ludicrous business of collecting antiquities. The Greek and Turkish laws forbidding the exportation of ancient remains from their territories eventually forced collectors to be satisfied with "treasures" obtained at high-priced art galleries or from equally high-priced smugglers and left the antiquarians the unsatisfactory pleasure of admiring ruins on their sites. The great pillage of art which began in the days of Sulla ended before the dawn of the twentieth century.

The historical trail of the collector of Greek antiquities is strewn with a series of events, both ludicrous and sordid, which attest to the overwhelming strength of human vanity. It is truly remarkable that ancient Greek sculpture should have been sought with such a passionate fury by so many different men at such widely varied periods of history for the same reason. The obsession for self-glorification seems an indestructible element in the character of all men.

BIBLIOGRAPHY

THE finest collection of manuscripts, books, pamphlets, letters and newspaper clippings concerning this subject was made by Joannes Gennadius (1844–1932), at one time Greek Ambassador to England. His invaluable collection is now to be found in the Gennadius Library in Athens. Some of the works which I found most helpful included:

CHAPTER I: The Loot of Sulla
4000 Years under the Sea, by Philippe Diole (Sidgwick and Jackson, London, 1954).
History of Greece under Foreign Dominations, by George Finlay, Vol. I, "Greece under the Romans" (Wm. Blackwood and Sons, London, 1857).
History of Rome, by Theodor Mommsen, trans. by Rev. William P. Dickson, Vol. III (Richard Bentley, London, 1863).
Lives, by Plutarch, Vol. I (Didot, Paris, 1877).

CHAPTER II: The Sack of Constantinople
The Age of Constantine the Great, by Jacob Burckhard, trans. by Moses Hadas (London, 1849).
"Ravages Committed in Constantinople by the Christian Armies", by Nicetas Chionates in *Travels in Various Countries of Europe, Asia and Africa*, by Edward Daniel Clarke (London, 1816).
Constantine the Great, by Lloyd B. Holsapple (Sheed and Ward, New York, 1942).
L'Empire Latin de Constantinople et La Principauté de Morée, by Jean Longnon (Paris, 1949).
La Conquête de Constantinople, by Geoffroi de Villehardouin (Paris, 1891).

CHAPTER III: The Favourites of James I
Life, Correspondence and Collections of Thomas Howard, Earl of Arundel, by M. F. S. Hervey (Cambridge University Press, 1921).
A Century of Archaeological Discoveries, by A. Michaelis, trans. by Bettina Kahnweiler (John Murray, London, 1908).

CHAPTER IV: Morosini's Lions
"Dispaccio di Francesco Morosini, Capitano Generale da Mar" (Venezia, 1862).
Raceonto Historico Della Veneta Guerra in Levante, by A. Locatelli (Giuolamo Albrizzi, Colonia, 1691).
A Journal of the Venetian Campaign A.D. 1687 Under the Conduct of the Capt. General Morosini (H. C. Taylor, London, 1688).

CHAPTER V: The Abbé Fourmont
Missions Archeologiques Français en Orient, by Henri Omont (Imprimerie Nationale, Paris, 1902).
A Journey into Greece, by George Wheler and Dr. Spon (London, 1682).

CHAPTER VI: The Dilettanti
Ionian Antiquities, by R. Chandler (London, 1769).
History of the Society of Dilettanti, compiled by Lionel Cust (Macmillan, London, 1914).
The Antiquities of Athens, by James Stuart and Nicolas Revett (John Haberkorn, London, 1762 through 1816).

CHAPTER VII: Marbles for a Scottish Mansion
The best general account of this subject is:
An Historical Guide to the Sculptures of the Parthenon, published by the British Museum (London, 1962).
There are a great number of contemporary pamphlets concerning the Elgin marbles among which the more interesting are:
"Memorandum on the subject of the Earl of Elgin's pursuits in Greece" (London, 1811).
"Notice of Memorandum on Subject of Earl of Elgin's Pursuits in Greece" from the *Classical Journal*, September, 1811.
"Memorandum on the Present State of the Negotiations respecting the purchase of the Elgin Marbles" (London, 1816).
"The judgment of connoisseurs upon Works of Art compared with that of Professional Men in reference more particularly to the Elgin Marbles" by B. R. Haydon, in *The Examiner*, 1816.

CHAPTER VIII: Marbles for Cambridge
Travels in Various Countries of Europe, Asia and Africa, by Edward Daniel Clarke, 6 vols. (T. Cadell and W. Davis, London, 1814).
The Life and Remains of Edward Daniel Clarke, by Rev. William Otter (George Cowie, London, 1825).

CHAPTER IX: So Much for Art
   Travels in Southern Europe and the Levant 1810–1817—The Journal of C. R. Cockerell, R.A., edited by his son Samuel Pepys Cockerell (Longmans, Green, London, 1903).

CHAPTER X: Aegean Treasures of the Louvre
   There have been many pamphlets published concerning the discovery and value of the Venus de Milo. Some of the more interesting of these include:
   Sur la statue antique de Venus Victrix découverte dans l'ile de Milo en 1820, by the Comte de Clarac (P. Didot, Paris, 1821).
   Dissertations sur les Venus l'Apollon et la statue découverte à Milo, by Chery Lenoir (Paris, 1822).
   Le Marquis de Rivière et la Donation de la Venus de Milo, by M. Etienne Michon (Imprimerie Generale Lahure, Paris, 1906).
   La Venus de Milo, by F. Ravaisson (Imprimerie National, Paris, 1892).
   La Venus de Milo, by Salomon Reinach (Paris, 1830).
   On the Winged Victory of Samothrace:
   Histoire de la sculpture grec, by Collignon (Paris, 1887).
   Monuments de l'art antique, by Olivier Rayet (Paris, 1880).

CHAPTER XI: Newton's Lions
   A History of Discoveries at Halicarnassus, Cnidus and Branchidae, by C. T. Newton (Day & Son, London, 1861).
   Travels and Discoveries in the Levant, by C. T. Newton (Day & Son, London, 1865).
   "Papers respecting the excavations at Budrun" presented to both Houses of Parliament by Command of Her Majesty (Harrison, London, 1858).

CHAPTER XII: The Temple of Artemis
   "The Temple of Diana at Ephesus", by James Fergusson, extract from "The Transactions of the Royal Institute of British Architects" (Trubner, London, 1883).
   Discoveries at Ephesus, by J. T. Wood (Longmans, Green, London, 1877).

CHAPTER XIII: The Woodhouse Collection
   "Correspondence as to the Woodhouse Collection of Antiquities", presented to the House of Commons by Command of Her Majesty in pursuance (Harrison, London, 1867).
   "Appendix to Correspondence as to Woodhouse Collection of Antiquities" by Command of Her Majesty (Harrison, London, 1867).

INDEX